LESZEK KOLAKOWSKI

GOD OWES US NOTHING

A Brief Remark on Pascal's Religion
and on the Spirit of Jansenism

THE UNIVERSITY OF CHICAGO PRESS

CHICAGO AND LONDON

The University of Chicago Press, Chicago 60637
The University of Chicago Press, Ltd., London
©1995 by The University of Chicago
All rights reserved. Published 1995
Paperback edition 1998
Printed in the United States of America
04 03 02 01 00 99 98   2 3 4 5
ISBN: 0–226–45051–1 (cloth)
ISBN: 0–226–45053–8 (paperback)

Library of Congress Cataloging-in-Publication Data

Kolakowski, Leszek.
    God owes us nothing : a brief remark on Pascal's religion and on
the spirit of Jansenism / Leszek Kolakowski.
        p.   cm.
    Includes bibliographical references and index.
        1. Pascal, Blaise, 1623–1662.   2. Augustine, Saint, Bishop of
Hippo—Influence.   3. Jansenists.   4. Semi-Pelagianism.   5. Catholic
Church—Doctrines—History—17th century.   I. Title.
B1903.K57   1995
273'.7—dc20   95-5768

Contents

CONTENTS

Acknowledgment

I am greatly indebted to my daughter Agnieszka; not only did she polish my incurably imperfect English but she made very many useful corrections in the text of this book. Her work was most helpful.

Preface

Does it make sense to write about Pascal after all the outstanding scholars of our century, after Brunschvicg, Strowski, Lafuma, Gouhier, Mesnard, to name only a few? The doubt is irresistible, but we can quote Bouillier's *History of Cartesian Philosophy*: "what can one say about Pascal that has not been perfectly said by Mr. Cousin in his two admirable prefaces and by Mr. Havet in his study and commentary to the *Pensées*?"[1] Bouiller's book was published in 1854, and since then an enormous number of works, both historical and interpretative, have been produced. The question, therefore, seems even more pertinent. On the other hand, great philosophers are, as it were, everybody's property. One may think and write about Spinoza after von Dunin-Borkowski and Gebhardt, on Aquinas after Gilson and Manser, etc. This kind of work never stops. Not because one discovers new texts or new biographical details; on these points the contribution of the scholars just mentioned is invaluable and perhaps definitive. Even though a slight probability still exists that some new documents will surface, it is most unlikely that they might revolutionize our knowledge. But the work never stops because nearly every generation has a Plato, a Kant, a Pascal of its own. Those wells of wisdom never dry up.

The present book is no more than a gloss, and it hardly needs mentioning that it deals only with some chapters of Pascal's legacy; as Pascal said, there is a meaning which makes the entire work of an

1. Francisque Bouillier, *Histoire de la philosophie cartesienne*, Paris-Lyon, 1854, vol. 1, p. 550.

author consistent, and it is the search for this meaning that induces us to reflect. We should admit, however, that this search is inescapably tainted by our attempt to find in it a major concept that we can apply to the experience of our own time.

The Jansenist context of Pascal's thinking can never be left aside; but it is no less obvious that to explain him by, or to reduce him to, this context would make of his work a footnote to a theological squabble which, important though it was in the seventeenth century, might seem only of historical interest. Jansenism attracted a number of eminent scholars—from Sainte-Beuve to the late Jean Orcibal—and I have nothing to add in historical matters. My purpose was to understand Jansenism both as a theological school that tried to cope with some of the insoluble mysteries of Christianity and as a reactionary model of Christian faith and life, a desperate attempt to ward off the grim menace of the burgeoning Enlightenment; I wanted to reflect on the meaning that unites its two sides. A few basic historical facts are briefly mentioned to make my essay more readable. Most of the comments on the secondary literature are relegated to notes in order to avoid unnecessary interruptions.

The present author's sympathies and antipathies are divided when he reflects on the conflict between Jesuit modernizers and Jansenist reactionaries. "So miserable is human destiny that the lights which deliver man from one evil throw him into another" (Pierre Bayle).[2]

2. In Paul Hazard, *La crise de la conscience européenne*, Paris, 1935, p. 108.

PART ONE

Why Did the Catholic Church Condemn
the Teaching of Saint Augustine?

We are going to talk about what is perhaps the most formidable and intractable puzzle of Christian thinking—the confrontation of divine grace with the human free will—not in order to depict its centuries-long and very confusing history or, God forbid, to contribute to its solution, but to see how this puzzle became the focus of a struggle between modernity and reaction embodied respectively in Jesuit and Jansenist doctrines in the seventeenth century, how Saint Augustine became a victim of this battle, and what role was played in it by Pascal.

> *Grace*: internal, external, habitual, sufficient, efficient, justifying, actual, prevenient, sanctifying, incongruous, perfect, imperfect, preparatory, stimulating (*excitans*), irresistible, versatile, equilibrated;
> *Grace*: of adoption, of regeneration, of inhabitation, of sanity, of medicine.

This is a list, by no means exhaustive, of adjectives and nouns employed in sixteenth- and seventeenth-century theological polemics to single out various kinds or various sides of divine grace. At first glance the list may look terrifying and suggest an extremely intricate battlefield which requires an enormous effort and erudition to be properly understood. In reality, while the controversy about grace was indeed obscured by a huge number of distinctions —invented for defensive or offensive purposes but adding little or nothing to the substance of the debate—the core of the problem was fairly simple (insofar as anything is simple in theology), and it is not very hard to grasp. Since, however, we are dealing with the problem of grace in the context of Jansenist-Jesuit strife, it seems reasonable first to state it as it was actually stated and phrased in this very context, and only later to reduce it to the basics, to skim over rapidly the antecedents of the quarrel and to try to reflect upon its meaning in the vicissitudes of the Counter-Reformation.

Within two centuries of the beginning of the Great Reformation, the Catholic Church issued a number of official doctrinal documents dealing, among other things, with the questions of divine grace, predestination, free choice, and the role of human will in people's salvation or damnation. The most important are: the bull *Exsurge Domine* (1520) condemning 41 heretical or scandalous propositions of Martin Luther; the decrees of the fifth and sixth sessions of the Council of Trent (1547); the bull *Ex Omnibus Afflictionibus* (1567) condemning 79 statements by Michael Baius; the bull *Cum Occasione* (1653) condemning 5 statements attributed to Cornelius Jansenius; and the constitution *Unigenitus* (1713) condemning 101 propositions of Pasquier Quesnel. The number of books devoted to the subject is immense; this was the core of the theological debate, the question par excellence which more than anything else—in theological terms—separated all churches, sects, and schools in Europe from each other. Lutherans and Calvinists, Arminians and Gomarists, Jansenists, Jesuits, Thomists—all defined their doctrinal stance first by giving their own interpretation of the canonical texts, in particular Paul's letter to the Romans: do we human creatures contribute in any way to our salvation and, if so, in what way? In no other concept are all the crucial aspects of Christian faith so concentrated as in that of grace: original sin, redemption, salvation, God the merciful, God the avenger.

Jansenists hardly ever called themselves "Jansenists," of course; the name was coined by their Jesuit enemies almost at the beginning of the controversy; it suggested a kind of a new sect set up by one recently deceased theologian. Jansenius's followers called themselves disciples of Augustine, whose authority had been unshakable in Christianity. They insisted that they—and their master, Jansenius—had nothing new to say; they simply followed and repeated the most traditional teaching of the Church, which conformed to the Gospels and to the epistles of Saint Paul and was

4

codified in Augustinian theology. The "Molinist" doctrine, on the other hand, was, they argued, a novelty in the Catholic Church, even though it brought back to life the most dangerous heresy of the Pelagians or semi-Pelagians (the so-called "Marsilians"). The Jesuit writers were indeed in an awkward position when they were challenged by the authority of Augustine, and most of the time they preferred to avoid the issue. When pressed on this point, they either issued gratuitous denials or sometimes—not often—pointed out that the great saint, much as he deserved respect, was not infallible, after all, and his writings were not dogmatically binding; they also averred that their own theory of grace was perfectly in keeping with the teaching of Thomas Aquinas, whose authority they often invoked. They accused the Jansenists, however, of being tainted with the horrors of the Calvinist heresy.

Good arguments may be advanced to show that both sides were right in their accusations. Jansenists were on firm ground in saying that they were faithful to the Augustinian teaching, and quite justified in scenting Pelagian errors in the Jesuit theology. The Jesuits were no less right in demonstrating the fundamental conformity of Jansenist tenets with Calvin's theory of predestination. This amounts to saying that Calvin was, on this point, a good Augustinian and that, by condemning Jansenius, the Church was in effect condemning—without, of course, stating it explicitly—Augustine himself, its own greatest theological authority. The pronouncements and the anathemas of the Council of Trent left some ambiguities which both Jesuits and Jansenists could plausibly interpret in their favor; the successive condemnations of Baius, Jansenius, and Quesnel, however, sealed the fate of the Augustinian tradition on this crucial point in the Catholic world. This was a momentous event in the history of Christianity and thus in the European history of ideas, not a long-forgotten quarrel of hairsplitting medieval minds.

Jansenius's *Augustinus* appeared in Lovanium in 1640, slightly over two years after the author's demise; the Jesuits, who had unsuccessfully tried to prevent publication, started their anti-Jansenist campaign immediately. They were not quite wrong in insisting that the other side had been the first to incite this squabble, but this was when nobody had ever heard of "Jansenism"; Saint-Cyran's attacks on Father Garasse appeared in 1626. There is no good answer to the question of when, precisely, to date the birth of Jansenism; much as the movement, later on, had a clear and strong awareness of a common cause and in fact acted, in many ways, as a kind of a party, it had never been set up in a formal way and could not do so without destroying itself. Saint-Cyran was arrested on Richelieu's order in May 1638 on the pretext of doctrinal error in the question of "attrition"; this was an important issue that was to appear time and again in Jansenist literature; it had a doctrinal and psychological—but not logically compelling—connection with the question of predestination and grace. In the same year Antoine le Maître—the nephew of Antoine Arnauld—left his worldly professional life to retire, as a layman, in the Port-Royal monastery, the first of the "solitaires." Once Arnauld's *Fréquente Communion* was published in 1643 one may speak of a conscious "movement."

Augustinus, Jansenius's magnum opus, is an immensely long theological treatise divided into three volumes. The first deals with the Pelagian heresy;[1] the second with the grace given to the first couple in Paradise and the state of fallen nature; the third with "the grace of Christ the Savior." Heretical ideas were to be discovered in all three volumes but especially in the last. The work is provided with a number of approbatur and with the customary caveat expressing the author's readiness to submit his views to the judgment of the Church. Quotations from Augustine's works fill a very substantial part of the text; among other fathers, Prosper and Fulgentius (both followers of Augustine) are quoted fairly frequently; only occasionally do we find reference to medieval authorities: Anselm, Bernard of Clairvaux, Thomas Aquinas, Bonaventure.

There is no need to depict here all the innumerable intrigues, plots, accusations, and counter-accusations during the almost thirteen years that elapsed between the printing of *Augustinus* and the papal bull. The first decisive attempt to obtain the official condemnation of Jansenius took place in July 1649, when the syndic of the Faculty of Theology, Nicolas Cornet, a pupil of the Jesuits and with a reputation for being their servant, tried to prompt the Sorbonne to condemn five anonymous statements which everybody knew he attributed to Jansenius. The maneuver fizzled out, in spite of the fairly strong influence the Jesuits had by then managed to build up at the Sorbonne; shortly thereafter, however, a collective letter was dispatched to the Holy See by a large group of anti-Jansenist bishops, demanding the condemnation of those very statements. The request did not attribute the authorship specifically to Jansenius but claimed that such opinions were being spread by some doctors. This unusual procedure proved efficacious.

The Apostolic See was apparently not enthusiastic about the resumption of a quarrel which had lasted for many decades, on an almost intractable question. Molina's celebrated treatise on the agreement of human free will with the gifts of grace and divine providence, the classic text of what Augustinians perceived as brazen, modern Pelagianism, was published in 1588, three years after the birth of Jansenius. It was attacked by Thomists, especially of the Dominican order, it produced a hostile commotion in various universities, and its doctrinal soundness was even examined, though without a damning verdict, by a special commission during the pontificate of Clement VIII. Under the next pontiff, Paul V, the Holy Office issued a decree prohibiting public discussion on the question "de auxiliis" and demanding that all books on the subject, even written in the form of commentaries on Saint Thomas, be first examined by the Inquisition. The injunction was twice repeated by Urban VIII but could not be properly enforced. Rome clearly wanted to avoid a major dispute that would set powerful orders against each other, spread to the entire body of the Church and split it. The condemnation of Jansenius might seem an accident in the sense that it was almost forced on the pope (who, for that matter, was not a theologian either by education or by inclination). But it was to turn out that, after decades of strong opposition in the most prestigious centers of Catholic learning, Lovanium and Paris, the Jesuit spirit of modernity did win. Both sides, the defenders and the attackers of the late bishop, sent their delegations to Rome to explain their position and to influence the tribunal and the pope.[2]

The Jansenist strategy, from the very beginning, was, first, to prove that the five statements were arbitrarily concocted by Cornet or by other Molinists, and could not be found in Jansenius's text (apart from the first statement, but this, they claimed, had been altered by their detractors to suit their sinister purposes); second, that all the statements, as phrased, were ambiguous and could be interpreted either in an orthodox or in a heretical sense; third, that the aim of the Jesuits was to obtain the condemnation of Saint Augustine on the pretext of a condemnation of Jansenius. They took the same line of defense both before and after the bull of 1653, even though, understandably enough, once they faced the formal condemnation they tended rather to emphasize the fact that nobody—in particular neither Jansenius nor they—defended the prohibited doctrine. Arnauld even argued that the papal constitution condemned the heresy in the abstract and not in Jansenius's sense, the latter's book being only an "occasion" ("cum occasione impressionis libri, cui titulus Augustinus Cornelii Iansenii . . .") for the decree.[3] This device was rather unconvincing; while the bull, indeed, does not use exactly the expression "in sensu Iansenii," it clearly says that its target is his opinions ("inter alias eius [Iansenii] opiniones") and includes a proviso that the pontiff does not thereby approve other opinions expressed in the book ("non intendemus tamen per hanc declarationem . . . aprobare ullatenus alias opiniones, quae continentur in praedicto libro Cornelii Iansenii"). One may imagine, certainly, a condemnation phrased in even stronger terms but the existing text leaves no room for doubt: five propositions, declared to be Jansenius's "opinions" are declared heretical (some of them being in addition "false," "blasphemous," "scandalous," "impudent," etc.).

It should be mentioned that the book had been condemned earlier on, in the bull *In Eminenti* in 1642; this, however, did not satisfy the Society of Jesus, because no particular tenet was included in the verdict and the point was rather to blame the author for breaching the order of silence imposed on theologians in the matters of grace and predestination (but the injunction had not reached Brussels). Jansenius himself could not, of course, be branded as a heretic, as the condemnation was posthumous, and one became a heretic, according to canon law, not just by having uttered a heretical sentence but by defending it, ecclesiastical warnings and condemnations notwithstanding; a heretic by definition has to be obstinate. Posthumous condemnation did not affect the person of the author, only the doctrine.

In the following remarks I confront, as basic texts (apart from *Augustinus*), first, a series of Arnauld's writings dealing with the subject; second, the two-volume attack on Arnauld by "the Calvinist Pope" Pierre Jurieu; and third, two works by Father Franciscus Annatus, the famous Jesuit polemicist (and, for a number of years, the king's confessor and one of the chief organizers of the persecutions); the discussion of the five propositions is one of the main themes of Jurieu's work, along with a lot of personal abuse. This confrontation is instructive, as all three men were immensely erudite in theology and in the history of the Church, and one hardly imagines that any of them might have missed any relevant historical or theological point supporting their arguments. Arnauld argues that the five statements taken in the heretical sense are indeed a part of the abominable Calvinist doctrine and are opposed to everything Jansenius taught. Whereas interpreted in the orthodox sense, if there is one, they simply express the Augustinian tradition which has always been Catholic theology par excellence. Jurieu insists, on the contrary, that the statements are not very ambiguous, that they are indeed Augustinian, that they reflect properly Jansenius's meaning and are, yes, Calvinist; moreover he says that Arnauld knows very well what is at stake; he himself accepts the Augustinian-Calvinist-Jansenist soteriology but, trying to remain in the papist Church for opportunistic reasons, he invents (mala fide) nonexistent differences between Jansenius and the reformed faith. Annatus, the first of whose two works under scrutiny was published before the bull and the second shortly thereafter, displays his fairness by making distinctions between Jansenist and Calvinist doctrines on some of the five points and opposes both doctrines to genuine Catholic dogma, conforming, as he avers, to Saint Augustine's teaching and to the "Sensus Alienus," i.e., to what the Jansenists said (wrongly) was the real target of the bull.

Ultimately the whole problem boils down to the perplexing difficulty in reconciling two tenets of Christianity: God is omnipotent and it is impossible to imagine that his will might be foiled by men; men are responsible for their damnation or salvation.

Does God Command Impossible Things?

The first proposition: "some of God's commandments are impossible for just people—with the forces they actually have—who will and try [to fulfil them]; and they lack the grace whereby those commandments would become possible."

This is the only phrase taken (almost) verbatim from Jansenius's work. He discusses the question in chapter 13 of the third volume of *Augustinus*. It is the Pelagian contention, he says, that "God does not order impossible things and therefore he gives to all sufficient aid [enabling them] to do what he orders"; indeed "nobody sins by doing something he cannot avoid."[4] This, however, is an impious and blasphemous expression of human hubris. According to Saint Augustine (numerous quotations confirm this), if it is true that God does not command us to do impossible things, this does not mean that whatever he commands can be obeyed by human powers alone; it is only wrong to say that "those acts are so impossible that man can perform them neither with his own nor with other powers if such powers come to his aid."[5] God often orders us to do something and takes his help away—not to drive man into despair but "to teach him that he ought to beg for help and for powers [enabling him] to do that, a help he feels he is lacking."[6] The Council of Trent did confirm the Augustinian teaching. Whatever God orders is feasible with his grace but this grace is not always there and not everybody gets it; otherwise we would not need to ask for help. And it is important to keep in mind that grace is refused not only to infidels and obdurate sinners but also to faithful and just people, who really do wish to abide by divine orders: they have will but not power. The paradigmatic example, both to Augustine and to Jansenius, is, of course, the denial of Peter, a supremely *iustus vir* who had the will to follow the commandments but was not provided with the divine aid to do it. One simple Augustinian sentence (among many) settles the matter: "I want you to will, but it is not enough that you will. You have to be aided so that you will fully accomplish what you will."[7] Even the Lord's Prayer, "do not lead us into temptation," implies that "it is not given to all not to be tempted above what they are capable of."[8] The self-conceited Pelagian contention that the will cannot be enslaved, and that we simply do not sin if we do not want to, is to be found among scholastics who fail to see that it is not enough to will, or to will not to, in order to overpower the temptation. "It is grace which causes that we not only will to do what is right but that we are able to do so." Bad will can be converted into good will only by the power of grace. God demonstrated, through Peter's example, that he punishes the pride of those who rely on their own powers. "And what is man without grace but what Peter was when he denied Christ?"[9]

Jansenius claims that Aquinas's theology does not depart from Augustinian tenets on this point. Did not he say that man is in duty bound to perform acts he is incapable of performing without grace, which God does not always confer (a just punishment for previous crimes or at least for original sin)?[10] Didn't he say that the sinner is guilty even if he cannot escape sinning, not unlike a drunken killer who is not excused just because he committed the crime as a result of being drunk, since he was guilty of having got drunk in the first place?[11]

The reference to Aquinas is somewhat doubtful; although he states clearly that it is not in our power to avoid all sins without gratuitously given divine help, he adds that we are able by acts of will to avoid particular sins in particular moments. Whereas according to the doctrine of Augustine and Jansenius no single act can ever be performed without this kind of grace. The full wording of the incriminating statement in *Augustinus* runs as follows:

> All this fully and most clearly proves that there is nothing more certain and better grounded in the teaching of St. Augustine than this: there are some commandments which are impossible not only to infidels, blind, obstinate people, but to just people as well—with the powers they actually have—who will and try [to fulfil them]; and they lack the grace whereby those commandments would become possible.

Arnauld's commentary on the first proposition may be summed up in two points. First, he says, Cornet's truncated version distorted the original meaning: Jansenius merely explains Saint Augustine's teaching; his detractors, in order to refute him, must therefore prove that it is not, as a matter of fact, Augustinian doctrine, which they obviously could not do. This part of the reply is rather weak. Ostensibly the original sentence, as it stands, is indeed of historical character: according to Saint Augustine's theology "some of God's commandments . . . ," etc. But no reader of *Augustinus* can fail to notice that what the author seeks to do is not only to expound what Saint Augustine believed—which could be done by any enemy of Christianity or by an atheist historian—but also to assert that this belief is undeniably, obviously in keeping with the Christian faith and thus *true*. Pelagians are deeply wrong on all points of their specific creed, Saint Augustine is perfectly right; Jansenius's writings are not a neutral historical description, they are the works of a dogmatic theologian. The sentence "aliqua praecepta . . ." unmistakably expresses Jansenius's own belief.

In his second remark Arnauld makes a distinction between two possible meanings of the proposition. It is obviously true and in conformity with Augustine (and that there are errors in Augustine cannot be said without heresy; it would amount to condemning the Church and the Holy See) to say that just men are sometimes deprived of grace and incapable of obeying the divine commandments even though they know what they ought to do and have a will to do it. But the same proposition, literally taken, might mean that there are commandments which the just man can never fulfill, grace or no grace. This is precisely the heresy of Calvin, who asserts that nobody, including the saints and prophets, no matter what grace he might have received, is ever able to abide by the divine law.[12]

This is what Arnauld wrote in 1646 before the papal bull. After the condemnation he had the solution ready: the bull condemned —and rightly so, in dogmatic terms—the Calvinist, not the Augustine, doctrine.

There is something desperate in this defense; one may even suspect that it was indeed written *mala fide*. Strictly speaking, one could perhaps force the suggested heretical meaning on the proposition, but there is not the slightest doubt about its real sense. God, to prevent the human race from trusting in its own moral powers, and to teach it humility, sometimes robs even saints of the grace which is necessary to obey his commandments. The wider meaning —that nobody, even with all possible divine help, is or ever will be capable of satisfying the law—is absurd in terms of Christian theology, and it is not the teaching of the Reformed Church. A Calvinist sentence quoted by Arnauld to prove his point—"neminem extitisse umquam qui legi Dei satisfaceret, nec ullum posse invenire" —says only that no human creature (presumably with the exception of Jesus Christ) can live entirely without sin. There is nothing specifically Calvinist in this saying; indeed, in Christian terms it is a platitude. It does not imply that some commandments are absolutely beyond human power, no matter how God might reinforce it.[13]

Other distinctions Arnauld tries to make in order to oppose the orthodox meaning of the first proposition to the heretical one are no less artificial and concocted *ad hoc*. "Volentibus," he says, might refer to people who have the perfect will informed by grace (and then the sentence would be false) or the imperfect will; "grace" might mean any kind of grace, including efficient grace, which infallibly achieves its goal, and then, again, the proposition would be heretical. Arnauld tries to convince his readers, or perhaps himself as well, that what the pope condemned was the Calvinist meaning of the first proposition and that no Catholic had ever held or uttered such an opinion. Alas, the supposed Calvinist meaning is a figment of his imagination: if "grace" could mean "efficient grace," the saying under scrutiny would imply that efficient grace is inefficient, which Calvin, of course, never suggested.

Jurieu, who analyses the first proposition at length, argues convincingly that on this point Jansenius confirms Augustinian teaching, accepted in the Reformed Church. Indeed the Thomists do not teach differently; the cause of the Fall is in man, not in God, but "the reason why God refuses efficient grace to a just man, and not to another, comes exclusively from the will of God."[14]

Let us then distinguish four doctrines:

According to Augustine, Jurieu, and Calvin, human creatures after the Fall can perform no morally good act (conform to divine law) unaided; for every such act they need the infusion of grace which is given to some and refused to others by the sheer wish of God, and not because some are more deserving of grace than others.

According to extreme Pelagian teaching, God enables us to do good if we want to and our natural status does not prevent us from fulfilling the commandments perfectly; if we fail in this, we can only blame ourselves; moral perfection is within our reach.

According to the semi-Pelagian teaching of the Jesuits, we do need divine grace to do good but "sufficient grace" is given to all, and it needs only our free will to make it efficient. Since this efficient grace is a constant condition of our life, we may say that moral perfection and our salvation depend on our effort and will.

According to Aquinas, we have enough grace to perform some good acts by our free choice, but the free choice does not suffice to avoid all sins in all circumstances.

Arnauld's defense is futile. What the pope condemned was not an imaginary statement of Calvin's. He interpreted the first proposition in the sense of Jansenius and Augustine. It was the teaching of Augustine that the pope declared heretical.

Father Annatus, in commenting on the first proposition, insists (rightly) that the proposition properly reflects Jansenius's views and that it was condemned as such. Orthodox Catholic doctrine says that "the grace which makes the commandments possible is such that it is up to free will to resist or to obey it" and, in addition, that the grace which is indispensable in order to abide by the commandments is never taken away. Father Annatus thus confirms the Jansenist rendering of the Jesuit position. He notes only that the Jansenists falsely accuse the Jesuits of claiming that grace is "subject to free choice." They, the Jansenists, call this a semi-Pelagian doctrine, but this is precisely the doctrine of which Calvin accused all scholastics, including Thomists and Scotists. According to the Calvinist heresy, just people, even if they act properly thanks to divine grace, sin in every good act.[15]

Does God Compel Us to Be Good?

The second proposition: "in the state of fallen nature one never resists interior grace."

The irresistibility of divine grace is one of the crucial problems in all the arguments about justification. Whereas the first proposition implies—without saying so in so many words—that a special grace (i.e., a grace going beyond what is given *promiscue* to all) is a *necessary* condition of any good act, the new one states that grace is the *sufficient* condition as well, i.e., that it always works infallibly and a person to whom it is given is helpless in resisting divine operations.

Jansenius, who deals with this question in several chapters of the second volume, is quite explicit about the difference between a necessary and a sufficient condition. We have to distinguish between two kinds of help God provides for the human will: "sine quo

AUGUSTINE AND THE JANSENISTS

voluntas velle non possit" and "quo fit." And it is clear that after the
Fall both the possibility of good acts and the will to perform them,
as well as their very performance, are God's gifts ("dat enim simul
et posse et operari"). And does not Holy Writ say that it is God who
elects us and not we who elect him? Adam enjoyed the kind of aid
that allowed him to make a free choice between obeying or disregarding the rules. The grace we (or rather some of us) are given is
more powerful; it acts invincibly, "giving us not only the power of
willing but the will to do what we can as well." When God gives,
people "most invincibly will the good."[16] Indeed, "Augustine frequently teaches—which may not be denied without patent impiety
—that once human nature has been thrown into the weakness of
sin, nothing good at all can remain in man, not a concession of will,
not an inclination or impulse, unless it is given to him . . . thus it is
necessary to admit that the very determination of will, whereby the
will determines itself here and now to agreeing, willing, making an
effort and acting, must be bestowed [conferri] by grace itself."[17]
The will "is so seized by grace that it can hardly be said to act.
Grace so implants itself in, and invades, the will that it does not
operate if the will wills but by operating it determines that it
will."[18] And "Augustine frequently says that man cannot resist God
who acts by grace." If he wants to save someone, no human free will
can resist. It is being acted upon "indeclinabiliter et insuperabiliter," and "the effects of divine mercy cannot be in human power,
otherwise God would be giving his mercy in vain, if man did not
will."[19] No divine law, no revelation of God's wisdom, no prophecies and no promise of reward (as Pelagians would have it) can
convert the human will to do good: only grace can do that.

Both Augustine and Jansenius seem unambiguous on this
point; once God wishes that a man do good, his will cannot be frustrated, his grace cannot be resisted.

Arnauld's salutary device consists in further *distinguos*. It is in
conformity with Scripture and universally admitted in the Church
(except by Molinists, who make the effect of grace dependent on
human will) that efficient grace cannot be overcome. Cornet, however, uses the ambiguous term "gratia interior," which might mean
the habitual kind of grace, or grace that has no justifying power, like
the habits of faith and of hope; it would indeed be a heresy to say
that one can never resist this kind of grace, for it would amount to

saying that people who have those habits never sin. As to the genuine efficient grace which changes our hearts, we can try to resist it, too; there are movements in us which go in the opposite direction, but this resistance cannot succeed, for this grace "never fails to produce the effect for which it has been given," in no matter how inveterate a sinner.[20]

Thus we can resist grace but never successfully; the grace infallibly overcomes our resistance.

The distinction, too, seems artificial. It was certainly not Jansenius's intention to say that people whom God wishes to enable to do good never experience, as a matter of fact, a contrary inclination or feel temptation. As Jurieu remarks, this would run counter to everyday experience. The sense of the condemnation is clear: it affects the very idea of efficient grace, the very concept of its irresistibility. It effectively approves the Molinist doctrine (or the semi-Pelagian heresy). Nor does Jansenius discuss the varieties of grace which God *intends* to be imperfect: a grace giving only "velléités," a weak impulse to the good, i.e., an impulse which inevitably —according to Augustine, Jansenius, and Arnauld—must be a failure since without grace in the proper sense, efficient grace, we can never perform a good act. It is always the same either-or; whatever we do, we do evil if we have no divine help (or if the help we have is of a kind not really designed to work, e.g., the very presence of revelation, of divine law, etc); if grace is given, we do good by necessity. There is nothing in between; either our acts are our own and then they are evil, or they are good and then they are acts of God operating through us irresistibly. Arnauld again invented a nonexistent meaning for the condemned statement in order to argue that this was the target of the bull and that neither Jansenius nor his followers were affected by the condemnation because they had never shared this heretical opinion.

But the Jesuit fathers knew better; the second proposition was declared heretical in the sense of Jansenius and of his great master.

Annatus admits that the directly intended effect of grace can in fact be frustrated. While in the "sensu alieno," human will is passive, like an inanimate object, and in Jansenist terms grace always achieves the total effect intended, true Catholic doctrine—of the Thomists, the Jesuits, and the great doctors of the Church—

teaches us that, as a result of the corruption of the will, grace may altogether fail to achieve its effect or achieve it only in part.[21]

On this point, too, the Catholic Church condemned the doctrine of Augustine.

Although Unfree, We Are Free

The third proposition seems, at first glance, somewhat obscure, but the intended meaning can easily be explained. It says "in the state of fallen nature, in order to earn a merit or to lose it, freedom from necessity is not required in man; freedom from compulsion is enough."

In other words, our acts are imputed to us, punished or rewarded by God, even if they are performed under "necessity"; only if they are performed under "compulsion" are they not thus imputed. The meaning of the sentence depends of course on the meaning of the distinction between "necessity" and "compulsion."

The real theological background of this doctrine is the same as that previously discussed: if we act by our own will—inevitably corrupted as it is after the calamity of original sin—we never choose between good and evil, we necessarily do evil; if we do good instead, we do this necessarily as well, even though it is God's infallible will, rather than our own, which makes us act. In both cases we act necessarily but in neither are we under "compulsion" (*coactio*), and in both cases moral merit or guilt are imputed to us: in the former case by justice, in the latter by mercy.

This conclusion cannot be logically inferred from the content of the third proposition, but the converse holds: if the said proposition is false, so is the just-summarized doctrine of salvation.

This doctrine *is* genuinely Augustinian and it is included in Jansenius's work. To make his point and to prove that his doctrine is shielded by the uninterrupted continuity of the tradition, Jansenius adduces an exceptionally long list of quotations from the most venerated authors, starting with the pre-Nicean fathers and ending with Aquinas.

The crucial point is simple: compulsion (*coactio, vis, violentia, compulsio*) occurs when I am doing something I *do not* want to do, something contrary to my *will*. If I am doing something and will to do it, I am free, even if my will has been shaped infallibly by God; this necessity is therefore compatible with freedom, or, as Saint Thomas would have it, "the simple necessity of will does not contradict freedom" (Sent. II, qu.10 art.2, ad1). And so, for instance, Jansenius says, "the will freely strives after happiness, although it strives after it necessarily. So does God, by his own free will, love himself, even though he does so necessarily."[22]

The target of Jansenius's critique is "libertas indifferentiae," the freedom consisting in my ability to make a choice between good and evil with nothing directing my will apart from this will itself. But if "freedom" implies that I can freely do good or evil, then God has no freedom, as he cannot—by necessity—choose evil; neither can faithful angels or Jesus Christ or the saints in heaven; nor can devils avoid doing evil. "Therefore it is wrong to conclude that an act of the rational will is not free if it is free from compulsion only . . . [on this wrong assumption] the freedom of man in his pilgrimage is a freedom not only from compulsion but also from immutable voluntary necessity, i.e., his freedom is indifferent to both [good and evil]."[23] "Freedom of human choice is free even if [man] inflexibly [or: unchangeably, *immutabiliter*] wants something or does not."[24] I employ the freedom of will on this sole condition that I *will* to do what I am doing.

While quotations from Augustine and other authorities seem to leave no room for doubt about the orthodoxy of the doctrine he defends, Jansenius is, of course, aware of the major inconvenience in his exposition. He points out that Pius V and Gregory XIII (the text says wrongly Gregory XV) declared heretical, among others, two statements (by Baius, although his name is not mentioned by Jansenius): "what occurs voluntarily, occurs freely even if it occurs by necessity" and "only violence contradicts the natural freedom of man,"[25] i.e., they condemned, or so it seems, exactly the same doctrine. Jansenius says, rather unconvincingly, that the condemnations, as they stand, seem to contradict everything the fathers taught us, consequently those statements must have had another meaning. This is an a priori argument derived simply from the principle that neither the apostolic Church nor the bishop of Hippo can err. And indeed, he says, even less convincingly, that those statements are false if "freedom" is understood as *indifferen-*

tia, because on this assumption what is necessary cannot be free. This artificial apology, trying to convert a statement into something it clearly is not, anticipates Arnauld's distinction.

According to Augustine, "the will, i.e. freedom, is not opposed to necessity but to nature."[26] Indeed, whatever is in our power to do, is done freely; therefore free will is perfectly compatible with the action of efficient grace: it is grace which allows our will freely to will that and not this. And if the will wills something "with such a determination that it cannot will the opposite, necessarily, by the sheer fact that it is the will that wills, it has the [proper] power, and by the sheer fact that it has this power, it is free."[27]

And in the second volume we read: "as to the necessity of sinning propounded by Augustine, and the abrogated freedom of doing good, they are not opposed to the freedom of choice, because Augustine teaches that both are in the same men."[28] The doctrine implying that freedom of the will consists in an indifference towards good and evil is a concoction of pagan philosophers. There is no ambiguity on this point: in doing both good and evil people are under necessity, they obey their *captivum arbitrium*, the will in bondage; in doing good they are "necessitated" by God's grace, in doing evil by their own depraved nature; they are nevertheless rightly praised or blamed because in both cases they do what they actually *will*, therefore they are not under compulsion. It seems that the condemned statement renders quite accurately the meaning of Jansenius and Augustine.

Arnauld's reply, as in other cases, makes a distinction between two senses of the proposition under scrutiny. Jansenius's critics suggest that according to him there is no necessity that can oppose freedom; it is indeed Augustinian doctrine that necessity rooted in the will does not deprive human acts of their merits or guilt, but Jansenius's critics read into his words the false—and Calvinist—claim that natural necessity, independent of human will, is compatible with freedom and makes human acts worthy of blame or reward. In reality both Augustine and Jansenius have in mind acts that are rational and caused by the will, and not irrational and natural ones in which our will takes no part.[29]

Arnauld is thus ready to admit that it is indeed false to say that we are free in acts performed mechanically as the result of natural reflexes. Then he can in good conscience declare that neither Augustine nor Jansenius or any of his fellow-Augustinians have ever defended this theory. His bad faith consists in suggesting that this was precisely the meaning intended by the papal constitution and that what the pope wanted to condemn was a silly idea, irrelevant to the theological squabbles of the time (or to any theological problems in the past). His distinction was cleverly devised insofar as it provided the Jansenists with a simple way out: to reject the condemned proposition. But he surely could not have been unaware of the pope's real target: the true meaning of Jansenius and Augustine. In the context of the debates of the mid-seventeenth century, Arnauld's explanation of the pope's intention is absurd, no less absurd than if the pope had suddenly decided solemnly to declare heretical the statement that two plus two is seven, a condemnation with which all the Augustinians would eagerly concur.

Again, Jurieu is right in his examination of the controversy: the Jansenists widen the meaning of the disputed doctrine by including in "necessity" (which does not abolish freedom) the involuntary movements that result from the blind forces of nature; and while they declare themselves ready to condemn this doctrine, they slanderously attribute it to the Calvinists, which amounts to saying that in the Calvinists' opinion dogs, horses, and stars are free. According to Jansenist theology, Jurieu says (rightly), the human soul is never in a state of indifference but is irresistibly attracted by good or evil; this necessity is compatible with freedom, otherwise the will would never be free.[30] Jurieu does not say clearly where he stands with regard to this (undeniably Augustinian) doctrine, but presumably he accepts it.

Father Annatus, in his analysis of the question, rejects the suggestion that the bull referred to the "sensus alienus" (i.e., the statement that merit or guilt is compatible with "natural necessity" as in involuntary movements or in the case of babies and madmen) and prefers the genuine Catholic solution: what is required for earning or losing merit is "freedom from any necessity that abolishes the ability of acting or not acting,"[31] in other words "indifferentia," the real possibility of assenting or dissenting. As in the previous, and the next, point of his exposition, Annatus, unlike Arnauld, does not evade the issue or try to make the Jesuit standpoint equivocal, but presents it clearly.

Can We Reject God?

The fourth proposition: "the semi-Pelagians admitted the necessity of prevenient internal grace for all particular acts including the beginning of faith; and they were heretics because they wanted this grace to be such that the human will could resist or obey it."

In other words, it is heretical to assume that it is in our power to choose to accept or to reject grace. This is, of course, similar to the second proposition: again, efficient grace—the core of Jansenius's and the Jansenists' teaching—is at stake.

A concise remark of Augustine's, among the thousands quoted by Jansenius, practically settles the issue: in rewarding his human creatures God crowns his own gifts (*dona sua coronat Deus, non merita tua* . . .). While Adam before the Fall could not do without grace, he was capable of having merit by force of his own free will (*non sine gratia sed non per gratiam*).

After the Fall everything changed, and this, Jansenius says, is what semi-Pelagians refused to see. They made two basic errors. "The first was that in their opinion the beginning of faith, prayer, remorse [lit. "gemitus," groaning], desires, and so on come from us, that is from free decision. . . . The next was their view that perseverance in faith was not a gift of God's grace but a function of the human will. . . . Indeed, both faith and perseverance in faith were imputed by the Marsilians to our power in such a way that they were not God's gifts; nor was God's direction of our thinking and willing needed to have and to keep them."[32] The will to persist in faith hinged, in their view, on human choice, not on grace. The Council of Orange (A.D. 529) clearly condemned the Marsilian heresy.

In the first volume of his work Jansenius is no less explicit: it is the opinion of mundane philosophers that one can attain the blessed life by virtue of one's own will, by natural means (as the Pelagians assert), or by law and doctrine (as the Jews would have it). Augustine teaches us unceasingly that even the soundest nature, let alone the corrupted one, needs divine help to prevent it from sinning, just as light is needed for seeing, even with the best eyes.

The Marsilians are ready to accept grace as a necessary condition (*sine qua non*) but not as a sufficient one (*gratia qua*). "Free choice suffices for doing evil, but it is powerless to do good [*ad bonum autem nihil est*] unless aided by almighty good." This is true not only after but before the Fall as well.[33]

In another passage the same idea is explained in more detail. God did not condemn anybody "until after he had seen, by his fore-knowledge, that [this man] would depart from justice." He wanted to save all, and he gave them for this purpose not only free will but good will, charity, and help in perseverance; perseverance was then under the control of the human will, and nobody was "efficaciter" predestined to reward or punishment. After the Fall, in spite of what "recentiores" maintain, this kind of divinely established equality (*aequabilitas erga omnes et singulos*) does not operate; God no longer wills to save all. The Marsilians, however, believe in a continuing divine "general will" and imagine that there is "no pre-destination of the elect except on the basis of the prevision of future events." But predestination, Jansenius explains, is gratuitous, for it comes before human acts or will are foreseen, and it is those acts and will which are caused by the infallibly working aid, *adiutorium efficax*.[34]

Arnauld, in analyzing the fourth anathematized statement, does not add much to his previous remarks on the irresistibility of grace. The statement as it stands is ambiguous, he says: if "preve-nient grace" is no more than the common "internal light" that pre-cedes human acts, the semi-Pelagians did accept it as a condition of every particular good work, including the first "movement of faith," but they rejected the grace which Augustine speaks of; the grace given by mercy and setting the will in motion. Their doctrine was heretical not because it implied that the human will can resist or obey grace—for it is self-evident that both are possible—but be-cause they alleged that the human will can foil God's will and make it void, or make it efficient by obedience, whereby grace becomes a tool to be used by the human will, the latter being the main cause of merit.[35]

Jurieu denies any ambiguity in the fourth proposition and, for all of Arnauld's *distinguos*, he appears to be right.[36]

Indeed, it is clear that, according to Arnauld, the semi-Pelagian heresy consisted in the rejection of irresistible grace, and it is no less obvious that this is what Jansenius's condemned state-ment attributes to the Pelagians. If it is heretical to say that it is heretical to reject irresistible grace, then the conclusion seems to be compelling: to believe in irresistible grace is a heresy according to the magisterium. But to Arnauld irresistible (efficient) grace is the gist of Augustinian teaching and of the perfectly established tradition of the Church. He therefore pretends that what the bull intends is to anathematize the claim that human nature never rebels against God's will. This, however, is a contention never made either by the advocates of the most extreme version of double predestination or by the most consistent Pelagians; it is indeed absurd in Christian terms, and Arnauld may safely assert that Jansenius and his disciples were never guilty of professing this theory. Human rebelliousness has been depicted and deplored time and again by all Christian writers; did not Augustine call our attention to the fact that the sway of the devil can be seen even in newborn babies who kick and cry and scream whey they are being baptized? What the argument was about was not whether or not there is in us a potential to revolt against God but whether or not we can do this successfully, so that God's will, manifested in his grace, can be frustrated by human resistance. That it cannot, and that grace works infallibly—within God's purpose—was undeniably the claim made by Augustine, Jansenius, and Arnauld. And this claim was declared heretical. Augustine's theology was condemned by the Church.

Annatus, in commenting on the fourth proposition, points out again that the sense genuinely targeted by the bull is: free will cannot *will* dissent from grace, whereas it can according to the Catholic faith. And the semi-Pelagians were not heretics because of their belief that grace leaves intact the free will's ability to dissent.[37] Characteristically, the Molinist apologist does not ask, as one would expect him to in this context, why then were the semi-Pelagians declared heretics? He noticed, no doubt, that, on this point at least, he was unable to define the difference between the "Marsilians" and the Jesuit theologians.

The Jansenists most vehemently denied the standard accusation of Jesuits that the Jansenist doctrine of grace had affinities with the Calvinist heresy. The most important distinction was supposed to consist in that, according to Augustine and Jansenius, the entirely gratuitous grace which justifies some by mercy, despite their crimes, and is refused to others by justice, operates after the Fall. Earlier on, when Adam could freely turn himself to good or evil, God separated the sheep from the goats conformably to his foreknowledge of their future behavior; whereas Calvin contends that this decision was made eternally, before the world was brought into existence. This might, however, be a distinction without a difference, considering that in the Jansenist view, if we take it literally, God must have *changed his mind* as a result of human sin, which he cannot do in any variety of Christian theology, and eminently not in the splendid chapter on time in Augustine's *Confessions*. God is timeless, and it is conceptually impossible that he at a certain moment should have decided about the future fate of people according to his foreknowledge of their conduct and later on, when the human race had so ungratefully requited his magnanimity, adopted other criteria of choice; for he knew everything in advance. If the Calvinist theory of grace is valid for mankind after original sin—and it *is* thus valid in the Jansenist faith (not that they could have ever admitted it, of course)—divine verdicts about the salvation or damnation of all individuals must have been ready eternally, that is, in human terms, before the Fall; otherwise we would have to assume that the disobedience of the ancestral couple surprised God and that he felt compelled, as a result of this unexpected event, to alter his plans. If indeed, after the Fall, God saved some people not because of their merits (nobody has any) but by imputing to them good deeds of which he himself is the only author (grace cannot be frustrated; people do *their* will, certainly, but as previously and infallibly shaped by God), the decision about the distribution of his gifts could not wait for the result of testing; there is no "before" and "after" in divine life.

For Whom Did Jesus Die?

The fifth proposition seems to be logically independent from the remaining four but it is the expression of the same doctrine of predestination. It reads: "it is semi-Pelagian to say that Christ died or shed his blood for all men in general." The *censura* which ends the bull adds the following clause to this statement: to say so is "false, insolent, scandalous, and if it is intended to mean that Christ died only for the salvation of the predestined [and what else could it mean?], it is impious, blasphemous, insulting, detrimental to divine piety, and heretical."

24

To be sure, everybody knew the seemingly unambiguous words of Paul: Christ "dedit redemptionem semetipsum pro omnibus" (2 Tim. 2:5): God wants to save all people (ibid. 2:4), God is the God not only of the Jews but of the heathens as well (Rom. 3:29), etc. But it turned out, as in many other cases, that what seems unambiguous in the canonical text may, by skilful exegesis, be made ambiguous and then unambiguous again but in a sense opposite to what it seemed to mean at first glance. (To be fair, one may add that some support, though not unambiguous, for the Augustinian position, could be found in John 17:9.)

It is very wrong, Jansenius says, to infer from Paul's words, as the Marsilians and the Jesuit Lessius do, that God gave all people "aid whereby they can be liberated"; they attribute to God a general will of salvation, indifferently applied to all men and resulting in "sufficient grace" for everybody so that people can make it fruitful or void by their own choice: "they destroy the entire efficiency of predestination and of divine decision." That Christ died for all means that the value of his sacrifice is sufficient to save all, but not that it works efficiently for all; therefore redemption does not apply to everybody. And Prosper states that "it may be said that he was crucified only for those who benefit from his death. . . . Christ is said to have brought redemption to all, that is to his entire Church scattered all over the world—to people of all tribes, tongues, and estates."

"The entire world is the Church and the entire world hates the Church. And so the world hates the world." Indeed, the world in the first sense is all the faithful. "Christ died for his faithful, for his sheep, for the salvation of his people" and not for infidels, even though his sacrifice was good enough to save all people and even demons. To those for whom he died he gave sufficient aid for them not only to be able to do what they ought to but actually to will it and to do it. It was for those people, predestined and elected, that he prayed to his Father, and not for those who were to die in injustice. The elect can be called "the entire world" because they live all over the earth. Only divine, and not human, will can cause people to accept grace.[38]

And so, conformably to Jansenius's interpretation, one may safely say that it is perfectly true that Christ died for all, since that is what the Scriptures explicitly assert, and it is no less obvious what this saying means, to wit, that Christ did not die for all.

Arnauld's apology adds little to these arguments; he says that even though no Christian may doubt that Christ died for all, the expression "all men" does not mean "all individuals without exception," as the Pelagians would have it. The Savior certainly did not want to save babies who died unbaptized, and the synod in Valence condemned the heresy of those who claimed that Christ died for all, including all who had been damned before his coming; he died exclusively for those who were to attain eternal bliss.[39]

Jurieu has no doubt about the issue. He confirms that, according to Jansenius, Christ did not die or pray for all, not even for "les justes temporels" (i.e., people who are able to perform some good acts but are not among the predestined and who, Jurieu assures us, will suffer particularly horrible punishment in hell, since they have made the wrong use of their justice, which in any case was not a real, i.e., justifying, virtue). Copious quotations from Augustine confirm his view that those who are justified were chosen by God eternally; God indeed wants to save all people but this means all those whom he predestined to glory. For the fifth time the Church condemned Augustinian theology.[40]

Annatus, too, makes the point very clear: far from being semi-Pelagian, it is truly Catholic to say that Jesus by his death conferred his grace on all people without exception and gave to all sufficient means for salvation. He does not mention, as in the previous case and probably for the same reason, how to define the difference between the Catholic (Jesuit) and semi-Pelagian view on this point. Jansenius's doctrine, in the very words of the heresiarch, states that Jesus thought no more of the salvation of anyone rejected than of the salvation of the devil.[41]

The Jansenists took comfort in the pope's answer to their delegation in Rome; they asked him to confirm that Augustine's teaching on efficient grace had not been affected by the bull, to which the pontiff replied "O, questo è certo."[42] This, however, meant little or nothing. No pope, at any time, could ever have admitted aloud that he had made Augustine the author of a heresy, even if, as in this case, this was precisely what he had just done. His denial could have been very useful and was quoted more than once in Jansenist polemical writings, but it was not enough to obscure the basic theological controversy.

Annatus suggests another, no more plausible interpretation:

the pope's saying implied that he had condemned the five propositions in the sense of Jansenius, not of Augustine, as was in fact the
case, because Augustine was indeed innocent of the heresy.[43] And
Jurieu remarks maliciously that the pope, who listened to long debates by theologians on the Jansenist errors, "understood of them
as little as if they had spoken to him in Arabic" and probably did not
even know the meaning of the propositions he reproved; indeed, he
adds, knowledge of canon law, not of theology, is what matters in
Rome.[44]

The Jansenists' tactic appears, with hindsight, the best devised or even the only possible one if they were to remain in the
Church. Had they opposed the papal condemnation, e.g., by appealing to an ecumenical council (as did some churchmen defending Quesnel after *Unigenitus*), they would probably have brought
upon themselves excommunication, thus reducing themselves to
an impotent sect, not to speak of the fact that they would have had
to wait for over two centuries for such a council to be convoked and
that the result, the dogma of papal infallibility, would in any case
not have been favorable to their cause. To avoid this fate they had to
accept the bull and to alter its meaning in such a manner that the
ostensible sense miraculously evaporated and what remained was
easy to condemn because—as they kept repeating—nobody defended such heresy. Once Arnauld contrived this shrewd maneuver,
everybody who for any reason sympathized with the persecuted Augustinians or simply disliked the Jesuits could happily repeat the
same remonstrance without any analysis of the contested doctrine
and without confronting it with the text of the censure; it simply
became a commonplace that "nobody every upheld the five propositions" and that the alleged heresy was a Jesuit invention. From
Racine[45] to Saint Simon[46] to Gazier[47] this was a standard line of
defense. Nicole even managed to write a book of over nine hundred
pages on the "imaginary heresy" of Jansenism without at any point
discussing this crucial issue.[48]

The Jesuits knew better; the pope did condemn the genuine
doctrine of Jansenius and this doctrine was virtually identical with
Calvin's. They were as right on this point as were the Jansenists in
saying that Jansenius had been a faithful follower of Augustine.

Bossuet simply remarked (rightly) that one should not ask
where the five propositions are to be found in *Augustinus* but rather

where they are not;[49] they are the soul of the book. It is worth mentioning that Voltaire, who was not noted for his pro-Jesuit bias, had no doubt that the heretical statements faithfully reproduced Jansenius's theology; the whole quarrel was to him, of course, like all theological quarrels, just a matter of ridicule, the meaningless squabbling of fanatics, but he was fair enough to blame both parties.[50] Sainte-Beuve, while reluctant to discuss theological issues, could not quite avoid this one in his voluminous history of Port-Royal. He mentions the problem briefly and recognizes that the five propositions "in a certain sense" are to be found in the incriminated work.[51]

Although the Jansenists probably had no other tactical option, they seemed to have made a laughing stock of the pontiff; it looked as if he had just invented a nonexistent heresy and fulminated noisily against some obviously absurd sentences which nobody had ever uttered.

While at the very beginning the Jansenists had tried to argue, indefensibly, that Jansenius was not the real target of the bull, they soon had to face the sad fact that the Holy Father condemned statements which, he claimed, were taken from Jansenius's work. They arrived at a salutary solution: the pope had been misled by Jesuits, who had made him believe that the heretical statements were extracted from the *Augustinus*. But the pope, being infallible in doctrinal issues, may be wrong in matter-of-fact questions such as whether or not a particular sentence is to be found in a particular book. This distinction between a question "de droit" and a question "de fait" was not invented by the Jansenists, just skilfully employed by them (Nicole apparently was the first to come up with this ingenious idea); they made it famous and it was to keep the Gallican Church busy for decades to come, and indeed to spark off the most abominable persecutions against Port-Royal. The anti-Jansenist party tried to blur the distinction—commonsensical as it might have seemed—and, lo, they succeeded! After three years of further intrigues and efforts, the new pope, Alexander VII, renewed the condemnation and fused *quaestio iuris* and *quaestio facti* into one, making their separation practically impossible. The new constitution, dated 16 October 1656, apart from confirming the bull of Innocent X, clearly stated that the propositions had been taken from the *Augustinus* and condemned in the sense intended by the author.[52]

The next years in the French kingdom were to be devoted to passionate quarrels about the "formulaire," a kind of anti-Jansenist oath which became obligatory for the clergy and nuns. It was imposed by the pope at the request of the king, and all the signatories had to declare "sincero animo" and swear by God not only that they condemned the nefarious propositions but in addition that those propositions had been taken from the *Augustinus* and their meaning had been thus intended by the author. We may leave aside the long and very complicated story of the formulaire, which became the main weapon whereby the Jansenist "sect" was to be destroyed. In vain the Port-Royal nuns argued that they had no theological training and had not read the book (no copy existed in the library of the monastery and, as Mother Angélique testified, their *directeurs* did not even allow them to read Arnauld's *Frequent Communion* because it was a matter of contention),[53] that many of them did not even know Latin, that they were ready to be obedient and to subscribe to all the doctrinal verdicts of the Church, but that matter-of-fact questions were beyond their competence. The Holy See and the king were inflexible.[54] And, as Pascal noticed in his remarks on the formulaire, "there is no difference between condemning Jansenius's doctrine on the five propositions and condemning efficient grace, Saint Augustine, and Saint Paul."[55]

Annatus, in his first anti-Jansenist book, made a daring, one may say heroic, attempt to demonstrate that the doctrine under attack had nothing to do with Augustine's theology. His arguments, however, display bad faith. According to Augustine the will is free by the very fact that it is a will and, by definition, if there is a *volitio*, its object must be in our power. Therefore, Annatus concludes, Augustine accepts freedom of choice in the sense of *indifferentia*: what is in our power can happen or not happen according to what our will decides.[56] This is clearly an abuse: the moot point was not whether there is such a thing as an act of will (Augustine never denied this, nor did Jansenius) but whether the will, involving a choice between good and evil, is or is not determined infallibly by God if it opts for the good. That it is so determined is Augustinian doctrine, which Annatus simply sets aside and makes the obviously wrong conclusion about "indifferentia" from the truncated presentation of Augustine's view. Augustine does not say, he adds, that divine foreknowledge abolishes freedom and is the cause of human sin,[57] this is true, but Jansenius does not say so either—that God might be the cause of sin was not the matter of contention, the point was whether or not good acts are caused by God (by the intermediary of the human will). Augustine says, "God foreknows that of which he is the author but he is not the author of everything he foreknows, and of what he is not the author, he is the just avenger."[58] This is true enough, but it does not support Annatus's apology; on the contrary, God is *iustus ultor* of that which he is not the author, because our sins are imputed to us; but he is the author of our good deeds. Throughout his book Annatus quotes Augustine saying that we are the authors of our sins and avoids the main issue: the irresistibility of grace. And he asserts that, according to Augustine, God gave man free will so that he could have merits of his own, not by necessity;[59] true again, but this applied to the status of man before the Fall and Annatus simply fails to inform his reader of what happened next: the loss of free will in this sense. It needs recalling that Augustine's early treatise on free will was subsequently corrected and explained in his *Retractationes* and that it is an abuse to quote it without restrictions. It appears, however, that this extraordinary attempt to convert Augustine into a semi-Pelagian and a defender of "indifferentia" was a rarity among Jesuits.

It has just been argued that both the popes and the Jesuits (and the Calvinists) were right in the matter-of-fact questions: the five propositions quite accurately summed up the sense of *Augustinus*; the Jansenists were right in their claim that *Augustinus* was perfectly faithful to its title.

What Was Wrong with Augustine?

Why did the Church condemn Augustine? As in most similar cases we can always argue that a series of accidents was at work: if Jansenius had died before the completion of his work . . . if the Jesuits had managed to prevent publication . . . if the pope had been more scrupulous in theological matters . . . if the king had been more cautious about the Jesuits' warning that his realm was threatened by a new sinister sect . . . if Paul V had published the virtually completed anti-Molinist constitution . . . etc.[60] The history of ideas is no less an infinite collection of unpredictable accidents than is political history. Still, we always try to employ our ingenuity to reveal a sort of "logic" in the sequence of events, and only enlightened by this "logic" do we boast of being able to grasp the meaning of events (or to impose meaning on them). There was no "historical necessity" in the fact that the papal bull was in fact issued in 1653, but there were powerful reasons why the Roman Church needed, in order to keep its might, to get rid of the Augustinian legacy. Jansenius unwittingly provided historical opportunity for the Church to "de-Augustinize" itself. It was a momentous event in the history of the Church when it exploited this occasion, adopting practically the Jesuit (or semi-Pelagian) doctrine in the crucial questions of original sin, grace and predestination, and thereby breaking—tacitly, needless to say—with a very important part of its theological heritage and shaping its teaching accordingly. Proviso being made for the notorious fragility of counter-factuals, one could even imagine that if the Church had (almost *per impossibile*) then adopted the Augustinian-Jansenist theology as the basis of its educational work, it would have embarked on the road to self-destruction.

Augustine not only codified the orthodox (since then) doctrine of original sin and divine grace but to a large extent created it. That the disobedience of the first man corrupted our nature, making us easy prey for all sorts of diabolic temptations and even bringing death into the world, was fairly clearly stated in the Scriptures. But that we, by the sheer fact of being Adam's descendants, contracted his actual *sin*, and not only the propensity to sin, was less obvious and its scriptural foundation was later on found to be faulty. Biblical scholars have known for a long time that the Vulgate mistranslated the celebrated Pauline expression "in quo omnes peccaverunt" (Rom. 5:12), thus suggesting that Adam was a kind of universal and that we are not simply his offspring but, in moral terms, his replicas, that we participate actively in his guilt; modern translations render this text not "in whom as all men sinned" but rather "inasmuch as all men sinned."

The early Greek fathers, unlike Augustine, did not need to cope with this problem and perhaps for this reason failed to elaborate a similar doctrine.

The doctrine of hereditary guilt, or of our unavoidable participation in the actual sin of Adam, is important insofar as it helps explain why all those damned by God are damned justly.

Let us sum up briefly the main components of the Augustinian-Jansenist theory of grace. First, we are, all of us, so hopelessly corrupted that we are absolutely incapable of doing anything good by our own forces; free choice, if it means a choice between good and evil, has been utterly wasted by sin; our will, insofar as it is ours, and not God's, can merely do evil and desire evil.

Second, divine grace is not only necessary to enable us to do good and to obey divine law, but, when it is given, it achieves its end infallibly. In other words, if God wants us to do good, we cannot successfully foil his will, for his will shapes human will and thus compels it to obey the orders. It is preferable, however, to speak not of "compelling" but of "necessitating" the will, because once the human will is thus molded by God, it really does will what God wishes it to will. Grace is therefore both a necessary and a sufficient condition of whatever good we seem to be capable of; efficient grace and irresistible grace are one and the same. This point has to be listed separately, as from the first principle we cannot yet deduce that it is impossible effectively to resist the operation of grace.

Third—and this seems to be logically implied by the two statements just quoted but needs to be made explicit—salutary grace is given gratuitously and distributed by God among human creatures according to his inscrutable will. After the Fall we contribute literally nothing to our salvation in terms of divine justice; we all deserve eternal damnation. If God wishes to save some of us, this is not because of our merits—nobody has any and nobody can deserve grace—but simply because he so wishes. Double predestination is just by definition, as whatever God does is just; there is no rule of justice other than his will. The saved are justified by mercy, the reproved are damned by justice.

Fourth—again this seems, if not logically compelling, at least a natural corollary of the former doctrines—Jesus Christ could not possibly have died for all men; he knew who would be damned and who saved and it is unthinkable that he should deliberately have shed his blood in vain or sacrificed himself for hell-dwellers-to-be.[61]

The arbitrary distribution of grace does not imply that the

elected are sinless or saints throughout their life; grace can be temporarily withdrawn to humiliate the just and show them the wretchedness of their nature when not aided by God. The damned, conversely, can occasionally display their ostensible virtues, but these will count for nothing on the day of judgment and will have no meritorious value. Those to whom God decides to refuse his help are simply left as they are, thrown back upon the resources of their depraved nature. Occasionally God might deliberately influence their will: just as Peter's denial was the paradigm of God's temporally withdrawing his help to the just, so God's "hardening the heart" of Pharaoh was a paradigm of the way he positively reinforced human obduracy in evil.

We have been talking of the grace that effectively makes us worthy of salvation in God's eyes. Otherwise everything is an act of divine grace, as God cannot act on someone else's order or request. The very creation of the world was an act of grace; so is the natural light which enables us to perceive and to know nature; so is revelation, which is accessible to everyone; so is the particular help given to the damned which enables them to perform seemingly virtuous acts. Those aids of which all people can have their share provide the abundance of God's grace but they have no meaning in terms of salvation; on the contrary, if God allows the unfaithful to gather some modest knowledge about himself—not real faith, to be sure—this is to deprive them of the plea of ignorance on the day of reckoning.[62] But the moot point was whether efficient grace carries salutary power.

To contemporary minds nourished on the tradition of the Enlightenment, the Augustinian doctrine appears no less bizarre than it did to the Pelagians of old, to Erasmus, to Erasmians, to Thomas More (in his anti-Lutheran treatise), or, for that matter, to Jesuit moralists. How indeed can we believe in a just and benevolent God who rewards and punishes his children according to his incalculable caprice, like a tyrant rather than a loving father? And how can he cast his children into the infernal abyss while knowing that their wrongdoings are performed under compulsion and that they cannot help what they do and what they are? Does not the very concept of sin imply that it is an avoidable act? The nefarious moral effects of the double predestination theory have been pointed out no less frequently: once people are taught that their salvation has

33

nothing to do with their conduct but depends solely on the Lord's unintelligible will, the whole point of moral education is hollow, and I may do whatever I please, since I know that God does not take my actions—right or wrong—into account; the very idea of moral responsibility becomes meaningless, except in the perverse sense that we are *morally* responsible for our remote ancestors, which makes a mockery of the rules of justice.

These standard strictures seem to be in keeping with common sense but they are, as it were, too easy to provide us with an insight into the theological, psychological, or social sense of the idea of double predestination.

What is at stake in theological terms is the *absolute sovereignty of God*. Of this the writings of Augustine, Calvin, and Jansenius leave no doubt. And sovereignty means not being bound by an external law. Pelagian or semi-Pelagian philosophy (and what is it but philosophy, a pagan contrivance designed to feed our *hubris?*) implies that we can, by properly ordering our conduct and forbearing from prohibited acts, become *worthy* of, or *deserve*, salvation, that is to say, we can *compel* God to save us; he simply has no other choice. If so, God is no longer sovereign; he is in duty bound to obey some rules, whether he wishes it or not. That he himself established those rules is no answer, especially in terms of the New Covenant. It is a symptom of sinful pride to blame God for being *unjust*, as if God's justice could be measured by our yardstick; what God does is just because he does it, and there is no higher standard of justice than divine will, no matter what its contents.

God's unlimited sovereignty does not run counter to his being the God of love. On the contrary, since the New Covenant abrogated Judaic law, we, as Christians, are under grace. This means that we must trust our Father and not bargain with him, not demand our due from him, not impudently make him accountable before a human court, not try to outsmart him.

The theory of double predestination is the theological expression of the Church that feels to be God's invincible *army*. The psychological message of this doctrine is not convenient permissiveness —"do whatever you wish, your conduct is irrelevant to your salvation,"—much as individuals might have employed this interpretation.[63] Both Augustine and Calvin erected clear barriers against this libertine exploitation of their theology: to be sure, God is not *paying* us for our merits, all the presumed merits are his gifts, but therefore those who enjoy undeserved grace show in their life that they verily are God's children; their virtuous conduct is not a *cause* of their salvation but rather its *symptom*.

A lot depends on the theologians' desire to be faithful to the principle of consistency. The simple saying "everything is in God's hands"—hardly contestable in Christian terms—might, when developed to its ultimate conclusion, imply the doctrine of double predestination. But it makes a difference whether the latter is explicitly stated or not. One may repeat, with conviction, the saying just quoted and believe in the freedom of the will, without being tormented by the feeling of one's own inconsistency. The situation is changed once the theology of predestination is unequivocally stated. Augustine did it, earlier fathers did not; Irenaeus might perhaps, anachronistically, be called a semi-Pelagian.[64]

Double predestination is a theological sword in the hands of a militant Church whose soldiers may rightly feel that they belong to the *assembly of the elect*. Certainly, in terms of Augustinian theology, the City of God is not identical with the visible Church, in which there might be, indeed there inevitably are, unworthy individuals, the future denizens of hell; only God will ultimately sort the wheat from the chaff. But to a faithful man of the Church the message of the doctrine is clear: *I am* among the privileged and I display in this life the signs of my being predestined to glory. Far from justifying passivity, indifference, or moral sloppiness, double predestination is well designed to encourage militancy. It is the ideology of a sect of warriors. It was thus in Augustine's time, as well as in the early Calvinist movement; fatalistic theology was, for early Islam, a source of belligerence and self-confidence; the Koranic message was not "do nothing because whatever is done is done by God" but rather "you are the instrument in God's hand, be brave, don't shun death; you are God's faithful son and remember always that whatever happens is God's will and must turn to the good." Later on, historical determinism had a similar function in the Communist movement; the intellectuals' argument, often employed in polemics by anti-Marxists, that "if everything is predetermined by historical necessity, why bother, better do nothing, history will take care of itself," was entirely out of touch with psychological reality. It was their very belief in the "victorious march of history," in which they were supposed to participate, that gave the believers a powerful mobilizing energy and the much-needed certainty of being on the right side. The apparent logic of inertia, *ignava ratio*, is contrary to the actual psychological impact of fatalistic and deterministic doctrines once they become the ideological expression of popular movements, and the Calvinists of the sixteenth and seventeenth centuries proved this no less than the Bolsheviks in our time.

This does not imply that the Church, as Augustine saw it, was supposed to be a tiny elite. It inherited the spirit of militant certainty from the time it had been an alien body among pagans, but in Augustine's day it was on its way to conquer the world. It was holy and spotless by its divine origin, not by the holiness of individuals. On the contrary, it was Pelagius who wanted the Church to be holy thanks to the Christian virtues of its members; it would thus have been reduced, had Pelagianism won, to a spiritual aristocracy, incapable of fulfilling its mission. His condemnation was therefore well justified; he might have deprived the Church of its institutionally guaranteed innocence. He strongly believed in personal responsibility, in human ability to avoid sin and evil by free choice; while he did not deny that God's help matters and that the gift of eternal salvation is ultimately his gift, he asserted in fact that a Christian is defined by his moral standards, not by baptism. And God's help consisted, in Pelagian terms, in the external means—revelation, commandments, examples—not Augustine's internal and infallible grace. This is obviously in keeping with Pelagius's denial of the inherited guilt.[65]

To be sure, the Church's prudence has always prevented it from talking about *double* predestination, such a doctrine having been in fact condemned on several occasions long before the Great Reformation, but it might be asked whether the distinction between single and double predestination was an empty one. The errors of Gottschalk provided an opportunity to phrase this distinction dogmatically, which the ninth-century Jansenius failed to make in his writings. The point is that after man had abused his free will and been reduced to *massa perditionis*, God chose from this mass, according to his prescience, those whom he, by grace, predestined for eternal life, and by the judgment of his justice, let the others perish; he had prescience of their sins but he did not predestine them to downfall (*ceteros autem quos iustitiae iudicio in massa per-*

ditionis reliquit, perituros praescivit, sed non ut perirent praedesti-navit).[66] Consequently there is only one predestination rather than two, and this predestination belongs either to the gift of grace or to the retribution of justice. The freedom of the will which we lost in Adam and regained thanks to Jesus Christ's sacrifice includes the freedom both to do good—preceded and aided by grace—and to do evil, when grace is missing (*et habemus liberum arbitrium ad bonum, praeventum et adiutum gratia, et habemus liberum arbitrium ad malum, desertum gratia*). God wants to save all people, as the apostle says, and whereas the salvation of the elect is God's gift, damnation falls deservedly on the damned. The canons of the Synod of Quiercy (A.D. 853) condemning Gottschalk's doctrine were apparently made dubious two years later at the Third Council of Valence, which stated that the elected are predestined to life and the impious to death (*fidenter fatemur praedestinationem electorum ad vitam, et praedestinationem impiorum ad mortem*),[67] divine mercy preceding the merits of the former, and condemnable evil preceding God's just judgment on the latter.

This confrontation of the Synod of Carisiacum with that of Valentinum III is perplexing and might suggest that whereas the distinction between Pelagian and Augustinian doctrine is clear enough, the one between single and double predestination is verbal rather than real. Indeed, conformably to the Augustinian legacy, God saves part of mankind by gratuitous mercy and casts whoever remains into the abyss by justice; he foresees, of course, the crimes of the latter no less than the merits of the former, except that the virtuous deeds of the elected are made *possible* (and presumably necessary as well) by grace, whereas the sinners' sins are their own, albeit necessary. If "predestination" is spoken of in the first case, this is for the following reason: while God *actively* helps those he has decided to take under his roof, and indeed has *caused* their "merits," he does *nothing* to aid the others and leaves them in their unreformed condition. Divine prescience makes no difference to the two categories of people, as obviously God does not need to wait impatiently for their respective conduct: he knows both. Thus his judgment and decision about the fate of both must have been taken eternally, and in this sense all people have been "predestined." Whether the expression "double predestination," which had been in existence since the seventh century (Isidore of Seville is credited with its coinage), is actually employed, is important for polemical rather than theological reasons. If the elected are *predestined* and the damned are not, this is because God has intervened in the life of the former, setting them straight and making them worthy of reward, whereas he has behaved passively towards the latter. Therefore, if we are to believe the dogmatic formulas, or the theologians' condemnation of "double predestination," what heretics seek to say is that God is the author not only of the salutary human acts but of the damnable ones as well; in other words he has actively *caused* the iniquities of the damned and *made* them offend him rather than simply staying idle. That God is the efficient rather than only the "deficient" cause of human sins is indeed neither Augustine's nor Jansenius's teaching. But neither is it the doctrine of Calvin. If it was preached by some later Calvinist theologians (like the Gomarists), it was not the official tenet of the Reformed faith and was in fact rebuked at the Synod of Dordrecht in 1618; in the annals of Christian theology it was a marginal extravagance. Therefore the distinction between "single predestination" in the Augustinian sense and the "double predestination" of the Calvinists is artificial.

However, libertine and occasionally "liberal" (i.e., semi-Pelagian) criticism cast doubt on the distinction from the opposite standpoint. The gist of this critique may be summed up simply as follows. Assuming that people are so congenitally corrupted that it is altogether beyond their capacity to perform any good acts, the distinction between efficient and merely "permissive" divine causality is dubious and precarious; since God wants to save all, as Scripture testifies, and since, of course, he has the power to do this, it is inconceivable that he should lend his hand to some and not to others, all people being in exactly the same situation in the relevant respects. If I see two people drowning and I can rescue both easily, with no risk to myself and no effort, I become guilty if I rescue one and let the other perish for no reason except my sheer wish; God, if he acted this way, would—according to this criticism—be a capricious tyrant and would bear responsibility, by omission, for the eternal death of sinners.

Again, the Augustinians do not need to be troubled by these arguments because the critics assume that God has *moral* duties towards his creatures, whereas in fact he has none; he simply *owes nothing to anybody*, he is not bound by human rules concerning reciprocity, debts and claims; no one may rightfully say "Lord, it is your obligation to give me this or that." The libertine murmur amounts to blaming God for not submitting himself to the requirements of human justice, i.e., for not surrendering his sovereignty. That he is the God of love does not mean that you or I personally *deserve* his love; none of us deserve it, quite the contrary, and if it is given to some, this is the Creator's gratuitous generosity; by justice alone we would all perish in infernal darkness. And one may argue that it would be absurd to say that love can be distributed according to justice; it cannot, by definition.[68]

The Pelagian doctrine had no significant support in the medieval Church; the Augustinian teaching on grace persisted as the highest authority and to some extent made its way into liturgy ("Rex tremendae maiestatis—Qui salvandos salvas gratis—Salva me, fons pietatis," we read in the *Dies irae*). When Saint Bernard says that, for salvation to occur, both grace (*quo fit*) and human free will (*in quo fit*), which gives consent, are necessary, this seems compatible with the Pelagian concept of freedom; but it is no longer so when he explains, a few pages later, that the pure act of willing comes from *liberum arbitrium*, whereas an act of willing the good is the work of grace. Thus the Augustinian doctrine is reasserted.[69]

Thomist theology, as has been mentioned, seems to leave some room for the free will to "cooperate" with grace, whereas this is rigidly excluded in Augustinian terms, and does not imply that whatever good there had been in human nature was utterly exterminated by original sin. Perhaps the difference is less fundamental than it appears, apart from the obvious difference in style.

Original sin, Aquinas says, which is inherited equally by all human creatures,[70] completely destroyed the original justice in us, but the inclination to virtue and the goodness of rational nature, albeit diminished, have not totally disappeared; they persist even in the damned.[71] It is true, however, both that the predestination whereby some are called to salvation has been eternally decided by God only and is merely "passively" in the elect,[72] and that God is the cause of the good which the elected are capable of, whereas those whom God has rejected are victims of their own guilt.[73] Divine foreknowledge of human merits is not the cause of predestination but the other way around: it is grace, resulting from predestination, that causes the merits. There is no other reason for election but the sheer will of God, even though it is true that God permits some evil in the world in order to make it more differentiated; evil contributes to the beauty of the whole. No injustice may be imputed to God on this account, since grace by definition is given gratuitously and never merited or due to anybody.[74] The end of predestination is attained infallibly, but free will is not abrogated, because it is through the will that predestination secures its objective in rational creatures. Whoever is predestined cannot die in mortal sin.[75] Neither does predestination make our prayers useless: they are included in advance by the economy of salvation, among its secondary causes.[76]

There are two crucial questions on which Aquinas is ambiguous: whether we are able to do anything good and avoid sinning by natural forces alone, and whether we can successfully resist God's grace and thus frustrate his aim. In the same article he quotes with approval Augustine's words that "men do absolutely nothing good without grace, whether by thought, will, love or deed," and then avers that some natural good has remained in corrupted human nature, and that people, although unable to attain the entire good in conformity with their nature, can nevertheless do some particular good acts. This sounds anti-Augustinian, no doubt. But his examples of good acts that we can do without grace are building houses and growing vines, i.e., acts that do not necessarily involve a moral choice between good and evil.[77] Then we are taught that after the Fall we are not capable, without grace, of loving God above all things and of fulfilling the divine commandments, let alone of meriting eternal life.[78] Without grace we cannot prepare ourselves for grace, i.e., turn to God.[79] Can we avoid sins without grace? It turns out that we are able to avoid the mortal sins but not all the venial ones; we do not necessarily sin all the time but our corruption prevents us from abstaining from all sin.

On "cooperative grace" Aquinas makes the distinction between operations in which God is the sole mover and those in which the human will acts as mover as well; in such acts the will is aided by God, who gives it strength, but this seems to imply that free will is nevertheless itself active in the same direction that God wills it to act. But then we read: "God does not justify us without ourselves, since when we are justified we consent to his justice by a movement of our free will. This movement, however, is not the cause of grace but the result of it. The whole operation is therefore due to grace."[80] Further, we are told that "God moves each thing according to its own manner . . . and it is proper to the nature of man that his will should be free. Consequently, when a man has the use of his free will, God never moves him to justice without the use of his free will. With all who are capable of being so moved, God infuses the gift of justifying grace in such ways that he also moves the free will to accept it."[81]

The preparation for the gift of grace is no less God's work than the actual gift: "even the good action of his free will, by which he is made ready to receive the gift of grace, is an action of his free will as moved by God." And this preparation operates infallibly because God's intention cannot be foiled.[82]

In the third book of *Contra Gentiles* we find similar ideas, sometimes elaborated in more detail. "Gratia gratum faciens" cannot, by definition, be deserved; election depends on the sheer will of God (*simplex voluntas*) and it does not behoove us to ask about its reason. This grace is necessary to persevere in virtue, as perseverance is beyond the power of free will; without grace we cannot love God properly or raise ourselves from sin. The "stupid opinion of the Pelagians," according to which man can avoid sin without grace, is refuted.[83] Divine providence does not abrogate contingency, because God's immense goodness consists among other things in his communication of his similitude to his creatures,[84] and it is proper that in rational beings he acts through their free will (*agens autem voluntarium assequitur divinam similitudinem in hoc quod libere agit*).[85] The preparation of the soul for divine aid itself comes from God's power.[86] It is grace which creates in us our love of God, and faith and hope for future bliss.[87] All this could have been said by Jansenius. But one point remains dubious. Aquinas says that while nobody's free will can bring grace, one can hinder oneself from receiving it; our failure of conversion to God is therefore rightly imputed to us because it is within the power of free will to obstruct or not to obstruct the reception of grace.[88] This strongly suggests that there is no irresistible grace which always works efficiently; at least on this occasion Thomas fails to restrict his explanation by saying that the very act of accepting aid has to be preceded by another preparatory aid, and that for want of this support rejection is inevitable, although still attributable to the sinner, like all his other misdeeds. If this is so, his doctrine on this point would not only be glaringly anti-Augustinian but it would run counter to the reservations just mentioned that are imposed on the concept of free will. It seems untenable, if the premises remain valid, to maintain that God's grace operates infallibly (to deny this would contradict his omnipotence) and that no good human acts—admittedly performed through free will—are possible without prevenient grace. Indeed, if it is in my exclusive power to accept divine help or to refuse it, and if therefore grace does not work irresistibly, then we may speak of positive human "cooperation" in the economy of salvation and not only of God's purposes being effected by the intermediary of the human will, which then to call "free" seems an abuse of the term.

It is thus understandable that both Jansenists and Jesuits could plausibly quote Aquinas to prop up their respective and mutually contradictory "soteriologies" with his authority. If, however, we prefer to clear the Angelic Doctor of the charge of self-contradiction, we must assume that he was—on this point, although not on many others—a genuine Augustinian after all, and that he simply chose not to repeat, when discussing the irresistibility of grace, his previous reservations to the effect that "free will," if it opts for virtue rather than sin (for the reception of grace, in this case) is itself informed by grace. The anti-Molinist instinct displayed by the Dominicans, the most exacting guardians of the Thomist legacy, seems to bear out this assumption.

We shall see that an analogous ambiguity can be spotted in the decrees of the Council of Trent.

A digression. The belief that everything is preordained by God is psychologically compatible with the belief that I am free in my actions. Personal freedom is an irresistible and elementary experience; it is not analyzable any further because of its elementary character. The former belief acts as a source of trust in life: God rules and orders everything, thus everything is directed toward a good outcome, even if we cannot know or see the cunning tactics of providence. This psychological compatibility proves doubtful when exposed to theological scrutiny, and the task is then to make a coherent, logically sound whole out of the two experiences (an analogous difficulty can be detected in the stoic moralists of old:

42

"my" unlimited freedom confronted with the universal rule of fate). An example. One of the most frequently quoted Old Testament verses, especially in Protestant countries, was the beginning of Psalm 127: "Except the Lord build the house, they labor in vain that build it"; the verse often adorned houses. Yet the builder knew that it was he who actually had built the house, that he had not sat idly, praying and waiting for God to do the job for him. Can he still believe that it was God, not he, who was the builder? Yes, he can, not only in the sense that God contributed to the work by omission, e.g., he refrained from ruining the construction by a natural disaster, but that he actually performed the task using the worker as his instrument; and the worker felt, at the same time, that he had not lost his freedom of action. It is too easy to say that the worker is simply mentally inept or a victim of "cognitive dissonance." The most elementary facts of experience—"I," existence, freedom— once converted into theoretical concepts, tend to resist logical examination and are therefore threatened with a verdict of theoretical annihilation; indeed, they have on many occasions been denounced as figments of the imagination. Still, they do not vanish from experience; they stubbornly refuse to evaporate, all philosophers' condemnations notwithstanding. To accept all-embracing providence without denying the irresistible experience of freedom is psychologically possible even for people who cannot be accused of having simply failed to learn their first lesson in logic; they do not necessarily feel mental discomfort because they believe in, or experience, both. But to unite both in a consistent "theory" seems hopeless, and when theologians ultimately admit that there is a "mystery" in combining providence and freedom, they do not claim to explain anything, but accept the inadequacy of "human reason." Rationalists normally shrug off the idea of "mystery" (as distinct from something not yet known) as a verbal cover for simple illogicality. However, when people think of ultimate realities, the experience of mystery, which often includes a logical helplessness, may be intellectually more fruitful than rationalist self-confidence that simply cancels metaphysical questions, relying on doctrinal dogmas. To be sure, we have only one logic at our disposal but we are not sure how far its validity can extend when dealing with those ultimate realities. We are often tempted to repeat the famous Augustinian remark on time: "I understand when you don't ask, but when I am asked, I do not know."

Nicole tried to cope with this question; to him we (e.g., the builder of a house) act as secondary causes. He argues that to neglect our duties on the pretext that God will do everything for us amounts to tempting the Lord. "Only God knows all the reasons why He conceals his operations under a certain order of causes that seem quite natural. We know but few of them. He cures men of their laziness, He forces them to work and to be watchful. He provides them with occupation and exercise; He punishes them by this laborious work; He makes them value more those things that cost more effort. But one may say that one of His main purposes is to hide Himself and to make His conduct unknown to those who do not deserve to know it."[89]

A Remark on the Antecedents of the Quarrel

From the condemnation of the Pelagians to the era of the Counter-Reformation the official and authoritative teaching of the Church was dominated by the Augustinian interpretation of original sin, grace, and predestination. Censures and condemnations more often than not came down upon those who yielded to the Pelagian temptation. Augustinian doctrine, although originating in the post-Constantine era, articulated the mentality of a Church which perceived itself as a tiny boat sailing towards the harbor of salvation in a hostile ocean of sin and heathen superstition, amidst adverse winds. It was adapted to the consciousness of an assembly of martyrs, of an intransigent sect. Should one not expect that the triumphant Church would abandon this mentality and adopt a more lenient and open doctrine, more or less compatible with the Pelagian message, albeit enveloped, of course, in a dogmatically acceptable idiom? In other words, should the Jesuit philosophy not have emerged centuries earlier than it did?

This is not a historical question, to be sure, rather a kind of historiosophical riddle. Pelagianism fitted into the attitudes of the nobility and the urban educated classes, people who wanted to feel that they had a large breathing space in their lives, who liked variety and change, were not afraid of the sinister sin of curiosity, and exercised their inquisitive spirit. There was more than a contingent affinity between the theoretical affirmation of liberty (in the sense of our ability to make unconstricted choices between various options) and "libertinage," not necessarily in the sense of debauched conduct but as a skeptical predilection to confront various answers to philosophical, scientific, or theological questions, a refusal to accept any barriers set in advance to our *libido sciendi*, a desire to apply our cognitive passion to the end. Belief in free will was a natural theoretical disposition in people whose existence was not confined within the narrow limits of lifelong, monotonous, unchanging toil, like the existence of medieval peasants and artisans, but left some room for individual initiative and stressed everybody's personal moral responsibility for his eternal destiny. The doctrine of predestination, on the other hand, was well adapted to the mentality of people who above all sought and valued moral security and whose main religious need was to be certain that they were possessed of truth and thus elected by God. Whatever the theological distinctions involved, the practical effect of belief in double predestination was the certainty of being among God's children. A part of the message of the doctrine was: you are safe; since you are a member of the true Church and listen to the divine word, you may rely on God's mercy.

And Augustinian theology seems to have been well adapted not only to the sectarian mentality of the early Christians but to the Church in power as well. If we are all, without exception, slaves of the devil, if nothing but evil remains in us after the calamity in Eden, if every act and every thought originating in us, rather than in God's inspiration, is fatally sinful, it seems natural to conclude that the infallible judge and guardian of morals, the Apostolic Church, must employ or encourage an efficient machinery of coercion—if not in order to increase the chances of salvation (which is entirely in God's hands), then to limit the number of human acts that offend God. In other words, there seems to be a pre-established harmony between Augustinian theology and the more or less theocratic claims of the Church. This is perhaps particularly salient in the case of Calvin, the most consistent Augustinian, but it is a platitude to say that the doctrine of the incurable wickedness of human nature has been a standard argument for various sorts of oppressive political orders under the guidance of the Church (proviso being made for the fact that the Church has never been theocratic in the extreme sense; it has not wanted to replace secular authorities but rather to control them).

This is, to be sure, only part of the truth. Molinist (or semi-Pelagian) theology was also employed to enhance the power of the Jesuits and of the Church. But this was in a new situation when the traditional pillars of stability had broken down and new ideological instruments were urgently needed (which is not to suggest that theological doctrines were necessarily planned to provide a religious order or the Church with a political weapon; more often than not ideologies are not deliberately and artificially concocted for immediate practical use). In a somewhat vulgarized rendition, the educational efforts of the Society of Jesus may be seen as an application of the contemporary advice "if you can't beat 'em, join 'em." This is indeed the concise formula for various forms of the Counter-Reformation, including Jansenism. The Jesuits operated in the upper layers of society, infected by a spirit of modernity of which some aspects could appear irreversible. The Molinist doctrine did not by any means imply that Jesuit priests, in order to hold sway over the ruling educated classes, should unreservedly endorse the corrupt conduct of their penitents, approve their sins and crimes, and explain that on closer inspection they were not crimes at all but at worst only minor misdemeanors, easily forgivable. It did, however, imply that human nature, God's work, while contaminated by original sin, could not be hopelessly rotten; that all natural impulses and desires could, if properly guided, conduce to good; and that a spiritual adviser or confessor, in order to mend a sinner's ways, should accompany him as far as feasible, show understanding for, and even solidarity with, his weaknesses and thereby direct him step by step towards virtue. There is no need to explain how easily this rule could be stretched and converted into universal forbearance; both Pascal in the *Provinciales* and two successive popes (Alexander VII and Innocent XI) in their condemnations of Jesuit "laxists" demonstrated it convincingly.

Reduced to their ideological basics, the clash between the two images of the human condition, and consequently two educational principles, can be thus expressed: is human nature an implacable foe of God, an eternal, contemptible rebel that must be destroyed, or is it a somewhat polluted object which could be tamed, ennobled, and set straight? Is violence or patient education a safer path for Christian upbringing?

The world-shaking controversy about grace in the sixteenth and seventeenth centuries might have been triggered by accidents, but it obviously touched the very foundations of Christian life.[90] The relationship between the natural and the supernatural, the way the border between them is drawn and thus the question of what can I do and what ought I to do to contribute to my salvation and to that of my fellow men: this is what Christianity is ultimately about. The quarrel had various theological, philosophical, psychological, and political ramifications, and we may say with the benefit of hindsight that it decided the very fate of the Catholic Church. Nicole was quite wrong in his claim (on the question whether the five propositions were to be found in Jansenius's work) that "nobody would ever have believed that the peace of the Church could be disturbed by this sort of trifle." What was at stake was the adaptation of Christianity to a new civilization that had been developing and maturing, surreptitiously, for several centuries. The *Liberum arbitrium* was one of its important instruments of self-expression, starting with Abelard.

The Jesuit doctrine was a unilateral continuation of the Christian humanism of which the main champion, at the dawn of modern times, was Erasmus. Erasmus's writings maintained a balance between two ideas which limited each other. He taught that, on the one hand, when corruption, simony, hypocrisy, cynicism, and all mortal sins seem to engulf the Church and threaten to destroy it, we must assume that it is up to us to direct our lives, always relying on God's help; we are truly responsible for our conduct, and sin has not robbed our nature of all good. On the other hand, we must never boast of our virtues, goodness, and achievements but rather be grateful to the Creator for having given us strength; we ought to trust not our own merits but divine mercy and benevolence. This was the moralistic expression of the doctrine of justification by faith, and it seemed coherent, at least psychologically.

When the point was to combine those two pieces of advice in abstract theological language, they seemed easily to collide. Erasmus perhaps did not need to bother about possible conceptual incongruencies in his preaching; he was a doctor in theology, to be sure, but he was not a theologian in the standard sense; he was a moral teacher, a writer, a philologist. Theology, however, had its rigors and required unambiguous yes-or-no answers: does our free choice, rooted in our natural forces alone, contribute at all to our salvation, yes or no? Is it in our power—ours, not God's—to cooperate with the grace of our merciful Savior, yes or no? If "yes," it would appear that ultimately our salvation depends on our own efforts; not that divine help is unnecessary, but it does not suffice: we have to add to it something from our own resources, all the while assuming that God's grace is, so to say, ubiquitous and evenly ("justly") distributed among the denizens of earth. And that is precisely the semi-Pelagian heresy. If the answer is "no," then the conclusion seems unavoidable: our eternal destiny has nothing to do with our deeds or misdeeds; God selects his flock according to his arbitrary choice, for reasons that are utterly and eternally inscrutable; and if I "deserve" to be appointed a sheep rather than a goat, this is in a perverse sense, because my meritorious contributions are entirely God's gifts. We may, if we wish, avoid talking about "double predestination," but only insofar as God does not compel us to sin or positively hand us over into the clutches of the devil but merely throws us back upon our own forces, which lead us inexorably into the abyss. And this is the Augustinian doctrine and the Calvinist heresy. The formidable dilemma could never be properly resolved in spite of enormous effort on the part of Catholic theologians to find a satisfactory intermediate solution, and it is well understandable that Jesuit priests were instructed to avoid discussions about predestination[91] and that the pope forbade theologians to continue the quarrel on the subject. In vain. Not surprisingly, in the squabble between Erasmus and Luther about free will, the latter had the advantage of a simple (or simplistic) consistency, whereas the former used common sense and the traditional evangelical image of a charitable and kindhearted Creator. Erasmus stressed time and again that we should not try to penetrate too deeply into divine secrets, for this would amount to feeding our pathetic pride, but rather to be satisfied with what the Gospels teach us and summon up our strength to abide by the commandments. Luther fulminated much more strongly, indeed furiously, against the corrupt Reason of theologians and the pseudo-wisdom of the Schools, but on this crucial question he exacted an unequivocal yes-

or-no answer, as the matter was simply "yes or no to Saint Paul," "yes or no to pagan wiseacres," "are you for Athens or for Jerusalem?" and ultimately "for God or for man?" He easily shrugged off all the seemingly commonsense arguments to the effect that it is inconceivable that God should distribute his grace "unevenly" or "unjustly"—as though grace could ever be given "justly," as though it were not gratuitous by definition, as though God were fettered by the human idea of justice and were our debtor, as though he could renounce his absolute sovereignty (if he had done so, we would be helpless prey for hell). God is merciful, of course, but when we peruse Luther's works we feel that we should tremble in the face of his mercy.

Luther may not, strictly speaking, have formulated in a neatly cut phrase the doctrine of double predestination, but only this doctrine could grow on the field he had cleared. It was not a matter of theoretical curiosity to him; it was a life-or-death question. Personal experience convinced him that to abide by evangelical commandments is simply unfeasible for us: Jesus wanted us to be perfect, not only in deed but in mind as well, and if we rely on our natural strength alone we can never be equal to his requirements. The despair which arises from this experience is salutary: we realize, however painfully, that in the struggle against Satan and temptations we are helpless; when we try to employ our natural virtues, everything we do turns to evil; driven to desperation, we begin to understand that God alone can save us and we rush to him, begging for aid. There is no way we could deserve salvation and there are no merits of our own that could buy out a soul from the depths of the inferno. Let us rely on a merciful God who can, in spite of our sins and not as a reward for our virtues, consider us justified by giving us the gift of grace. In faith we are pure and so are our works; they carry no justifying force in themselves, but they express the reality of our conversion.

This is, of course, a genuinely Augustinian insight, and it would take quite a skilful dialectician to argue that it does not imply the grim doctrine of double predestination (proviso being made for the ambiguity, just mentioned, of the word "double"): God chooses whomever he wishes and no human merits contribute to his selection; gratuitously given faith makes us justified, and no foreknowledge of human conduct precedes the divine offer (except in the spurious sense that God foresees the fruits of his own generosity).

Wretched creatures that we are, we manage to pervert or to forget the pellucid teaching of Paul and Augustine, and it was this obliviousness which so profoundly corrupted the Church. The reliance on human "works" became a foundation of the entire educational, nay, financial system of Rome; the traffic in indulgences was perhaps the most striking but only one of many signs of depravation. The scandalous humanist belief in the "virtues of heathens," so glaring in Erasmus's writings, is a nefarious effect of the same contempt for sound Augustinian theology; a pagan by definition cannot be virtuous in the proper sense, i.e., have virtues inspired by faith, and the sham virtues that originate in our corrupted nature can only add to the weight of our sins on the day of judgment. The scholastic trust in human reason in divine matters was another symptom of the same hubris that had been blossoming under the sway of the morbid Pelagian heresy.

Erasmus failed to explain how the idea of justification by faith can be compatible with the belief in the freedom of will, being content with advising us not to try to fathom the mysteries of faith; in all matters relevant to our salvation the Gospels are clear enough, and anyway it is our life, not our theological erudition, that we will be called to account for before the supreme Judge. His theoretical reflections were at the service of a moral reform of Christian people and of the Church, but as a moral teacher he could get away with not probing to the very end the formidable riddles of theology, on the issue of predestination no less than on that of the Trinity or of the divinity of Jesus.

Luther, however, believed this question too serious and too urgent to be left undecided, and he wanted to be consistent. Not that he believed in the power of reason or of "human logic"; quite the contrary, he knew it to be irreparably polluted by our devilish arrogance. But this was not a matter for reason to decide, but for the incontestable words of Holy Writ, unpardonably distorted by corrupt prelates. Here there is no place for prevarication and evasive language, no references to Jerome (patron saint of humanists) in order stealthily to undermine the authority of the great doctor of Hippo.[92]

It would be out of place to dwell on the clear link between the theological idea of justification by faith and the project of the urgently needed reform of the Church in the first decades of the sixteenth century. The meaning of the controversy about grace seemed clear in Christian terms, both educational and political. Let us repeat: far from encouraging dismissive or indifferent attitudes to our own conduct, the belief that our salvation is totally in God's hands, and to no degree in our own, makes people aware that they must take the matter of salvation with extreme seriousness; instead of relying on comfortable mechanical devices in our quest for justification, we should rather ask ourselves whether in our life and behavior the marks of election can be detected. The advocates of unconditional predestination wanted to awake a spirit of genuine piety, as opposed to easy "works." The idea of a democratic Church that did away with its complicated institutional hierarchy and got rid of a great deal of its ceremonial adornment was a natural consequence of this doctrine: the Church is no more capable of forgiving our sins and making us just than is a priest or a pope; only God can do that. The yearning after the legendary purity of the Church of the Apostles, the refusal to believe that we can bargain with God about the price of redemption, try to outwit him or pretend that he owes us a reward, the readiness to surrender to his mercy, the theology of justification by faith, the scorn for the "pagan saints" of humanists and for scholastic learning and logical skills, the mistrust of the arts unless they are at the service of piety—all this forms a whole in which the psychological, political, and theological (or philosophical) strands are tightly interconnected.

The doctrine of double predestination, implicit in Luther, was made explicit by Calvin. His Augustinian radicalism is expressed bluntly and unrestrictedly: we have no freedom of choice between good and evil, whatever we do without grace is a sin and, although unavoidable and necessary, no less condemnable as such, because it is voluntary; we have no merits of our own, grace precedes all good works and our election has nothing to do with our works but is rooted in the gratuitous mercy which God bestows on some; his choice is just because there is no measure of justice save God's sheer will; but for grace, we all deserve hell; but grace is displayed in people's conduct, therefore predestination does not release us from the obligation to abide by God's law.[93]

In Calvin's texts there are many phrases which unreservedly

state that human creatures are absolutely incapable of performing any good act. The Jansenists delighted in quoting them, as they could triumphantly show how fundamentally their master's doctrine differed from the Genevean heresy: according to Calvin nobody, no matter how much aided by grace, can do anything good, whereas Jansenius's orthodox Augustinian theology says that while we are unable to do good without grace, with grace we not only can but infallibly do obey the commandments. This is a precarious apology; the context of Calvin's seemingly unqualified verdicts about our corruption leaves no room for doubt about their meaning: we can never, ever do good without divine help, but once we get it (undeservedly, of course) we can and we do—by necessity though not by compulsion. This is the same Augustinian doctrine that Jansenius adopted.

In the so-called second (or radical) Reformation the question of predestination, to the extent that it mattered (in some currents other issues dominated: Christology, the Eucharist, the Trinity, the priesthood), was roughly decided either in pantheist or Pelagian terms; strangely enough a convergence can be detected in those two tendencies. In the former the terms of the question of evil have changed: whatever happens is God's work, and, of course, no evil can be produced by God; what we call evil is the attraction of nothingness, the self-directed energy of my "I-hood," and it is up to me whether I surrender to this diabolic allure or resist it. It is a choice between Being and Nothing, and the choice is mine. The Pelagian temptation is expressed in doctrines that clearly assert human responsibility for salvation or damnation; without denying the necessity of grace they simply assume that grace is evenly distributed and it is up to us to use it properly. And this is the Molinist philosophy. The dissidents of the Reformation were systematically accused of being crypto-papists; this they certainly were not, insofar as they accepted the democratic concept of Christian life: they were as opposed as their critics were (or even more) to a hierarchical idea of the Church, to the doctrine of the Apostolic succession, and to the *ex operato* interpretation of the sacraments. Like the Jesuits in the Roman Church, they represented within the Reformed countries the embryonic spirit of the Enlightenment and the commonsense (later Cartesian) belief in free will.

But the complicated history of the "Reformation-within-the-Reformation" need not bother us in the context of the prehistory of Jansenism, which had to define itself by its attitude to the Augustinian legacy, to Molinist modernism and to the post-Tridentine Church, and to a lesser degree to heretics of the Calvinist, Lutheran, or Zwinglian persuasion.

The history of the official doctrinal Catholic reaction—before the Jansenist quarrel—to the problem of free will, predestination, justification, and grace is clouded by ambiguities which will be useful briefly to mention.

The condemnation of Luther, which might retrospectively, and somewhat anachronistically, be seen as the first official act of the Counter-Reformation (a number of reformers had been condemned by then, to be sure, and the Great Reformation had not yet taken shape), is a haphazard collection of sentences concerning mainly the sacrament of repentance, papal authority, indulgences and purgatory, but few of them deal with the theological problems of sin and grace. Some confirm the incurable sinfulness of human nature (the sin remains in babies after baptism; the seeds of sin, even without any actual sin, prevent the soul of the dead from entering heaven; the just man sins in every good act; the best work is a venial sin)[94] and one is unmistakenly Augustinian in content: "the free will after sin is a mere name [*res de solo titulo*] and when it is doing its own [*quod in se est*] it commits a mortal sin."

What is striking in the final Tridentine codification of the doctrine of justification is that it seems to be even harder on Pelagian errors than on the horrifying new heresy of the Reformation. Of the final anathematized statements the first three are clearly Pelagian, but almost all of the remaining thirty condemnations are aimed at the new theology of justification by faith and at double predestination. But when we peruse the more elaborate decrees on justification it appears that the room they leave for our "cooperation" in the process of salvation is not only minimal but could, on a permissible interpretation, be reduced to nothing.[95] Among the five causes of justification none is attributed to human effort: the final cause is God's glory and eternal life; the efficient cause is the merciful God who gratuitously sanctifies his children; the meritorious cause is Jesus Christ; the instrumental cause is the sacrament of baptism, and the formal cause is God's justice whereby he makes us just. On the last point the decree mentions, to be sure, that the divine gift of justice is distributed according to the will of the Holy Ghost and conformably to everybody's "proper disposition and co-operation." And in the fifth chapter of the same decree we learn that man is not inactive when his heart is touched by the enlightenment of the Holy Ghost because he can reject the inspiration, although he cannot move himself towards justice by his free will. The claim that human free will is merely passive, does not cooperate by its assent with God, and is incapable of rejecting this call is condemned; and so is the statement that man's good works "which he performs by God's grace and Jesus Christ's merit" do not really deserve an increase of grace. We are also taught that "what is called our justice—insofar as we are justified by its being in us—is God's because it is instilled in us by Christ's merit" and that God's "goodness towards men is so great that He wanted His gifts to be their merits."

What is curious about these decrees and anathemas is that they may be compatible with and, with some additional premises, reforged into the Augustinian (and thus, in anticipation, Jansenist) soteriology, whereas with other additional premises they can look like a part of the Molinist, semi-Pelagian doctrine. Certainly, we are not "inactive," because we can use our free will to reject divine aid; it seems therefore that there is no irresistible grace (the efficient grace of Jansenius). But if it is a matter of free choice to reject the call of the Lord, it must be true that the same free will can opt for its acceptance. This is not clearly said, however, and one can guess that the opposite is true, because we are not able to turn towards justice by an act of free will. It seems therefore that we need a special kind of grace in order to accept grace and that, if we turn our back on God's offer, we do so inevitably if this additional grace is not offered to us. And if the rejection is inevitable, so is the acceptance; hence "free choice" indeed becomes, in spite of verbal protestation, a mere word without reality. This reading is reinforced by the passages just quoted that say God wished to see his own gifts as our merits; his arbitrary generosity does not alter the basic fact that our good deeds are not of our making (unlike our wrongdoings, for which we are fully responsible) and that we do not positively contribute to their happening. We must never boast of, or rely upon, our own moral force, but we are not like inanimate objects; the first part of this explanation reflects our real situation, but the second may be suspected of being no more than a verbal decorum. Jansenius would not oppose it.

To make the same Tridentine pronouncements compatible with semi-Pelagian theology is perhaps a more demanding task—and more stretching of words is needed—but it is not unfeasible. The anti-Pelagian canons condemned all who said that man can be justified before God without grace, by natural forces alone, that grace makes salvation easier but is not necessary in order to acquire it, and that one can have faith, hope, and charity without the inspiration of the Holy Ghost and repent sufficiently in order to merit the justifying grace. All this may be absorbed by semi-Pelagians if supplemented by the assumption that grace is distributed equally (or "justly") among human creatures and, although necessary, does not suffice for salvation (or is not irresistible) because it is up to us to make proper use of it by employing our free choice. And the doctrine of irresistible grace is nowhere unequivocally stated in the decrees.[96]

When we say "Molinism" and "Jansenism" in interpreting the Council of Trent we are of course guilty of anachronism. The ambiguities of the sixth session "on justification" are basically the same as those we can detect in Erasmus's writings and it is permissible to imagine that Erasmus, had he lived a dozen years longer, would have approved, somewhat reluctantly, the final verdict: we are responsible for our sins, but as to our virtues, we should thank God for giving them to us, rather than boast of our perfection. But perhaps he would not have been enthusiastic about the work of the conciliar fathers, because he advised us to be abstemious in fathoming God's ways and operations, to be satisfied with the knowledge that guides us in moral issues, and to relegate the subtle theological speculations and squabbles to the realm of adiaphora (in fact, more often than not, such disputes were to him positively harmful, rather than just useless).

Alas, in the same year that Erasmus died (1536) the first edition of Calvin's *Institutiones* was printed. What was ambiguous, or suggested but not expressly said, by Luther became clear, explicit, complete. The Tridentine formulas were still indeterminate, but this incompleteness could not last endlessly. After the Calvinist codification of the doctrine of predestination, the space for intermediate or ambiguous solutions was narrowing down. Indeed the quarrel between Jansenists and Molinists only revealed what had already been true for some decades: if you don't shirk theological clarity, if you genuinely condemn the Calvinist heresy, you have no other option but to be a semi-Pelagian in all but name; if instead you condemn semi-Pelagianism and faithfully follow the great doctor, the hammer of heretics, you will be in great trouble when you try to explain just how the doctrine you follow differs from the horrors of Calvinism. Inevitably, your adversaries will accuse you of being a semi-Pelagian in the former case and of being a crypto-Calvinist in the latter. And in both cases there will be no shortage of good arguments. For a long time the Church took refuge in ambiguities, trying to patch up the issues and refusing to say clearly which side it was on. The Jansenists eventually compelled it to make a choice.

In spite of the long-lasting reluctance of the popes to address themselves in a clear-cut way to the issue, and their unhappiness over the continuing squabbles, some changes can be noticed in the period preceding the Jansenist debates. With all its ambiguities—including the possibility of later making it compatible, by skilful dialectical exegesis, with the Jesuit concept of free choice—the Tridentine verdict, at least in its main thrust, was directed against Pelagian teaching, and the language of the decrees strongly suggested that the emphasis was now on grace, God's sovereignty, and the corruption of human nature. The Church apparently tried to respond to, and absorb, the challenge of reformers and rebels by taking over some important elements of their critiques. That is what we call the Counter-Reformation: the Church reforming itself by assimilating and thus neutralizing the ideological weapon of its foes and making it its own weapon—in this case a cautious, and not irreversible, return to the Augustinian concept of Christianity.

But the condemnation of Baius (1567), shortly after the conclusion of Trent, marks a departure from this path. The unusually long list of errors (the criticism of Baius started earlier; the Sorbonne censored some of his doctrines in 1560) is clearly anti-Augustinian in spirit. The condemned propositions not only stress, inter alia, the total impossibility of good acts not aided by grace; they include the idea that the free will, without God's help, is able only to sin; that whatever a sinner does is a sin and all the works of infidels are sinful; that no sin is venial by its nature but each deserves eternal punishment; that it is Pelagian to think that anything coming from natural forces can be good or that any use of free will can be other than evil. The condemnation of the first of Jansenius's five propositions is already there: "the sentence that God has commanded to man nothing impossible is falsely attributed to Augustine, since it is Pelagius's [doctrine]"; the third is clearly anticipated in Baius saying that "man sins damnably in what he does necessarily," that "only violence is opposed to man's natural freedom," and that "what is done voluntarily, is done freely, even if it is done necessarily." Baius even taught that every crime can infect the criminal's descendants, not unlike original sin.[97]

This was the strongest condemnation of undeniably Augustinian tenets before the anti-Jansenist bull, and the followers of Molina had some authoritative sources to succor their cause.

Let us repeat: this process of de-Augustination of the Roman Church was not going on in the heaven of pure concepts; what was at stake was the Church's ability to adjust to the new, emerging civilization. To impose on the upper classes of French society the discipline and deadly seriousness required by the Augustinian doctrine was no longer possible. The doctrine of double predestination, implying roughly that "nothing is under our control," had never suited the tastes of the aristocracy. And this great affair develops in mid-seventeenth century France: this is the Cartesian or post-Cartesian world, teeming with libertines and skeptics; *libido sciendi* and curiosity are flourishing; the educated layers of lay society assert their freedom of inquiry, all warnings and censures notwithstanding. It is not safe, to be sure, openly to proclaim atheism, but skeptics know many ways to express themselves clearly and without great risk, and perhaps never in history was the doctrine of the afterlife and immortality so frequently and openly challenged and disdained in poetry as it was then.[98] The post-Tridentine reforms may have worked relatively efficiently among the secular and regular clergy, but they could not affect the mentality and the habits of the upper classes, and the royal court was what it was. The Augustinian moral stringency and inflexibility were simply not for ball-rooms or comedy-goers. One could not tell the upper classes that curiosity is a dreadful sin, that theatre is a diabolic contrivance, that flirting with one's neighbor's wife is irrevocably a straight path to eternal fire, and that we ought to give our belongings, apart from bare necessities, to the poor.

Apart from libertines, indifferent to tradition and dogmas, some of them cautiously and some openly defying the old intellectual order, there were deists and believers in a natural law that was quite independent from positive divine prescriptions: Cartesians who saw in the philosophy of their master secular reason endowed with unlimited autonomy and an utter contempt for history and "memory" (the proper organ of theology, according to Jansenius); critics who demanded that Scripture be examined like any literary text, by philological and historical analysis and ultimately left nothing of its binding force (all the fideistic protestations of Richard Simon notwithstanding); and scientists who step by step were ruining the meaningful order of the divinely ruled universe and, in investigating nature, wanted to rely upon experiment and mathematical instruments only.

It would be unfair to say, as Jansenist writings suggest, that the Jesuit moralists did not take Christianity and the Christian commandments seriously. They did. They were a powerful organ through which the Church could operate in various new cultural settings where the use of flexibility was effective and the enforcement of harsh rules inherited from the Church of the martyrs was impossible. In fact, as Pascal noticed in the fifth *Provincial Letter*, there were among Jesuit writers both "laxists"—later twice condemned by the popes—and fairly rigid moralists, and confessors had at their disposal a variety of manuals, all of them "probable," to be used in various social circumstances. The clientele of the Jesuits were not atheists and libertines, but rather nobility engaged in all sorts of worldly business, people of questionable morals, to say the least, by strict Christian standards, but who still wanted to believe that there must be a much less strenuous and less exhausting method of eternal salvation than the Augustinians would suggest. The "easy devotion" was a way to keep them in the Church and under the Church's partial control (especially in matters concerning the education of youth) and ultimately to lead them to God who is *really* merciful—that is to say lenient—and understands human weakness. The Jesuits in a sense believed in the power of grace more than the Augustinians did: to be sure it is up to us and our free will to make grace efficient, but this is not a very laborious task precisely because God is so lavish in distributing his gifts, and nobody is left helpless by him, whereas in Augustinian doctrine he distributes his grace sparingly and according to quite incomprehensible rules.

One might well compare the way the Jesuits operated in French society to today's social and religious function of liberal Reform Judaism in America and elsewhere. The reform synagogues, too, may be accused of not taking Jewish law—that is to say, the Jewish religion—seriously, but they work in a specific cultural setting, quite unlike the shtetls of Eastern Europe of old. One could not expect many thousands of urban and suburban American Jews, businessmen and professionals, rigorously to observe innumerable, immensely complicated, and cumbersome Jewish rules; this is feasible only in poor, stagnant, ghetto-like communities of which examples are still in existence among the Hassidim both in Israel and in America. To say that a true Jew must not pick out from the law those rules which do not inconvenience him in his daily routine while leaving aside all the others, sounds plausible, but it amounts to saying that, if the law is not significantly relaxed (even though God, so far as we know, did not divide his law into convenient and inconvenient parts or say that the latter are unimportant), those Jews who cannot abide by all the rules without radically changing their lives are effectively banned from Judaism. While Reform synagogues might seem, to the guardians of orthodoxy, centers of regrettable departure from God's way or simply of betrayal, they are probably the only instrument which can keep a large number of Jews within the confines of Jewishness, loosely defined but not unreal.

In the same sense, the role of Jesuit educators, preachers, and writers was a dual one: they did not produce the new, undemanding morals, they found them ready-made, and had to make very numerous concessions to the "world," for the alternative—enforcing high standards—would amount to expelling those in the "world" beyond the borders of the Church, losing all influence on them, and ultimately leaving uncountable souls hopelessly in the clutches of Satan. And they knew what they were doing. On the one hand the Society's casuists dangerously loosened the Christian tradition by adjusting it to modernity; on the other hand they were instrumental in bringing about the necessary mutation in the Church and enabled it to survive and to reform itself in the new civilization, thanks to a newly gained flexibility. The Jesuits did not invent casuistry: it had been a normal and indispensable procedure, consisting in the application of general moral principles to particular cases, each of them somewhat different from the others and in a sense unique. In terms of the Church's tradition there was nothing wrong with casuistry as such, indeed it has always been needed in making moral judgments, and in the work of confessors in particular; it is simply the art of differentiating. It was the Jesuits who gave the word its bad name, or rather the Jesuits as depicted by Pascal.

Thus expressed, the idea of casuistry seems simple and innocuous: in judging people and people's sins we ought to know the details, as no two cases are absolutely identical. But things look less simple against the background of the theology of the Reformers and the Augustinian legacy. The Reformation did not want to differentiate. As has been said, it produced, or recreated, another psychological pattern in the human encounter with God. Whatever we do without faith offends God, whatever we do once elected by God sings his glory. The distinction between venial and mortal sin is either insignificant or outright harmful; we must turn to God and pray to him in the awareness of our sinfulness, which we should know to be incurable by human effort. The auricular confession of all particular sins is useless, indeed it is one of the novelties that profoundly corrupted the Church. Given this attitude, the art of casuistry must have looked like an attempt to haggle with the Lord, to quarrel with him about the most convenient interpretation of the law, to find loopholes in the commandments and stretch their meaning in order to find an easy path to salvation, and ultimately to reduce man's relationship to God to a purely legal, or rather commercial, one, when our sins and merits can be computed like items on a price list. God and man, however, do not relate to one another as seller and buyer but as father and child, and the child ought to appear before the father in humility, fear, and trembling. A most unpleasant surprise on the day of reckoning awaits those who imagine that they might, by a shrewd maneuver, induce (or compel) God to give away salvation for nothing. Their God was distinctly male.

The Jansenists could not, of course, directly question dogmatically established tenets of the Catholic faith, like the distinction between venial and mortal sins. But they went in this direction as far as dogmatically feasible, and further than was safe. They really wanted us to live always as repentant sinners, never losing our feeling of awe in the face of God, never forgetting our wretchedness and guilt. The distinction between attrition and contrition seemed to them suspect for the same reason. The concept of free will in the traditional sense was horrifying to them, as it implied that ultimately we save ourselves, that is, we seem to arrogate to ourselves divine privileges.

But the Zeitgeist seemed to be on the side of the Jesuits. Or rather a strong wing of the Zeitgeist, because moral repugnance to the practices of the casuists—not necessarily implying the full endorsement of the theological position of Jansenius—is known to have been quite strong among both the clergy, especially the secular clergy, and the French educated classes.

A Note on the Provinciales

Much as casuistry might be innocent in principle, its degenerate forms were to become famous, immortalized and ridiculed through Pascal's masterly pen. The *Provincial Letters* have been a classic of French literature almost since they were printed in 1657. The later condemnation of the excesses of Jesuit moralists by two consecutive popes has been less famous, and the actual texts of "laxists" are hardly read nowadays (in fact Pascal himself had hardly read them, except for Escobar; the excerpts were provided for him by friends, as he confesses).

No unprejudiced reader can fail to be won over to the side of the author when he peruses the *Provincial Letters* or to be amused by quotations from various Jesuit writers who seem to have a ready-made excuse for all kinds of human depravities and crimes. Did not Father Le Moine argue that no action is sinful unless God inspires in the agent the knowledge of his weakness, the desire to be healed, to pray and to beg for his help—so that people who simply do not care a damn about God cannot commit a sin? Did not others argue that one becomes a murderer only if one takes money in order to kill someone in a treacherous way? Or that a monk may take off his habit without incurring excommunication if he does so for a shameful reason like going to a brothel? Did not Escobar say that it is not simony if, in buying an ecclesiastical benefice, the buyer does not give money as a reward for a spiritual good but only as a way to move the will of the seller? And is it not true that, according to Lessius, if someone slaps you in the face, it is permissible to kill him? That there is no sin, in the view of Escobar and Molina himself, in killing a thief who tries to steal from you a thing of the value of one ducat (écu) or less? That there is no usury if the creditor takes money from the debtor not as a matter of justice but as a sign of gratitude? That the possession of money is legitimate even if it was acquired by disgraceful acts like adultery or murder? That a woman of good society has more right to demand money for secret fornication than a whore because her body is more precious, in the opinion of Father Fillintius? That, as Father Barry assures you, if you always carry a rosary, the door of paradise is wide open to you, no matter what you do otherwise? That laziness is indeed a mortal sin, but should be defined as sadness at the fact that spiritual things are spiritual? That we have no obligation to keep our promises if we have no intention of keeping them in the first place, in Escobar's judgment? That any man, as Father Barry states, may go to a brothel in order to convert fallen women, even if it is very likely that he will commit a sin there? That almsgiving is a duty, but only from our excess, and hardly anyone has an excess, not even kings, as Vasquez says? That, according to a number of fathers, a judge is not allowed to take money for dispensing justice—unless it is received simply as a sign of generosity—but he has no duty to return this money if he took it for giving an unjust verdict? And that, if you have sinned—which is no mean feat under these conditions—your confessor is in duty bound to give you absolution once you say that you prefer to defer your repentance until your sojourn in purgatory? And that a confessor would be commiting a mortal sin by refusing absolution to someone who can find an excuse in a probable opinion, even if this opinion is much less probable than the opposite one, and all opinions are probable if they are expressed by a serious author from the Society?

The list is long and well known. It was extended by quotations included in *Les Écrits des Curés de Paris*, written in part by Pascal and later, to some extent as a result of those very *Écrits*, in three censures of the Holy Office of 1665, 1666, and 1679 (the first two in the pontificate of Alexander VII, the third in that of Innocent XI). The condemned statements, altogether 110 of them, include the permission to duel, to kill one's unfaithful wife, to kill false witnesses, as well as the judge, to take a false oath, to murder a thief to avoid the loss of one ducat, to cause abortion, to steal in serious need, to take interest on a loan (as a sign of gratitude, not as something due by justice), falsely to accuse another person of a crime in defense of one's own honor, etc. The doctrine of probability is condemned, as well as the claim that it is enough to perform an act of faith once in one's life. That a son may, without sinning, revel in having killed, when drunk, his own father because he will inherit the father's wealth is considered scandalous *ut minimum*, as is the permission to a married couple to perform the *opus coniugii* for pleasure alone, and the judgment that to copulate with a married woman is not adultery if the husband accepts it.[99]

All this has provided much amusement, thanks to the *Provinciales*. They became an instant best-seller and have never ceased to be one. It was certainly a hard blow to the Society, which abounded in learned scholars but had apparently nobody with a remotely comparable literary talent. (It is known, for that matter, that Pascal was not always reliable, and often unjust, in presenting moral and theological doctrines of his adversaries; his pamphlet—and this was a pamphlet, not a theological study—suggested that some ridiculous opinions of a few fathers were typical of Jesuit writings, whereas most of the casuists were not "laxists" in any strong sense.)

Still, if we look at the *fatum libelli*, we notice that the victory of Jansenism in this particular battle was quite dubious, if not pyrrhic. The *Provinciales* became not only an item in the standard canon of French letters but above all a part of the libertine-liberal-anti-clerical-Voltairian canon. It functioned as a pamphlet that unmasked "Jesuit hypocrisy" and, by extension, the hypocrisy of the Catholic clergy and, by a further extension, the hypocrisy of the Christian religion. Its specifically Augustinian background and Jansenist inspiration could easily pass unnoticed. This was not, needless to say, the author's intention, quite the contrary; but to know what Jansenism was about, people should have read Saint-Cyran, Arnauld, and the Master himself. It was not the ascetic, austere, dread-spreading Augustinians who were to make obligatory

reading of the *Provinciales* in the lycées, but rather cynical, skeptical, vivacious followers of eighteenth century *philosophes*.

Both the "laxist" writers and their Augustinian foes knew, of
course, what made Jesuit piety attractive: it was easy and undemanding. Who would not prefer to be perfect, or at least worthy of
salvation, for such a low price? Who would not, having a choice,
take the guidance of an obliging, friendly confessor, rather than of a
severe, inquisitive accuser? We may well assume that Molière's
Celimène attended mass every Sunday, sat occasionally in a confessional and took communion without necessarily having any strong
religious convictions, but perhaps remembered once a year that she
would die one day and vaguely believed that God would take her
under his protection. A Jesuit adviser was just what she needed. If
she had been under the supervision of a Jansenist priest she would
have either committed suicide or, more likely, stopped visiting the
Church and her confessor altogether, and so would her friends.
The drawing rooms and the court would have slipped beyond the
clergy's control and the thundering of Augustinians would not have
helped.

Both the Jesuits and the Jansenists contributed to the enfeeblement of Christian values, the former by their leniency, the latter
by their intransigence; and both contributed to keeping those
values alive, the former by making Christianity so easy, the latter by
making it so difficult. The Jesuits were accused of not taking Christianity seriously, the Jansenists of making it so exacting as to be
practically inaccessible to the overwhelming majority of mortals.
The former certainly prevented many people from abandoning the
Church altogether, the latter reinjected into the Church the memory of its origins and tried to revive the spirit of God's army, sol-
diering on fearlessly amidst all adversities and never ready to
compromise.

Bossuet, in his funeral eulogy of Nicolas Cornet in 1663,
spoke of "two dangerous diseases" that affected the Church. Without mentioning Jesuits or Jansenists by name he deplored their
terrible excesses: on the one hand "the inhuman leniency, the mur-
derous pity" which made life so easy to sinners, and on the other
the extreme rigor which could tolerate no human weakness and was
constantly shouting anathemas; the former makes vices lovable and
contributes to corruption, the latter makes virtue repugnant by es-

tablishing perfection as an obligatory standard for all. We should, Bossuet says, keep the middle way without sliding to the (Jesuit) left or to the (Jansenist) right.[100] But appeals to moderation are of little weight when so much is at stake.

The most striking examples of the laxists' permissiveness concern events characteristic of the nobility and the aristocracy, but it would be unfair to accuse them of a class bias; there is advice specifically addressed to servants (on stealing or on helping their masters in adventures not quite recommended by the Gospels), to judges, etc.

It needs stressing that the anti-laxist verdicts of the Holy Office were unlike the condemnation of Jansenism; they mentioned no names and they targeted only specific items of casuistry. No theological issues were at stake and the Molinist theory of grace was not involved or even hinted at.

There is no need to seek a preestablished harmony or a compelling logical connection between this doctrine of grace and Jesuit casuistry. The reasoning might go in opposite directions: if divine grace is there as a constant support, and if ultimately our salvation depends on us and not on God's incomprehensible choice, this might be a good reason for appealing to individual responsibility and effort (as in the Pelagianism of old), rather than for promising salvation so cheaply; similarly, the Jansenist doctrine might have seemed to favor moral carelessness by making all our efforts irrelevant to the divine selection. In both cases, however, psychological realities run counter to what common sense might have expected at first glance. If there is a technical way to open the door of paradise, it is natural to make it as easy and uncomplicated as possible; if salvation is a matter of contract with God, the temptation is quite natural to give it the least cumbersome interpretation possible. Neither is there a preestablished harmony between the original constitution of the order and Molinist theology; but anti-Augustinian teaching appeared early, even during the Council of Trent, where Lainez, the general of the order, argued against efficient grace.[101]

It is plausible to argue that the two antagonistic worldviews may be contrasted in terms of the way in which they perceived continuity and discontinuity between the world of nature and the realm of divine operations. This is not, of course, how people then phrased the problem in their polemics, but it is a useful interpreting device. To the Molinists, unilateral successors of Renaissance humanism, the divine is a familiar environment, almost an extension of the cosy world of experience; grace is just there, omnipresent, and our natural skills are there to manipulate it properly to our benefit and God's satisfaction. In the world thus arranged life is basically pleasant. For the Jansenists (and the Calvinists, for that matter) there is a terrifying abyss between nature and the divine, and there is no way we could breach the gap by relying on the resources of our incurably corrupt and rebellious nature. The abyss is ontological, moral, and cognitive. In ontological terms, God is the absolute ruler of the universe, not a partner or a contractor or a seller of heavenly commodities; his will is definitive and irresistible. In moral terms, it is known that our inborn rebelliousness has to be defeated by divine violence, and not employed for good purposes; our task is to humiliate ourselves in fear and trembling before God, accepting his will in advance, unreservedly. In cognitive terms, we must admit that we face a profound mystery when God is spoken of, and no natural cognitive powers can pierce it; God deigned to reveal to us something about himself and that is what we ought to be satisfied with, whereas philosophical efforts to fathom what is beyond our comprehension are no more than signs of our vanity and conceit.

The Molinist doctrine, not surprisingly, implied that all natural energies, faculties, and passions are good in themselves and can always be directed towards the good if properly steered by spiritual guides; nature is to be ennobled, not crushed. The main method, therefore, is to accommodate oneself to human reality as it is; in order to set it right one must first of all show solidarity with it, accompany it and try to improve it nonviolently, step by step. This seems a sensible, humane, and efficient way of education. The question is, however, how far the priest is ready to adjust himself to the sin in order to combat it eventually; critics—by no means only Jansenists—objected that the shrewd Jesuit complaisance, designed to better the sinner, ultimately meant nearly total tolerance for sin. The attacks on Jesuits during the famous quarrel about Chinese rites were quite analogous: the fathers, purporting to convert the pagans, tolerate the infiltration of their superstitions, customs, and language into Christian ceremonies and conceal from the converts-to-be those fundamental truths that they would find too hard to swallow, thus producing a half-Christian, half-pagan cult.

The clash was about the spiritual foundations of Christianity, and it may be seen as a reenactment, in a specific cultural setting, of a never-ending conflict hidden in the roots of Christianity, in the ambiguity of the very idea of creation. Nature is God's splendid work of art and as such it must be good and admirable. But by creating nature God revealed the infinite rift between the creator and his product. Nature manifests God but, when contrasted with the infinite maker, it will always appear miserable and worthless, even apart from its pollution by original sin. If we optimistically stress the continuity between God and the world, we are liable to be tempted by Molinist philosophy; if we perceive the awesome gulf separating God from everything that is non-God, we will find cogent the Augustinian-Jansenist image of the universe; if we try to be in the middle, we are probably ready to be convinced by Thomist arguments; if we oscillate between two extremes, we will be in the company of mystics. What matters here is that both extremes are rooted in the Christian idea of the infinite ruler calling into being finite things. It is therefore reasonable to assume that conflicting worldviews will emerge in the Christian world as long as it deserves this label. The Jesuit-Jansenist contest, even if accidentally triggered, expressed this tension in a language that was shaped by the then recent history of the Counter-Reformation: as a problem of grace versus free will. We can find in today's Christianity the same conflict, focused on other questions and expressed in another language.

The doctrine of efficient grace was incontestably the core of Jansenism as a theological party. Other ingredients of this theology must briefly by mentioned to answer the question: who, and in what sense, won the contest?

The sacrament of penance was the second important criterion whereby people of the "party" could recognize one another.

How to Avail Oneself of the Heavenly Bread

It is commonly admitted that the *Fréquente Communion* by Antoine Arnauld (first edition in 1643) became, perhaps not intentionally, a kind of founding manifesto of the Jansenist party and the crucial document that consolidated the movement and gave it a clearly distinguishing theoretical or ideological expression; this is what party manifestos have always been for. Even though anti-Jesuit writings by Saint-Cyran had been in circulation for a decade and a half and the opus magnum by Jansenius for three years, Arnauld's text, written at Saint-Cyran's instigation, provided potential adherents of Jansenism with a doctrinal basis in which they could find a well-articulated contrast between their—i.e., Augustinian—idea of Christianity and Jesuit novelties. Unlike Jansenius's work, the *Fréquente Communion* was written in French and addressed to the general educated public, not only to theologians, its length notwithstanding (Arnauld was totally incapable of being concise in his writing; in this he was similar to his great Calvinist opponent Pierre Jurieu). It immediately became a best-seller.

The question how often people should receive Holy Communion might appear of secondary importance to today's Catholics, but Arnauld, by analyzing the uses and abuses of two sacraments—penance and the Eucharist—managed to oppose to each other two radically different concepts of Christian life and methods of seeking salvation. The text was provided with forty-five *approbatur* by bishops and theologians, quite an impressive part of the Who's Who among French (mainly secular) clergy; its target was the Jesuit "Christianity made easy," and its arguments use quotations from the fathers and councils, occasionally from modern reformers (especially, and not surprisingly, Charles Borromeo; Jansenius is quoted briefly two or three times), as well as references to the customs observed in the early Church. The immense theological erudition of Arnauld is harnessed to show that the Jesuits want to tempt us into the "broad path" and that such people, as John of the Cross said, must not be believed even if they perform miracles.

According to Jesuit authors, the Eucharist is a celestial medicine designed to cure the sinful state of our souls; it is natural therefore that the more grievous our sickness the more we need this divine aid, and that the more we feel robbed of grace, the more quickly we have to rush to God. The blood of the Savior annuls our sins and we ought to seek, everyday and without fear, participation in his merits. Once we commit a mortal sin, we go to the confessor and receive absolution, and immediately thereafter we should approach the Lord's table. True repentance is hardly mentioned in Jesuit teaching, Arnauld avers, whereas it is essential in Church tradition. The Jesuit priests believe that they may not refuse absolution to people who declare that they prefer to postpone their repentance until their sojourn in purgatory.

Arnauld argues, quite convincingly, that this approach is both sacrilegious and contrary to well-established tradition. Without the proper spirit of repentance, without penance, the divine bread turns into poison for those who recklessly rely on its salutary effect. And did not Basil say that those who deserve the Holy Sacrament have to be dead to sin, to the world, and to themselves, that they must acquire "perfect sainthood"? Did not Ambrose warn us that whoever wants to eat life, eats it to his damnation unless he changes his own life? Only if you share the virtues of the Christians of old, only if you attain a state of innocence, charity, and ardor of the Holy Ghost, may you take communion frequently, warns Bonaventure. Even those who have already abandoned their evil conduct but are not yet completely cleaned by the pure love of God, not perfectly united with God and not altogether perfect, have no place in the Church, according to Denis. And Cyprian teaches us that "perseverance in piety, in virtue, in faith, in good life and in good works" is the absolute condition of being admitted to communion.[102] The recipients, as John Chrysostom says, have to be "lofty souls having nothing in common with the earth."[103] "Extreme purity" is required for participation in Jesus Christ's flesh and one ought to approach the sacrament in "awe and trembling."[104] Some great saints voluntarily abstained from communion, considering themselves unworthy because of venial sins they had committed.

In the first centuries of the Church public penance was customarily required not only for mortal and publicly committed sins; the devil doesn't care whether a sin is public or secret: his aim is to tear away a baptized person from his place among God's children. It is the priest's duty to delay absolution after confession until the sinner has atoned for his crimes by a proportionate penance, shed his old self and changed into the new. We must not just rely on absolution; since only God can forgive our sins, we must beg his forgiveness in pain and tears, in sackcloth and ashes, with mourning and fasting, recognizing the enormity of our misdeeds, mortifying ourselves both in body and in conscience, never despairing about divine mercy but neither assuming that God has already forgiven us. We must not hope for conversion on the death bed after a godless life: *poenitentia morituri moritura.* Penitents who deplore their sins without abandoning them and those who abandon them without deploring them are equally unworthy of absolution, let alone of communion; so are those in whom the confessor sees no real improvement and who seem likely to revert to their old habits. Many sinners dread hell for no better reason than their amour propre; yet God does not let us into his kingdom as a reward for amour propre.

The results of this easy, undemanding Christianity were only too predictable: a catastrophic decline in moral standards and omnipresent corruption in all areas of life. Everybody is willing to rush to the confessional and no one to do penance; there have never been so many confessions and communions and never so much depravity and disorder. "Who does not know that for 20 years fornication has been regarded as a slight failing; adultery, one of the worst crimes of all, as a piece of good fortune; fraud and betrayal as virtues of the Court; godlessness and libertinage as strength of mind."[105] Corruption in marriage and family, corruption among the youth, fondness of luxury, gambling, blasphemy, cheating in trade, usury, simony—this is the picture of the age (it is not obvious what those "20 years" refer to—perhaps to the beginning of Richelieu's power).

Sancta sanctis, holy things for holy people—this adage aptly sums up the tenor and the content of Arnauld's passionate plea for the restoration of the Christianity of the fathers. He is well aware, of course, that lamenting the decline of Christian virtues among the faithful has been standard in theological and devotional writings since the third century. But he seems to believe that the world had never sunk so deep into the abyss of sin. What he wants is clear: a Church of saints, or rather a sect of saints. The inevitable decline in the number of those who will be accepted into the communion of the Church does not bother him at all. Gideon drove away all the cohorts from his army and only 300 were left to fight and win; "and is it not certain that 300 Christians who live in the zeal of faith bring more glory to the Church than 30,000 men who are similar to the cowardly soldiers of Gideon?"[106]

The sacrament of Holy Communion builds or restores the communion not only with Jesus Christ but also with his mystical body, the Church. Under the conditions set up by Arnauld, if one took them seriously, the Church would inevitably dwindle to a tiny sect of the perfect, with no prospect of influencing the impure world, let alone of conquering it. It would perhaps go back to the catacombs. It would certainly become what the rigorists wanted it to be and what they thought it had once been, in the good old days: a healthy but foreign body in a world dominated by evil. Perfect sainthood, extreme purity, innocence and Christian zeal, being dead to the world, a blameless life—this is what is expected from any Christian willing to remain in communion with the Church, not just from the monks of the contemplative orders; there is no gradation of merits, no attenuating circumstances, not the slightest leniency for human weakness; the same spirit that was displayed by the great martyrs of the early Church is now required as the general norm. A provincial synod, Arnauld reminds us, made a praiseworthy decision in imposing ten years of penance on a priest who was guilty of fornication and volunteered the self-accusation. François de Sales suggests that no more than one among 10,000 *directeurs des consciences* is up to the task.[107]

Arnauld, and all Jansenists, when accused of demanding the impossible and of imposing impracticable requirements on people and priests, replied: what is at stake is eternal salvation and on this point there is no bargaining or looking for easy solutions; it is a deadly serious thing, indeed the only thing that really matters. The Jesuit fathers could certainly not be accused of neglecting eternal salvation; on the contrary, they wanted to make it as widely accessible as possible. Indeed they made it easy. They were not accused—not even by Jansenists—of being self-indulgent and benefiting themselves with their easy-to-follow routes to eternal bliss; their personal moral discipline was not an issue. But they obviously wanted to maintain and extend the Church's sway over the royal court and upper classes of any society where they operated, and this they could not do without accepting social conditions or "human nature" for what they were. One may safely say that the need for less exacting, to put it mildly, rules of Christian life was too imperative not to be met; why the Society assumed this task is a separate question. It was known that Louis XIV, whose conduct was notoriously less than edifying by Christian standards, lived in terror of hell. One can hardly imagine the arch-Christian monarch being unable to find confessors ready to bring solace to his tortured soul and to let him continue.

The Jesuits were well aware of being innovators; Arnauld quotes his adversary Father de Sesmaison, S.J., who wants to build "une Église d'à présent," a modern church. He himself was well aware of being what we would call "reactionary" in the strict sense: he wanted to go back to the Church of the Apostles no matter what the price, and if this meant reducing it, like Gideon's army, to 1 percent—from 30,000 to 300—so be it. Naturally enough, he was the implacable enemy of all who, in religious matters, sought any foundation other than the divine authority and the fathers. He allowed reliance only on "this truth established in the Tradition which recognizes no visions, no revelations, no reasoning and no particular opinions but is the arbiter of all visions, all revelations, all reasoning and all true and Catholic opinions."[108]

While the Church is incorruptible in faith, the conduct of the majority is not only corruptible, it is bound to grow worse the nearer we come to the end of the world. God visited his unfaithful flock with various calamities, proportional to their weakness; he let the devil bring about the heresies of Luther and Calvin and he let the Turks invade Christian kingdoms. One must not pass over in silence the decay in the Church; better to provoke a scandal than to abandon the truth, as Saint Bernard says (*melius est ut scandalum oritur quam veritas relinquitur*). And it is the calling of bishops to restore proper discipline.

The Jesuits did not deny the magnitude of corruption among Christians but their therapy was quite different: precisely because virtue has become so feeble, the healing power of sacraments has to be distributed more lavishly. The Jansenists—as well as many Thomist theologians and many bishops and priests who, without necessarily sharing the doctrine of Jansenius, remained loyal to the tradition—argued that the Jesuit medicine exacerbated the sickness they claimed to cure: it let people continue in their wicked habits with impunity and degraded absolution to a mechanical formality.

How to Repent: Saint-Cyran's Answer

The question of contrition was a natural corollary to, indeed a part of, that of the sacrament of penance. Contrition is real (perfect) repentance; the sinner, with his heart ground to ashes, deplores and regrets his wrongdoings not for personal gain but because they offended God; repentance arises from love of God. Attrition, or imperfect repentance, is a sinner's regret and sorrow rooted in his fear of damnation (*gehennae metus*) and shame. The former kind of repentance is thus disinterested, concentrated on God alone, while the latter is selfish.

The moot point was not the superiority of contrition but rather whether attrition had any value at all (or whether it was even a sin itself) and, correspondingly, whether perfect repentance was necessary for forgiveness or, perhaps, attrition sufficed. As to absolution, the controversial issue was whether it had a "declarative" or an "operative" value (the Jansenists tended to reject the latter interpretation).

The strongly worded statement by Luther to the effect that the sinner is made a hypocrite and a worse sinner by a repentance that consists of (or perhaps even simply includes) sorrow over the loss of eternal bliss and the incurrence of eternal damnation was condemned in Leo X's bull, and the anathema was repeated in the 14th session of the Council of Trent. The more detailed explanation makes a distinction between contrition and attrition: the latter, if it includes the will to abstain from sin and the hope of forgiveness, is God's gift and helps the penitent pave his way to justice. Attrition cannot per se lead to justification without the sacrament of penance but it prepares the sinner for the illapse of grace.[109]

This amounted to rejecting the concept of attrition as a sin; it was supposed to be helpful but the question of whether attrition can be sufficient to deserve forgiveness (with the sacrament, to be sure) was not clearly resolved.

After decades of quarrelling among theologians and bishops, the cautious Holy Office (in 1667, under Alexander VII) issued a decree ordering both sides—those who asserted the necessity of an act of love of God for the reception of grace in the sacrament of penance and those, more numerous (*quae hodie inter scholasticos communior videtur*), who denied this necessity—not to censor and insult each other until a definitive decision came from the Holy See. Such a decision, however, was not to be taken, except that the previous verdicts were more or less repeated; among the errors of the Lovanian Jansenists, condemned in 1690, we find again the statement that attrition is not a good and supernatural movement, and in the *Unigenitus* (1713) the "contritionist" doctrine is indirectly reproved in the claim that the stronger the repentance originating solely in the fear of torment, the more it results in despair. This saying is clearly connected with another heretical sentence of Quesnel: "only love speaks to God; God listens to love only."[110]

The uneasiness of the Jansenists in the face of the approval of attrition as a worthy, albeit imperfect, way to God is well understandable; they argued that the very distinction between two kinds of repentance was unknown before Trent, and that the fathers had been unanimous in making genuine love of God an absolute condition of genuine repentance, the sheer dread of eternal fire depriving, in their view, our mechanical *miserere* of any redeeming value. (But among great medieval theologians there was no unanimity.)

It all goes back to the very foundation of Jansenist theology; it is based on the "everything or nothing" idea, aptly expressed in another false statement of the Lovanians: "every deliberate human act is toward the love of God or of the world; if the former, it is the Father's charity; if the latter, the lust of flesh, thus evil."[111]

This was indeed the soul of the writing and teaching of Saint-Cyran, the second spiritual father, after the bishop of Ypres himself, of the prospective Jansenist movement. His faithful disciple and the author of a long biography and apology, Claude Lancelot, quotes his master's words: "everything we do that is not for God is for the devil; he takes it for himself" (this was said on the occasion of his comments on Virgil who, Saint-Cyran asserted, condemned himself by producing such beautiful poems, because he wrote them for vanity).[112]

While Jansenius and Saint-Cyran spent many years together studying the fathers, especially Augustine (who, according to their testimonies, was hardly read then) and shared both the Augustinian worldview and the sadness at the sight of corruption and dissolution in the Church, they were quite unlike in character and attitudes. Jean Orcibal, who probably knew more about Jansenism and Saint-Cyran than anybody ever has, even says that their correspondence, which he edited, is a dialogue of the deaf: whereas Jansenius was an intellectual who sought an answer to a precise scholarly question, Saint-Cyran was interested in practical issues, in the restoration of Augustinian spirituality and thereby of the primitive Church.[113]

Obviously, Jansenius was not just a dispassionate historian; he spent over twenty years on his huge work on grace because he believed that subject to be an issue of paramount importance for combatting the modern Pelagians in the struggle for the purity of Christianity. But his work has indeed mainly a historical rather than a devotional character. Saint-Cyran, though a very learned man, was, in his lifestyle, an extremely powerful spiritual guide, a moral teacher, devoted to the people he met, exerting an almost irresistible influence on them, a confessor, a master of souls (a "charismatic personality" as he would be called today, thus being lumped together with company he would not necessarily enjoy). There is a mystical streak in him, unlike in the later generation of Jansenists; commerce with God was to him a daily occurrence, he often felt his guidance in the "movements of his heart"; God instructed him directly, sometimes in dreams; he lived, as it were, in a divine environment. He occasionally employed typical mystical idiom, e.g., speaking of annihilation as a going into nothingness, which by nature is suitable to us, and advising us not to think of the past or future. He stressed nonetheless that one must never abuse the Pauline freedom from law as a pretext for disobedience to the Church and tradition or rely on private revelations that might well be diabolic temptations.[114]

In an essay on grace and justification which Orcibal published from a manuscript, Saint-Cyran repeats the main Augustinian tenets about predestination, and theologically he does not differ at all from Jansenius. Grace, which is a "movement [directed] towards God and a holy disposition to charity," produces in a Christian man "all the good he does during his life." The sheer fear of hell does not come from grace. The state of indifference which enabled Adam to do good or evil according to his will was lost and his descendants could only make a choice between various sorts of evil; their will "is capable only of sin." Just people, after redemption, "are determined to do good, being pushed by God into a blissful necessity of doing good." The grace of the just is not deserved; our good deeds are no less than miracles. Predestination is "God's eternal love which God accords to some children of Adam—after having seen them fall into damnation as a result of the sin of their fathers; God abandons other people and gives them nothing but the hell they deserve, whereas the love he confers on others provides them eternally with the eternal bliss of paradise." "For this [choice] there is no other reason except the will of God, who wanted to save some and not others, but by a discipline and an order of conduct that one learns in the Church."[115] This includes practically the entire content of the first four condemned propositions.

As a *directeur spirituel* by calling, a healer of souls, Saint-Cyran was interested in theological issues mainly in a practical pastoral perspective.[116] The question of genuine repentance was, of course, crucial to him and it was on the pretext of heresy on this point—and not on the theology of grace—that Richelieu ordered his arrest on 15 May 1638. This was one of the most important dates that contributed to the self-awareness and self-assertion of the Jansenist movement.

Saint-Cyran had by then had a long priestly and literary career, including his early humanist period when he defended a number of "laxist" tenets (in such matters as suicide, the use of the sword by priests, and usury); his studies at Louvain under the supervision of the learned Lessius, S.J., one of the leading Molinists; his conversion to rigorous Christianity; his close friendship with Bérulle, with whom he shared both the dream of the primitive Church and little respect for monastic vows (a human institution, unlike priesthood). In 1626, long before anybody had heard of the "Jansenists," Saint-Cyran initiated a sort of anti-Jesuit crusade by attacking Father Garasse, the famous Jesuit polemicist and the author of a number of works in which he wrote against Calvinists, Gallicans, and libertines. Garasse was a larger-than-life specimen of Jesuit humanism; he believed in the enormous power of natural reasoning in divine matters and in almost unlimited possibilities of human nature to achieve moral perfection; one of his remarks, particularly outrageous to the Augustinians, was that the most exacting commandments of the Gospel were fulfilled by pagans, relying on their natural forces alone. He fought against libertines not because of their humanist doctrines but because of their skepticism; to Saint-Cyran, as later to Pascal, skepticism (in this case Charron) was a kind of ally in the anti-Pelagian battle insofar as it humiliated the conceit of secular reason, and in general unmasked the misery of the human condition and human achievements, whether intellectual or political.

Both Saint-Cyran and Jansenius passed down to their spiritual heirs a contempt for philosophy and speculative—as opposed to scriptural—theology, their profound mistrust of everything that is of purely human origin, their strong conviction, based on the fathers and the epistles of Paul, that the truths God has deigned to reveal to us about himself and his judgments are infinitely beyond our mental capacities—they have to be accepted humbly and praised simply because they come from God and not because we can measure them by the wretched standards of our logic and justice. The Jesuit writers' fondness for antique pagan literature and mythological imagery, tawdry adornments which they employed in their writings, repelled the Augustinians as being no more than symptoms of the same theological disease: the Pelagian belief in the value of human culture, "human" meaning created by human ingenuity and not by the inspiration of the Holy Ghost. Saint-Cyran spoke about the dangers of music and song, even if they were pious, and later castigated the craving for knowledge (which he himself eminently displayed) and lamented the excessive spread of education.[117]

Thus Saint-Cyran clearly articulated the terms of the war he was declaring on modern Pelagians. The war was to last for more than a century and it deeply affected the fate of Christianity. In the first skirmish the Augustinians won; as a result of Saint-Cyran's strictures and the subsequent censure of Garasse's book by the Sorbonne, the Jesuit order silenced their prolific fighter and sent him to Poitiers, where he died in piety in 1631.

It did not necessarily take a clever Jesuit theologian to notice some unmistakeable analogies between this germinal Jansenism and the spirit of the Great Reformation: fundamentally the same

theory of grace, the same scorn for secular science, philosophy, reason and scholasticism, the same desperate striving after the purity
of the early Church, the same spirit of seriousness and austerity.

An aversion to mechanical piety and "contritionism" were
organic parts of this attitude in Saint-Cyran. Since the Holy Office
wisely forbore from issuing any definitive opinion in this matter,
neither those who asserted the necessity of contrition nor those
who believed that attrition was enough could be accused of heresy.
This was Saint-Cyran's line of defense. He demanded, as a minimum condition of absolution, that the penitent bemoan his
offenses to God and sincerely resolve not to sin any more. Lancelot, who included a treatise on contrition in the first volume of
his *Mémoires*, quotes a number of fathers to support Saint-Cyran's
view; Chrysostom said that those who are more terrified by infernal
pain than by the fact of having affronted God, thereby deserve to be
sent to hell. God wants to be loved for his own sake and not for
one's own benefit; this is included in the very idea of love ("what is
not loved for itself, is not loved at all," according to a concise and
perfect formula of Augustine).[118]

Richelieu, as a number of historians point out, had more reasons to harass Saint-Cyran than for the latter's alleged heretical
"contritionism." Apart from the fact that the cardinal was himself
the author of a catechism in which attrition was declared sufficient
for absolution, both personal and political animosities were involved. Saint-Cyran was an independent spirit enjoying great respect among the educated middle classes and this in itself made him
suspect. Both Jansenius and Saint-Cyran opposed Richelieu's anti-
Spanish ventures and the help given by France to heretical Hol-
land. The cardinal let himself be convinced (wrongly) that Saint-
Cyran was the real author of a book by the Oratorian Father
Séguenot, who strongly defended the "contritionist" doctrine and
argued that genuine and worthy repentance must originate in perfect charity and be free from selfish and servile considerations; even
worse, he dared express his lack of respect for monastic vows, as
they belonged rather to the Old Covenant. He was also arrested, a
few days before Saint-Cyran. The cardinal was, of course, a su-
perbly skilful and sober politician; but this does not mean that in
religious matters he was no more than a cynical manipulator. He
lived in terror of hell and he is said to have requested from the theo-

logian doctor Lescot (the same who was to be Saint-Cyran's interrogator after the latter's imprisonment) a written certificate stating that he, the cardinal, would be saved.[119] Besides, the memory of religious wars and uprisings was by then relatively fresh and nobody could be assured that hot theological disputes, even if they started on the pages of abstruse Latin volumes, would not end up on real battlefields at a time when social peace was fragile and frequently disturbed.

The budding new movement—soon to be known under the name of Jansenism but already conscious, at least germinally, of its identity—might have looked like a threat to the crown, not because it was politically disloyal or anti-monarchist (Arnauld was a fervent royalist) or hostile to the church hierarchy, but because it was not under control.[120] It was the Jansenists who initiated the conflict by their attacks on the Jesuits and, for all their learning, seriousness, and piety, they displayed a spirit of intransigence or even fanaticism, an ability to compromise with nature, with human weakness, with modernity, with new forms of secular life. They argued, quite convincingly, no doubt, that, far from developing a new theology, let alone a new philosophy, they were simply trying to revive the spirit of the fathers and the tradition of the early, and thus the most perfect, Church, and that it was the Jesuits who brought forth dangerous novelties, previously heard from Pelagian heretics only. But to statesmen this argument was pointless; they were not interested in the intricacies of the theology of grace, whether Augustinian, Thomist, or Molinist; they wanted to avoid a religious split of unpredictable consequences. It was not difficult to convince the king and his servants that a new and potentially powerful sect threatened the realm with a religious war which should be prevented at any price. Once this spectre of a "new sect" gained credibility, no theological or moral arguments could stop the process of persecution that was eventually to crush it—at least on the surface of things.

There were several items in Saint Cyran's original accusation (finally, only the "contritionist" heresy was left) and most of them are reported in the somewhat ambiguous reply of Vincent de Paul to the request of Lescot. According to this testimony Saint-Cyran was a man of perfect virtue, but Vincent did not want to listen to his advice concerning the Congregation des Prêtres de la Mission, and

he never called Saint-Cyran "mon maître." Only once did he hear
Saint-Cyran saying (one of the charges) that God had destroyed
the Church five or six centuries ago, but by this expression he
wanted only to deplore existing corruption. He had never heard
Saint-Cyran stating that the Tridentine Council was illegitimate
(another charge) or that a just man ought to obey no other law but
the internal movement of grace, much as he used to talk about
those movements and to quote Paul's *iusto lex non est posita*. Neither
had Saint-Cyran argued that the Jesuits should be destroyed; he
had rather praised the first fathers of the order, but he blamed some
of the later writers of the company because of their opinions on
divine grace.[121]

Whatever Saint-Cyran might have said in private, the Jansenists, while they never publicly questioned the Tridentine decrees
—this would have amounted almost to self-excommunication—
and quoted them when it was appropriate, probably felt some discomfort about some of the council's statements; apart from the at-
trition/contrition distinction, the canons on justification were not
unequivocally Augustinian and left room, as has been mentioned,
for semi-Pelagian interpretations, which Jesuit theologians did not
fail to exploit.

Orcibal, who makes the distinction between Lovanian and
Saint-Cyranian variants of Jansenism (after the Arnaldian and
Quesnelian varieties), argues that it was Saint-Cyran, rather than
Jansenius, who endowed the movement with its characteristic
ethos; an ardent seriousness, and a hatred of undemanding and self-
ish religiosity, and of compromises.[122]

Much as they might have differed from each other in character and in the focus of their respective interests, one may safely say
that Saint-Cyran expressed Jansenius's theological intransigence in
terms of educational, devotional, and pastoral work; they were two
sides of the same coin. It is plausible to think that the harassment
and persecutions of Jansenists in general, and of Port-Royal in particular, did not result simply from the incompatibility of the theological tenets of Augustinians and Molinists. The course of events
was to some extent influenced by the militant and sectarian spirit of
their campaign. Had they not systematically expounded their beliefs in a strongly polemical anti-Jesuit context, thus declaring war
on a very powerful organ of the Church, had they not tenaciously

clung to the literal exactness of their theology, had they employed more cautious and less bellicose language, they would perhaps have got away with their doctrinal bias; François de Sales held virtually the same views on contrition as did Saint-Cyran, and even the Augustinian dogmas on predestination and grace could have been phrased in a manner that would not give the impression that a new "sect" was in the making. (The simple saying that "God's will cannot be overpowered" could not have been attacked.)[123] But then there would have been no "Jansenism," only one more devotional school advocating a more rigorous and less indulgent approach to moral issues. Jansenism arose from a sense of urgency, or even despair, from the feeling that Christianity was in mortal peril, that depravity in the Church imperatively required immediate action.

No doubt in their anti-Jansenist war the Jesuits behaved abominably and cruelly; especially their mean and vindictive treatment of pious and defenseless women of Port-Royal who were never involved in any theological squabbles caused widespread and understandable indignation.[124] But the Jansenists were not only superior to their adversaries in theological orthodoxy and literary skill; they were self-conscious, indomitable fighters. What they wanted was not just to express their theological and moral views but to defeat their semi-Pelagian foes and eventually to conquer the Church.[125]

A Note on Philosophy

The battle was not supposed to be waged on the field of philosophy at all. Jansenism was usually no less antiphilosophical and antischolastic than the launchers of the Great Reformation, and for the same reason. Jansenius in his opus magnum says that the proper faculty of philosophy is the intellect, whereas the organ of theology is memory (without making a distinction between natural and revealed theology). This in itself was not a condemnation. Soon we learn, however, that there must be *limes ac modus* in examining divine mysteries and that one must always submit humbly to divine authority—conformably to the exhortations of the Scriptures. To apply human reason in this matter is highly dangerous; and we know that both Paul and the early fathers fought against "human philosophy." Scholasticism is no more than human (read: pagan) wisdom; "those scholastic truths or those miserable questions . . . are entirely a product of human thought," there is nothing certain and established in them, new opinions come to refute old ones, etc. And indeed, if you apply Aristotelian doctrine to things divine, you end up with the conclusion that the mysteries of the Trinity, the Incarnation and original sin are all false: the first because of the principle of identity, the second because two completed natures cannot have one hypostasis, the third because there is no sin without will.[126] And in his commentaries on the Psalms Jansenius's namesake and theological forerunner, the bishop of Gand, stated that all knowledge is vain if it is not based on divine light and the Church's teaching.[127] Saint-Cyran's aversion to philosophy was, if anything, even stronger; and Pascal, much as his work was to be absorbed into the Western philosophical canon, considered philosophy a futile business and did not want to be a philosopher. To be sure, Arnauld was a philosopher in the full sense, not only a theologian,[128] but he followed the Pauline warning "*sapere ad sobrietatem*" and cannot be accused of trying to fathom God's secrets by "human logic" or of expecting that faith can ever result from rational investigation. He was a semi-Cartesian; he saw nothing wrong in the cogito and approved the proof of the immortality of the soul in the *Meditations.* But according to the *Port-Royal Logic* he wrote with Nicole, the rational side of Christianity is that we may trust those who have proved that they deserve trust, and that the fulfilment of prophecies and of divine promises provides us with such proofs.[129] This is rather an encouragement to believe on practical grounds and not a claim that religious truths could be rationally established in a scholastic or Cartesian manner, let alone that reason might create genuine faith.

Infants in Hell

Among the characteristic tenets of the Jansenists—after the theology of efficient grace and predestination, the "contritionist" approach to the sacrament of penance, the general spirit of moral rigorism (one must live in separation from the world), their antischolastic, antirationalist, and anti-Pelagian zeal—there is one that might seem bizarre or freakish but is consistent with their world-view and gives an interesting insight into its meaning. According to a doctrine quite unequivocally stated by Augustine, unbaptized children who die without committing any actual sin suffer eternal torments in hell just because of not being baptized.[130] Jansenius strongly supports this opinion in various parts of the *Augustinus.* He blames the Pelagians for believing that newborn babies are pure like Adam before the Fall and that if they die in this state they receive eternal bliss,[131] and he repeats the Augustinian doctrine without allowing for any exceptions: dead unbaptized babies are eternally damned.[132] This is an argument to uphold the Augustinian notion of predestination: God does not want the salvation of all. And in 1623 Jansenius approved and praised a treatise exclusively devoted to this issue, by a fellow Augustinian, the Irish Franciscan Florentius Canrius.[133] The author argues that children are infected by sin while still in the womb of the mother, and that if they die with original sin not erased by baptism they "go into eternal fire" (*ituros in ignem aeternum, sensus poenam patiuntur, aeternam dolorem, aeternam tristitiam,* etc.) To make his point very clear, he says that in spite of the opinion of "some theologians," there is no "*medium locum felicitatis naturalis,*" nothing between celestial bliss and infernal torture, no place whose little dwellers will suffer only separation from God's beatific vision but otherwise enjoy natural happiness ("some theologians" include, as was known, Thomas Aquinas, who is not named, however).

This rather frightening doctrine seems to have been adopted by the Jansenists (and, earlier on, by Baius) as a matter of course; Saint-Cyran professed it, as did Arnauld,[134] and as did Pascal, as we see from his remark on original sin and hereditary guilt ("what is more opposed to our miserable justice than eternally to damn a child, who cannot have a will to commit a sin in which it seems to have had so small a part that it was committed six thousand years before it was in existence").[135] That, according to Calvin, dead babies may be justified without baptism is to Arnauld a proof that Calvin was not an Augustinian, contrary to what the Jesuits suggested.[136]

One may add that, according to common belief, the elect will feel enormous delight at the sight of the torments of the damned and so we should suppose that if the parents of the unlucky babies happen to be themselves baptized and saved (and babies frequently died just after birth), they will jubilate on seeing their offspring devoured by everlasting flames (this is an extrapolation: I have not seen this point specifically made by any Jansenist author).

This doctrine seems to fit the Augustinian notion of the primeval calamity: since original sin, besides utterly corrupting our nature, made us actually guilty, and since baptism, without healing our nature or enabling us to perform good acts by our will, erases this guilt, it is natural to think that, before receiving the sacrament, these poor little creatures are entirely in the possession of Satan and deserve to accompany him to the realm of darkness. And this is a matter of justice, considering that the infernal abyss is where we belong by nature.

But there is another side of the story. We all deserve damnation according to the rules of justice but we know for certain that God saves some of us as an act of his mercy. How do we know that his mercy cannot extend to unbaptized children? Is it simply because they were not baptized, and the elect must be born again *ex aqua* as a minimum condition? But some unbaptized adults seem to have been saved. Augustine himself mentions the most extraordinary story of Saint Dismas, the good thief crucified next to Jesus: he was the only person in history to whom the Savior explicitly said that he would be in paradise—and the same evening at that (but Augustine suggested that the criminal had been baptized either in prison or on the cross, by water flowing from the Savior's body).[137] And Ambrose mentions catechumens who suffered martyrdom for faith before baptism and believes that God adopted them among his children.

In other words, it seems possible that some adult unbaptized sinners can be saved; why not unbaptized babies, free of any actual sin? Should we say that the former received the "baptism of desire" and were rewarded as a result? But this is impossible in terms of the same Augustinian theology: nobody can be saved as a reward for good deeds or good desires, as there is nothing a human creature can do by his own will to increase, however slightly, his chances of being naturalized in heaven; if some pious desires arise in the human soul, this is not the work of nature but an act of the gratuitous mercy of God. If the inscrutable divine will mercifully elects some and justly rejects others, why should this choice be limited to adult sinners and be inapplicable to infants?

The mystery of the Augustinian approach to this question is this: that God is absolutely sovereign, nothing and no one can limit him or impose any rules on him. His will makes the norms of justice, rather than being subordinated to such norms; otherwise the latter should be preexisting and independent of his decrees. He can, if he so wishes, accept anybody into his kingdom and convert his most hardened foes (again, the paradigmatic example of Paul). But, if we are to believe the Augustinian theology, he *cannot* save babies who, apart from the infection of Adam, are innocent. This is really a strange doctrine. God is sovereign but, as far as babies are concerned, he seems to be helpless, as if there were simply an iron law independent of his will which prevents him from rescuing them.

And if indeed it is fair to say that the teaching on the fate of unbaptized babies, while consistent with Augustinian "anthropology" insofar as it adds even more color to the image of a human world obsessively focused on the story of original sin, is inconsistent with the belief in the absolute sovereignty of God, we may argue that, apart from giving an interesting insight into the way God rules his messy farm on earth and into the very nature of the Lord, this reveals a possible tension between the two main pillars of Augustinian theology, God's illimited sovereignty and man's total corruption; it looks as if the latter limited the former or had precedence.

God is merciful, and this means: we are at God's mercy. We ought to love him, all of us, but only those of us to whom God himself has mercifully conferred the proper skill are able to perform this supreme duty. Ultimately it seems that our love of God is, as Spinoza would have it, a part of God's infinite self-love.

So it is in theological terms. But the more important reason why unbaptized children are inescapably damned is institutional; indeed it might have been seen as a matter of *stantis vel cadentis Ecclesiae*. What is at issue is the indispensable role of the Church as the mediator between God and his creatures. If it is possible to be saved without baptism, then the celebrated formula of Cyprian, "no salvation outside the Church," in the sense in which it was interpreted until recently, is not valid; the Church is not necessary for salvation, therefore it is not necessary altogether. The charismatic concept of the institution and its legitimate continuity become doubtful. Only God saves, of course, but he makes his choice, according to Augustinian theology, from among the congregation of the faithful, the members of the Church. Nobody from outside the visible Church belongs to the invisible one, to the communion of the predestined. A necessary condition of salvation is institutional. For this reason the validity of baptism is to be defined in institutional terms only, and the long and arduous battle of Augustine against the Donatist heresy was crucial in keeping intact the continuous, exclusive right of the Church to define the validity of the sacraments and the Church's perfect purity, all the misdeeds of churchmen notwithstanding. Baptism is valid if it is conferred by a validly ordained priest, who might be a heretic or a great sinner ("Whom Judas baptized, Jesus baptized"); the grace of sacraments comes from the Savior, not from a priest.[138] And the Church is *columba casta*, a pure dove, whatever might happen. God-instilled faith in Jesus Christ—explicit, not merely implicit—is certainly a condition of salvation but it can have its effect only among the baptized. On all these issues the Jansenists were loyal Augustinians.

The Gnostic Temptation

Original sin and the corruption of nature as the main conceptual framework (or "hermeneutic device") that makes the human condition intelligible and to which all sides of our life have to be referred, cannot be explained simply by the Latin mistranslation of a sentence in an epistle of Saint Paul. The famous sentence was indeed routinely employed to support the Augustinian interpretation of the catastrophe that made us what we are, but this very interpretation was a powerful expression of a more deep-seated worldview which may be called the *gnostic temptation*, and this temptation is almost unceasingly present in Christianity.

The word "gnosis" covers, of course, numerous groups, sects, doctrines, and heresies, some of them heterodox Christian, some not Christian at all, and if we rely on historians who succeeded in extracting from this *moles indigesta* a few basic recurring topics, we notice immediately that the very foundation of the gnostics' soteriology is not only incompatible with, but radically opposed to, Augustinian teaching, namely, their belief that a special kind of enlightening knowledge which we can gain by our *own effort* will bring us salvation. The temptation thus refers not to soteriology but to cosmology, to the very way the dichotomy world/God, good/evil, light/darkness, is drawn. To be sure, no Augustinian, under the threat of self-excommunication from the Church, could openly embrace the Manichean or Cathar doctrine and suggest that the body as such is evil or that we are imprisoned in flesh as a punishment, let alone that the material universe is a mischievous contrivance of God's everlasting enemy. But the Augustinians—by no means only the Jansenists—went in this direction as far as dogmatically conceivable, and sometimes stopped at the very brink of the unspeakable Manichean heresy. In various ways they spelled out their unshakeable feeling that the world we live in is not the world we really belong to, that our home is elsewhere, that we are pathetic creatures condemned to wade through the mud of this valley of tears and that the only thing we ought to think about is the moment we will end our journey. They really felt coerced into sharing the citizenship of two incompatible and hostile realms— the divine and the bodily—and there was no shortage of New Testament quotations to reveal this hostility: the Savior said that he was not of this world (John 8:26) and his favorite apostle warned us that we must not love the world, lest we perish with it (I John 2:15–17).

It has been mentioned that the clash between Augustinian and Pelagian or semi-Pelagian thinking, as we see it with the benefit of hindsight, was rooted not only in various social and cultural conflicts but in the conceptual fission of the idea of creation. It was this split which, to a large extent, was responsible for the birth of neo-Platonic metaphysics.

The Jansenists were on the "dualist" side of the cleft. Understandably enough, they were mistrustful of Aquinas's hylemorphic philosophy, despite the fact that the definition of the rational soul as the form of the human body had been dogmatically nobilitated at the Council of Vienne. The Thomist universe was a place of perfect and pleasant hierarchically ordered harmony; in the substantial unity of soul and body this harmony is displayed. We are not torn between two opposite poles of attraction, we have our satisfying niche in the cosmic order; the human being is neither soul nor body but a compositum, and the dogma of the resurrection of bodies is perfectly in keeping with this philosophical insight.

But in the Augustinian world—and emphatically so in its Jansenist variant—we are torn asunder between our belonging to two inimical cities; in every moment of life we face a frightening choice: world or God, darkness or light, evil or good, Satan or Christ, flesh or spirit, and all those dilemmas amount to one. Much as the Jansenist thought might have been "Christocentric," the resurrection of the body was not one of their themes. Nor was the essential goodness of matter or the mystical adoration of God in every grain of sand, in every leaf of grass.

Gnosis, according to one of the best-known historians of this phenomenon, "reveals [to man] his true nature, his genuine and permanent being, it makes him know or recognize *who* he is, what he is in himself and never ceases to be. . . ." It assures him that "he does not belong to the world, that he is not 'of the world' even though he is 'in the world', that he goes where he came from, that the place and the state he goes to have to be the same, that they were originally and previously his own, in principle and beyond the world and the becoming." A gnostic feels that he has been "thrown" into the world and his supreme desire is to deliver himself from carnal life; he experiences his own body as an alien thing, a prison or an oppressing chain, a source of suffering and nothing more.[139]

It is arguable that the clearly unChristian part of the gnostic legacy—the belief in a special kind of salutary knowledge that opens the path to deliverance and that it is up to us to acquire—survived in the utopian mentality, whereas the other part—the painful experience of not-belonging to "the world," of being an alien—persisted as a standard tenet of the Augustinian wing of the Christian sense of life.

Curiously, the gnostic temptation was reinforced by an impulse coming from an entirely difference source: Cartesianism. Human reality, defined in terms of *cogitatio* alone, was opposed by Descartes to the material universe that was governed inflexibly by a few simple mechanical laws; the world became soulless and godless, having no final causes, no moral qualities, and no mystery, transparent to the eye of a scientist, whereas human existence, in metaphysical terms, became bodyless. Thus we had to confront two areas of reality, severed from, and alien to, each other, naturally incommunicable.

Certainly, the conclusions are not gnostic at all, quite the opposite: the lifeless universe was not a terrifying cave, a sinister cage from which we ought to try to escape and with which we must have as little to do as possible; it was rather a territory to be conquered, a field on which the human will to power would assert itself. But the radical separation of the human soul from the cosmos, once it was inserted into the Augustinian context, could and did give the diluted and adapted gnostic tradition a new, unexpected stimulus. How the Cartesian feeling of the total "otherness" of the world converges, and makes a consistent alloy, with the Augustinian contempt for the terrestrial realm can be seen in Pascal. "We are not of matter and we do not belong here," is both the gnostic and the Augustinian message (with different theological interpretations, of course); "we are not of matter, but, being infinitely higher than it, we have to compel it to serve our earthly needs and aspirations," is the Cartesian appeal. Benevolent God created the universe, no doubt, and supports it continuously, but for all practical purposes, in investigating the world we may safely forget him; the world our reason deals with carries no traces of the divine presence.

Hans Jonas, in discussing the legacy of gnostics, contrasts their image of the cosmos with the typical views of pagan antiquity: the latter, including in particular Plotinus, believed in the affinity of man with all cosmic energies; to the former, on the contrary, man and the cosmos were fundamentally, irreducibly alien to each other.[140]

One is tempted to see an analogous contrast between the Renaissance and Baroque civilizations. Jean Mesnard, for example, discusses the cultural mutation that occurred in France around 1630, after about half a century of slow preparation.[141] He points out that the Renaissance *vision du monde*, embodied by la Pléiade, was based on the quasi-Platonic, optimistic belief in universal harmony and in the network of correspondences between microcosmos and macrocosmos. This image of cosmic unity, vaulted by a benevolent providence, is replaced by the new one, from which stability, peace, and harmony seem to have vanished; what dominates is disquiet in the face of a world that is alien, hostile, and threatening; an individual asserts his dignity against the world, and their incurable heterogeneity is expressed, among other things, in the revival of Stoic philosophy, in the exaltation of the individual will affirming itself in its tragic opposition to indifferent nature. Mesnard even notices an infiltration of the new life-perception in the Molinist emphasis on the human will in the work of salvation (not quite plausibly perhaps; to the Molinists, however often they might have quoted Stoic sages, the world was a cozy home, rather than a place of tragic conflict). A component of this new attitude is the emergency of classicism, a return to sober and precise language, devoid of artificial frippery, an emphasis on abstraction and rationality. Descartes fits into this picture, according to Mesnard. He fits, certainly, but only in part, and the same may be said of Augustinians and Molinists: no major philosophical or religious current perfectly embodies the baroque world-outlook.

We are naturally prone to seek an explanation of such cultural mutations, and usually there is no shortage of plausible-looking causes. In the case under scrutiny we can also list a number of agencies that operated earlier or simultaneously with the cultural changes we are trying to understand: religious wars; the development of absolutism and centralization; the enfeeblement of parliaments; geographic discoveries that opened new vistas on the world and produced increasing uncertainty about the unshakeable and everlasting validity of Christian and European values; the Turkish encroachment on European soil; Copernican cosmology and Galileo's physics. But we are never sure about what really came first— social, political, and scientific changes, or transformations in mentality (*Lebensgefühl*, as the Germans would have it). Assuming that a mutation did in fact occur from the prevailing Renaissance mentality, as it was expressed in literature, the arts, and religious thought, to the spiritual world of the Baroque (and chronology is never consistent in such matters; some ideas the gnostic tradition is credited with can be found in Greek and Roman mysteries, in medieval Augustinism, and among the early pioneers of the radical Reformation in Germany), was it not a mutation in the modern sense, a simple turn of events due to chance?

A proviso is needed at this point, although it is obvious and uncontroversial. The Jansenists were not "crypto-Calvinists" as their enemies suggested. Their doctrine of predestination was indeed very close to, if not identical with, Calvinist teaching, for all their efforts to prove the opposite. But in such important matters as the interpretation of the Eucharist and of penance, the sacrament of priesthood (to which they attached special weight), the apostolic succession, the cult of saints and of the Holy Virgin (prominent in Saint-Cyran), and the very concept of the Church, including the hierarchy and the papacy, they were emphatically, unequivocally Roman. They were a bona fide part of the Catholic Church and an important organ of the Counter-Reformation. Their leading figures (including Arnauld and Nicole) wrote powerful anti-Calvinist pamphlets.[142] Later on, they applauded the revocation of the Edict of Nantes. The Church was not primarily and originally defined by a particular view of the relationships between grace and nature—a fragile area of subtle, and never-ending theological distinctions— but by a theoretical framework which asserted exclusive legitimacy of the Church as the immutable *corpus mysticum*: the continuity of the priesthood, the primacy of the bishop of Rome, the "real presence" of Jesus Christ's body in the holy sacrament. On all these fundamental points the Jansenists did not need to evade contentious issues (unlike in the question of efficient grace) or to seek refuge in ambiguities; they were wholeheartedly Roman. Neither did they believe in the inamissibility of grace or in the certainty of salvation.

And they were a powerful organ of the Counter-Reformation in that they took over some aspects which, in cultural terms, gave the Reformation its strength: moral rigor; a spirit of seriousness and of discipline; a piety that was concentrated on the doctrine of original sin, of human corruption, and of the day of reckoning; the image of God as being, above all, the stern Judge; the great weight they attached to the reading of the Bible and an attempt to make the Scriptures accessible to all the faithful. "The Jansenists resemble heretics in the reform of morals but you [i.e., Jesuits] resemble them in evil," as Pascal was to say.[143] What this evil was supposed to be is not explained.

As to the universal accessibility of the Scriptures, the Jansenists shared some, but not all, of the reasons advanced by the Protestants. The principle that everybody ought to, and should have, the opportunity to read the Bible was, during the Reformation, part of the attempt to depose Church tradition as a separate source of authority, and thereby practically to break the continuity of the ecclesiastical organism. The latter would then risk becoming a secular institution for religious purposes, rather than an infallible keeper of the eternal truth, and the abolition of the sacrament of priesthood completed the break. The Jansenists cannot of course be accused of such a sinister motivation. On the contrary, they never tired of quoting the decrees of various councils and papal pronouncements, and their attachment to tradition was genuine and unwavering. But their insistence upon the accessibility of Scripture—time and again supported by appeals to the practice of the early Church—was well in keeping with their spirit of seriousness and their belief in predestination as they understood it.

The reluctance of the Church to make the Scriptures accessible to all was based on obvious reasons: it was the book of heretics, and free reading could only result in further heresies, in false and dangerous fantasies which poorly educated Christians would spin from a superficial acquaintance with the text; and such a license would blur the distinction between priests and the simple faithful. Jesuit writers were very explicit on this point. Father François Garasse, in his antilibertine *summa*, says that some people infer from the Bible that they should obey God only, and not earthly powers, or that God did not divide people into rulers and subjects. "Badly understood Scriptures can more easily lead a mind to atheism than any form of human persuasion." Women especially should be kept away from this dangerous text—and from all learning, for that matter (a learned woman is a greater horror than a bearded one); the virtue of a young girl would be seriously harmed if she were allowed to peruse the Song of Solomon or the story of Susanna, etc.[144] Plenty of similar warnings may be found in Jesuit literature, as in the popular and often reissued handbook by Martin Becanus.[145]

The Jansenists could not be moved by such arguments; to them the word of God was obviously addressed to his entire flock, and to withhold it from people for opportunistic or political reasons runs counter to God's intention. And if you are a beneficiary of divine grace, you will not err in understanding the Lord's message; if you are not, nothing will help you anyway.

Just as the Jansenist counter-reformation, in order to fight the Calvinist enemy with his own weapon, assimilated those aspects of heresy which were relevant to moral life, and inevitably contaminated itself with some of its dangerous theological tenets, the Jesuit counter-reformation took up the tradition of secular humanism and tried to baptize it or to make it into an instrument of the Church. And they, too, were infected by the adversary they wanted to neutralize by assimilation. This is a common phenomenon in the struggle of ideas.

Jansenism was not strictly speaking a "sect," not only because its followers considered themselves faithful carriers of the genuine Christian tradition (most Christian sects made identical claims) and indeed of the spirit of the Roman Church, but because they were never, in fact, separated as a group from the Church. Jansenius's statements were condemned long after his death, so he himself could not have been declared a heretic. Nor were Saint-Cyran or Arnauld or any of the leaders, all censures, imprisonment, and persecution notwithstanding. Jansenism was not a sect but a reactionary party within the Church (they would be described as "fundamentalists" in today's parlance). It was clear on various occasions that Rome was unhappy about the quarrel and would prefer to silence Molinists and Augustinians alike; the combative mood of both camps made this impracticable, and the Church took a step the extraordinary importance of which it may, as I have argued, have been unaware: by condemning by proxy the teaching of Augustine, it demolished the main theological barrier between itself and modernity.

It has been pointed out—by Sainte-Beuve among others—that Jansenius's constituency was the educated middle class (including some of the secular clergy), parliamentarians, lawyers, and, in general, the *noblesse de robe*. This does not imply that there was a *vinculum substantiale* between Jansenist theology and the specific class interests of the *noblesse de robe*; Goldmann's attempt to establish this link and to prove that Jansenism was no more than an expression of this particular interest is ingenious but unconvincing and artificially concocted; it starts with the dogmatic assumption that every ideological movement of any importance must reflect the aspirations of a specific social class.[146] The monarch, as a result of Jesuit intrigues and pressures, wanted to eradicate the movement not because he perceived it as a class enemy but because he feared—perhaps not quite irrationally—that a large-scale clash, no matter on what seemingly trifling or intricate issues, might bring danger to the state and the crown, since almost the entire educated and active population of France was entangled in the quarrel, on one side or the other.

Nicole, after Saint-Cyran, depicted the unique ethos of the hard Jansenist religiosity with particular clarity and explicitness, and it may be worthwhile to single out the main points of his preaching.

First, the stress laid upon faith as an act sui generis, never to be confused with beliefs that are commonly referred to by this name. Genuine faith is to be distinguished from (1) the faith of demons, based on proofs; (2) human convictions supported by these very proofs; (3) beliefs based on false assumptions, as in Muhammed's religion; (4) "a faith that God could give to all people by the light of intellect alone."[147]

Faith must be present in all our acts without exception: we get up in the morning because God orders us to take up our duties; we eat not for pleasure but because God orders us to sustain our life, etc. So the truth of faith cannot be left to, or even discussed in terms of, reason. If even one single point of faith were submitted to the judgment of reason, we should have to acknowledge that all of them must be thus submitted, and consequently we would die without faith; we must surrender ourselves to the Church.[148] If Nicole occasionally speaks well about reason, this is only when reason is contrasted with passion, never when it is contrasted with faith.

Second—and this is the crucial point—there is no faith without love towards God; no faith without charity. This point was later condemned in the *Unigenitus* but it was repeatedly attacked before then. It was, indeed, suspect on two grounds: because the unity of faith and love implied that impeccably orthodox beliefs are worthless and cannot be seen as a separate virtue; and because it might easily suggest that once you feel you love God you do not need to bother about dogmas. This is precisely what some dissidents in the Reformation did, and argued on this assumption that the Church had better be abolished altogether.

Third, love towards God must always, incessantly, and unconditionally fill our entire soul, our being. "God, strictly speaking, requires from men only their love; but He requires it in its entirety. He does not want men to have any attachment elsewhere; they must not find rest in any creature as no creature is their end."[149] We may love creatures, in particular other people, only by reference to God, never for themselves. "The serfdom of men in God is total and embraces all moments of their lives; therefore they are in duty bound to act for the sake of God in all moments of their lives."[150] "God must occupy the entire soul of a Christian."[151]

It is always either-or: craving or love; no motivation except love of God is of any value. People should not worry too much about the death of their nearest and dearest; indeed, Chrysostom threatened those who did with excommunication.[152] Everyone should "withdraw from the world" to the extent necessary in order to obey God.[153] The condemnation of amusements, curiosity, idleness, honors, luxury, wealth, etc. is routine, of course; but one wonders where to place the distinction between venial and mortal sins. We are taught, for instance, that women who bare their hands or arms commit a mortal sin, as they arouse evil lust in men, which amounts to "spiritual homicide."[154] Marriage itself cannot be condemned as such; "marriage regulates lust, but it does not make it regular; lust in itself is always irregular and it is only by force that it is kept within the limits prescribed by reason."[155]

Nicole (himself an exquisite stylist, called by Bayle "one of the most beautiful pens of Europe")[156] is particularly harsh in condemning literature and theater; he devoted a separate treatise to the subject. "Since it is certain that if dramas could agree with the rules of Christianity, it would doubtlessly be those of Mr. de Corneille, there is no better way of revealing the dangers they all carry than by showing that the dramas of this very author are most contrary to the Gospels, that they corrupt the mind and heart by the heathen and profane feelings they inspire."[157] "An author of romances or a dramatist is a public poisoner, not of the bodies but of the souls of the faithful; he should be considered guilty of infinite spiritual homicides, whether he effectively committed them or could have caused them by his pernicious writings. The more effort he makes to cover the criminal passions he depicts with a veil of honesty, the more dangerous he makes them, and the more apt to corrupt simple and innocent souls."[158] "By its own nature the theater is a school and an exercise of vice because it is an act in which [the author] necessarily has to excite in himself vicious passions."[159] All temporal things are just shadows without substance, employed by the great seducer, and the theater is the "shadow of a shadow, the figure of a figure."[160]

When Racine, by then the young author of two tragedies, produced his celebrated letters and castigated his former teacher for such extravagant views on the theater, he proved that he had failed to grasp the spirit of Port-Royal, where he had received his first schooling. He asked what was wrong with innocent amusements, poetry, and theater. But to the Saint-Cyranians everything was wrong with these things; there is simply no such thing as an innocent divertissement, for to amuse oneself is no less than to abandon God, even for a short time. Should we weep all the time and never laugh? asked Racine. Yes, exactly—was the Saint-Cyranian reply.[161]

Strongly phrased "contritionism" is a natural ingredient of this mentality. Since love of God is the supreme commandment, and all commandments must be obeyed out of this love, it is clear that the servile fear of punishment, since it is selfish, is worthless, and that if we forebear from evil acts for no better reason we still sin against God; our apparently good acts don't count before the Judge if they are prompted by anything but pure love of God (and since, as Nicole repeatedly says, very few people love God, it is safe to suppose that very few will be saved; this was, for that matter, a standard belief of the Jansenists).[162]

It is worth noting that Nicole, like most of his fellow Jansenists, is suspicious of mystical language. He fulminates against Desmarets de Saint-Sorlin, writer and anti-Jansenist pamphleteer, who earlier in his life, as he himself acknowledges, practiced the most abominable craft (he wrote novels and plays), and then keeps talking about mystical "anéantissement" and claims to be a God-anointed prophet. Nicole's point is that persuading people to desire spiritual annihilation is in effect telling them to follow their whims of the moment, and that this allegedly privileged state, because it is supposed to blot out the memory of the past and anticipation of the future, abolishes moral discipline. Moreover, if I pretend to know that I have emptied myself and that only God operates in me, I fall into heretical Calvinist hubris, for this kind of certainty is impossible.[163] A strong mistrust of mysticism is important in the description of the Jansenist mentality insofar as it shows their emphasis on moral discipline and distinguishes them from all kinds of "enthusiasts" and fanatics—including the Compagnie du Saint Sacrement —whom Nicole repeatedly castigated, associating them with German Anabaptists, Quakers, etc. His strictures on mysticism are the same that led to the condemnation of quietism (he directed a strong attack against Mme Gyuon and her followers). But on the question of grace he was not an orthodox Augustinian.[164]

This insight into Jansenist mentality may be supplemented by the pedagogical rules elaborated by Jacqueline Pascal, Blaise's younger sister, for Port-Royal's school for girls.[165] An extreme and very detailed form of discipline is recommended in order to teach the pupils to think of God only. From the tender age of four, when the children entered the school, they were required to spend as little time as possible on things like combing their hair and dressing, because their bodies were to become food for worms. They were trained in self-mortification and taught to do gladly all the work they most disliked, for the less their work was pleasing to them, the more it pleased God. Their movements were strictly regulated; they were not to look about when in chapel; most of the day they were to keep silent; they were never to write letters or notes to each other without the permission of the mistress; in the refectory they had to keep their eyes lowered; under no pretext could they touch, kiss, or hug each other; they were taught humility, trained to confess their defects publicly, and taught that for a God-loving soul nothing was of little importance: everything was great. Consequently, they were not to place much weight on the distinction between light and heavy sins. Only edifying religious books were, of course, permissible.

The point is not to what extent such rules differ from those established and enforced in schools run by other orders, but that they are unmistakably Augustinian and naturally arise from the idea of the utter depravity of human nature. For them to be properly justified in theological terms it is not enough to believe that we should constantly be thinking of God and referring to Him our thoughts and deeds; it is in addition necessary to admit that our corruption is total and incurable, that our main task is to pray to the Lord to heal us and that whatever comes from nature is rotten and hostile to God. No concessions must be made to the body and to the profane life, to natural emotions and natural desires, even seemingly innocent ones.

If we ask whether this hostility to the profane is an essential part of the Christian legacy the answer is probably yes, but only on an Augustinian interpretation of original sin. But theologians may argue—and some did—that this was an idiosyncratic interpretation, not necessarily justified by the canon of the New Testament. "Secular Christianity" is an oxymoron; but a Christianity that accepts, within wider or narrower limits, the right to self-rule of the realm of the secular is not. The trouble, however, is that these limits cannot be defined in advance nor can an agreement be reached about how to enforce them on the basis of the original canon; cultural conditions settle the limits, not an immutable text of the Gospels. Therefore the Jansenists might have been right in fearing that any concessions would have a self-propelling tendency and set in motion further demands, so that once a "limited autonomy" of the profane is conceded, it easily degenerates into the attitude of "anything goes." To speak of Christianity in any recognizable sense is, then, pointless, and the distinction between the two realms simply disappears; where there is no Sacred, there is no Secular either. Ultimately this is what the entire battle between Christianity and the Enlightenment has been about.

The battle between the Jesuits and the Jansenists—i.e., modernists and reactionaries respectively—was of course fought on a field where all the players were strongly committed to the Church and the Catholic faith. But they all knew that they lived at a time when the norms of their world were being relentlessly and mercilessly undermined by the new civilization—in science, in customs, in philosophy, and in art. Naturally enough, in view of the danger, each side within the Church perceived the other as enemies *intra muros*: the Jesuits, in the eyes of their foes, had entered into friendly negotiations with the devil and thus, whatever their true intentions, let him take his place triumphantly in the temple; the very identity of the Christian Church was thereby jeopardized and open to question. The Jansenists, in the eyes of the opposite side, were trying to make the Church into a besieged fortress, closing their eyes to reality, losing contact with the world, depriving the Church of any efficient tools to convert the pagan environment, and ultimately leading Christianity to disaster. Both were faced with an eternally recurring dilemma that never has a satisfactory solution: all concessions to the enemy are risky, but so is an intransigent attitude that allows no concessions. In this sense both were right.

To be sure, Jesuit "modernity" extended only to some areas of the new age: customs, social life, morality, theology, the general climate of humanism; they were reactionaries in matters concerning science. In this field it was Pascal who was modern. They condemned the new science in the name of revelation and, at the same time, extolled the power of reason *in divinis*; their trust in the rationality of the Christian faith and their sympathy with the humanist belief in natural religion were thus inevitably shallow.

What was at stake in the Molinist-Jansenist quarrel in philosophical terms is reducible, like all important questions ever debated in the history of Christianity, to the question of the relationship between the realm of nature, physical experience, and profane life, and the higher, divine reality that elusively manifests itself through nature. The Jansenists, driven by their gnostic temptation, saw this relationship as a radical discontinuity; profane life was for them a collection of obstacles and ambushes that we must overcome on the path to our home. That our earthly existence is a time of trial is, of course, a standard Christian tenet, but more premises are needed to conclude that the only thing that is of any value in this life consists of disciplining our wretched nature and that our attachment to anything but God is a terrible sin of idolatry. Such an attachment—or a belief that anything that is not eternal could deserve attention or love—is a never-ending temptation for souls crammed into the cage of flesh. It is consistent, from this perspective, to admit our own helplessness and to expect liberation only from the Savior.

It is not enough, for the Jansenists, to be a good Christian, to observe the commandments and to believe; they want us to be *nothing but Christians*, to deprive us of all that does not have a Christian meaning or, even if it does, is not generally perceived to have one. Everything, at every moment, must be directed towards God; whatever is not so directed is, in a strange sense, unreal. Disinterested curiosity, earthly love of any kind, the arts, our profane joys and pains—all this is unreal unless it has acquired a modest reality by being related to God. Tears, as Saint-Cyran taught—after Chrysostom—are for lamenting our sins; any other use of them is an abuse.[166] This might strike us as harsh—a mother weeping for her dead child would be committing an act of religious abuse—but it is perfectly consistent with the Jansenist mentality.

Can this mentality be called "theocentric" in the proper sense? This is by no means certain, because a genuine theocentric attitude includes oblivion to one's own salvation, whereas the spirit of Jansenism is focused on salvation as the supreme good, after God. The Augustinians had only scorn for people who say "Eternal salvation? Yes, but. . . ." There is no "but."

"Contritionism" and exhortations to love God in an entirely disinterested and unconditional way would seem logically to include wholeheartedly accepting hell for God's sake, as did Catherine of Siena or Theresa of Avila; but this was not a Jansenist theme.[167]

It is natural to suppose that, within this mental framework, a true Christian is a rarity, an exception, and that the overwhelming majority, by these standards, are actual or future hell-dwellers. Again, this was an all-or-nothing philosophy, a program to reduce the Church to a sect of the perfect, a recipe for disaster.

Jansenism was a religion not only without smiles or laughter but also without art and even without intelligence, for all the intellectual brilliance of its leaders and the genius of Racine, Pascal, and Philippe de Champaigne. It was a sad, oppressive religiosity concentrated on one task, however hopeless in the cultural conditions of the time: to quash corrupt human nature. But although the Jansenists often behaved fanatically, they were not just unreasonable fanatics obstinately defending a dogma. They were justifiably worried about the fate of Christianity, not merely and not mainly about the actual corruption in the Church and the moral standards of the faithful, but about the powerful trend to water down what had always been the proper meaning of the Christian religion. Christianity was built around the belief in salvation which Jesus had brought by his life and by his suffering on the cross. If it is supposed—as the semi-Pelagian doctrine suggested—that the unfaithful, e.g., the ancient pagan heroes and sages, could achieve meritorious virtues, if the unbaptized can perform salutary deeds and perhaps achieve salvation as a result of their own natural forces, then, indeed, "Christ died in vain," then one no longer needs Christ in order to be saved, and Christianity is useless, or reduced to a secular philosophy.

The Jesuits might have argued that they preached nothing of the kind: they stressed the omnipresence of "sufficient grace." This is true as far as it goes. But the Augustinians perceived in this doctrine—and not without reason—an effective way to consign Christ, and thus Christianity, to oblivion. For it teaches that God gave us grace and now everything depends on us; for all practical purposes this ubiquitous grace may be forgotten (just as God may be forgotten in Cartesian physics, although we are told that he created the world and sustains it in existence); we should rely on our own forces. Thus the cross is discarded and "Christ died in vain."

Priests and theologians knew what was at stake, but the Augustinian-Jansenist solution seemed to many of them unacceptable because it robbed all human effort of any value and destroyed whatever freedom remained in us: by nature we are like demons, and God, by miraculous intervention, transfigures demons into faithful angels, compelling them to be good. So some theologians, especially Dominicans, looked for a Thomist *juste milieu* to save both human responsibility and the cross. Time and again it turned out, on closer inspection, that this was a very arduous, if not an impossible, task, and the middle solution could survive only if one were inconsistent or reluctant to follow the problems through to the end.

Bayle commented briefly on this issue in his article on Jansenius, accusing all sides of the quarrel—Jansenists, Thomists, Calvinists and Molinists—of bad faith: "Someone said that questions of grace are like a sea without shore or bottom. He would perhaps have been more right if he had compared them to the straits of Messina, where one always risks being crushed on a rock while trying to avoid another one; *incidit in Scyllam cupiens vitare Charybdim.* Everything boils down to this: did Adam sin freely? If you answer 'yes' you will be told that his fall had not been foreseen; if you answer 'no', you will be told that he is not guilty. You can write a hundred volumes against either of these conclusions and still you will be forced to admit either that the infallible prevision of a contingent event is a mystery that is impossible to grasp, or that the way in which a creature without freedom can nonetheless sin is totally unintelligible. This is enough as far as I am concerned; since one has to admit one or the other of these incomprehensible things, what is the point of writing so much?"[168]

This is, of course, in keeping with Bayle's notorious scorn for theological subtleties: once we see that a problem is clouded by impenetrable mystery, we should forebear from discussion. But nobody—not even the pope—has proved successful in commanding silence on issues which, however mysterious, deal with our ultimate destiny.

Winners and Losers

Who won this deadly contest? The question is not meaningless, although the answer obviously depends on the timescale we adopt and on the very meaning of the word "win."

In the most direct sense the Jansenists were defeated, that is to say condemned by the Church; the later "anti-laxist" papal statements were incomparably less menacing, and their targets were some very specific moral propositions of unnamed Jesuit moralists rather than theological doctrines. To be sure, Jansenist attacks called public attention to the casuists' excesses and contributed to their censure; this, however, resulted in the withdrawal of some scandalous texts or in silencing some particularly frivolous Jesuit fathers. The Jansenists' indignation was to a large extent successful: the laxist style disappeared. But the order survived; its later dissolution had nothing to do with the seventeenth-century quarrel.[169]

The last great wave of persecution of the odious Augustinian "sect" came in the last years of Louis XIV with the ultimate physical destruction of the Port-Royal monastery (including the desecration of tombs) and the bull *Unigenitus* (1713). By then the great protagonists of the original Jansenism were dead. The bull was, if anything, of greater importance than the sixty-year-old *Cum Occasione*. The most Christian king himself, as was commonly known and as Clement XI informs readers in the preamble, frequently and with great zeal pressed the pontiff and demanded from him the condemnation (perhaps to his sorrow). We also learn from the preamble that false prophets, of whom Pasquier Quesnel turned out to be an outstanding specimen, are no less than Satan's disciples and followers (*mendacii parentis exemplo ac magisterio edocti*)—rather strong wording. Of the 101 false dogmas,[170] those concerning grace are so unmistakably and glaringly of Augustinian origin (some are literal quotations) that even the editors of Denzinger's *Enchiridion* deemed it proper to note, in their brief commentary, that many of Quesnel's heresies indeed show an affinity with the works of the Hipponian but that a genuine Catholic may not attribute to the latter any infallible and absolute authority (as Calvin, Baius, and Jansenius did) because his authority depends on acceptance and interpretation by the Church's magisterium. This is the most unambiguous admission from a semiofficial source that the teaching of Augustine on grace really was heretical.[171] Nothing remained of efficient grace, of course. It is heretical to say that in the new covenant God gives what he commands (prop. 3 and 6,7,8); that without Christ's grace we cannot profess him and with it we can never deny him; that grace is irresistible and that the divine will to save a soul must achieve its goal (10–21, 30–31); that all grace is given through faith, which is the source of all other graces (26–27); that no grace is conferred without the Church (29); that Jesus Christ shed his blood for the elect (32); that a sinner without grace is free only to do evil (38); that even the natural knowledge of God, like that of heathen philosophers, comes from God, and without grace breeds only vanity and presumption (41), etc. The Augustinian "all or nothing" principle, so emphatically assimilated by the Jansenists, is expressed by Quesnel in the daring and seditious claim that there are two kinds of love: love towards God and love towards the world and ourselves (44), and that there is no sin without the latter and no good works without the former (49). "Contritionism" is clearly asserted in the blasphemous proposition that to abstain from evil through sheer fear of punishment is to commit evil in one's heart and to be guilty before God (60,61,62).

Some of the condemned propositions might sound strange to readers who no longer remember the old quarrels: why should it be impious and pernicious, for instance, to say that "where there is no charity, there is neither God nor religion" (58), that "God rewards only charity, as charity alone worships God" (56)? And why is it that only a disciple of Satan can say that "those who want to approach God should not come to Him with bestial passions or be driven by natural instincts and fear like animals, but by faith and love, like children" (66)?

Yet the Church is rarely, if ever, reckless in such matters; the target of these condemnations was the idea, variously expressed by Augustine, Luther, and other early Protestants, and strongly supported by some Pauline antinomian sayings, of the unity of faith and love. And this idea was to be condemned for two reasons, one everlasting and the other circumstantial.

The temptation had always existed in Christianity to take a literal and unqualified view of the Pauline opposition of law and grace and to believe that all that matters in Christianity is faith (in the sense of "trust"), that true faith necessarily includes love towards God, and that he who is blessed by faith possesses all virtues and enjoys the status of God's child. All merits, all rules, all commandments, and all Christian values were concentrated in an undifferentiated act of faith/charity; whatever else is needed follows automatically, just as sins automatically follow the status of the sinner, and even the most heroic act of self-sacrifice is a sin if grace is missing. In other words, if you have true faith, you do not need to worry about anything else.

Taken unrestrictedly, this idea might amount to a denial of the Church: since grace is given to chosen individuals and makes them worthy of salvation, an ecclesiastical organization seems redundant. This is of course the extreme version, frequently to be found among the German prophets of the "inner word," and one which no Jansenist could be accused of preaching: on the contrary, the Jansenists never tired of praising the Church, the priesthood, the sacraments, and the hierarchy. But they preached—perhaps inconsistently—the irresistibility of grace and the vanity of all merits that are not rooted in faith. And the tension between the Church as the channel of grace and the same Church as a legalistically ordered earthly organ is ineradicable: it is part of the Church's own self-definition; it is perhaps a particular case of the universal tension between structure and meaning. In order to survive as an identifiable body and to perform its task as the guardian of moral order, the Church could not be satisfied with the idea of an unverifiable, heaven-sent faith; it must operate according to clear rules and tell its flock what exactly they are supposed to do or forbear from doing in order to be accepted by God. It has to have a hierarchy of sins and merits, to explain which sins are pardonable and which are not, which deeds are merely good and which really meritorious, etc. The "all or nothing" doctrine might be justifiable by some New Testament texts, but as an educational device it was inoperable, except perhaps in the early Church of martyrs. God is not a peddler of salvation; you don't negotiate with him about eternity. This is what the Augustinians seemed to teach. But life is too complicated, all of us are admittedly sinners, and it is most important to know the hierarchy of sins and merits: I might be imperfect in matters concerning adultery, but on the other hand I am good at celebrating the Sabbath, attending the Lord's table, and abstaining from blasphemy; should this not count? A moral price list is indispensable for a Church that sees itself as the master of souls and overseer of human conduct. And above all, to love God, to love him truly, is both a necessary and a sufficient condition of Christian life. And love is something one really has to feel, rather than merely profess; if I am not capable of experiencing it, what am I to do? Will I go to hell? Even if I am otherwise a model of a virtuous Christian? Then again, some people are heretics and some doctrinally pure—not a mean distinction; should it be a matter of indifference whether or not I am obedient in matters of creed? If not, I may count my obedience and adherence to the Church's dogmas a kind of virtue, a merit. Consequently a distinction is needed between "faith" in the sense of an intellectual act of assent and "faith" in the sense of real love and trust, and we ought to admit that the former without the latter *is* meritorious and will add to my credit on the day of judgment.

This is the everlasting, commonsense reason explaining why the Augustinian doctrine of salvation as well as the 101 errors of Quesnel were condemnable and why the condemnation was well-grounded. The circumstantial reason was the same as the one we have already mentioned in describing the meaning of Jesuit modernity; in the new world, full of novelty and excitement with the expansion of secular art, poetry, drama, history, and philosophy, new territories on the map of the earth as well as on the map of the spirit, with the endless expansion of human curiosity and creative effort, it was a hopeless task to convince people, in particular the educated classes, the nobility and the court, that they should live as if they were nothing but Christians, a pure embodiment of the spirit of the Gospels, that they should stifle their curiosity and their mundane interests. Christianity had to make itself, if not "easy," at least much easier, in order to survive. One could not resurrect as a universal norm the ethos of the apostolic time when the faithful really lived in the shadow of imminent apocalypse. But that is precisely what the Augustinians tried to do—to their doom.

Since many theologians, priests, and bishops were outraged by the apparently careless and frivolous casuistry of some Molinist writers without sharing the Jansenists' theory of efficient grace or their rigidity on the issue of contritionism, one may be tempted to ask why it was the extremists rather than the moderates who led the battle. One could, after all, be an earnest reformer and be scandalized by extravagances of the "easy devotion" without either being a dogmatic Augustinian or exposing oneself to the accusation of not taking Christianity seriously; a number of great names in the history of French "spiritualité" and theology of the seventeenth century can be quoted in this context. A combative spirit and a zealous self-righteousness can be found among extremists more often than among moderates, to be sure; this is included in the very nature of extremism. But this does not necessarily imply that "History" regularly puts extremists in the forefront of wars; sometimes She does, sometimes She doesn't. In all ideological and political conflicts an extremist wing is involved but often it survives on the margins and contributes little to the final outcome. It was not so in the case under scrutiny. Can we say that this was mere accident, perhaps the character of individuals, the extraordinary role of the formidable tribe of Arnauld? And would there have been Jansenism without Jansenius, perhaps with the name Arnaldism? It is difficult to ignore such questions, but they are, alas, unanswerable.

Another part of the bull deals with the question of access to the Bible. It was known that the Catholic Church had been very reluctant to allow, let alone encourage, laymen to read the Holy Scriptures, and the reasons for this unwillingness are obvious; that their interpretation was reserved for the clergy and that it was not for the common people to fathom the arcana of the Revealed Word had been stated more than once. But since the *Unigenitus* it became heretical, offensive to pious ears, injurious to the Church, impious, etc., to say that reading the Bible was for everyone, including women, and that it was contrary to God's intention and to apostolic practice to forbid it (props. 80–86). A common practice is one thing, a solemn anathema by the highest authority is another.

Three of the condemned propositions (90–92) have an indirect political meaning and might even be seen as a boomerang that hit the instigator of the bull, the king himself. According to the bull it is heretical, seditious, impudent, etc., to say that excommunications must be issued by the supreme pontiffs with at least a presumed consensus of the entire body (of the faithful); that the fear of an unjust excommunication must never prevent us from doing our duty and that we never leave the Church, even when we seem to be expelled from it by human malice, if we are attached by love to God, Jesus Christ, and the Church itself; that to suffer excommunication and anathema peacefully is to imitate Saint Paul, and by no means to rise against authority or to split the unity of the Church; and that Jesus heals the wounds inflicted without his authority by the inconsiderate haste of the supreme pontiffs.

Such a violent reassertion of absolute papal authority was generally, and rightly, perceived as a heavy blow to Gallican liberties. The commotion in France was much stronger and wider than after *Cum Occasione*.[172] Opposition to the bull was widespread both among the clergy, including a number of bishops, the archbishop of Paris among them (he had been, in fact, one of the targets of the Jesuit plot), and among lay Catholics. It is assumed that the bull fused Gallicans and Jansenists together into one camp; previously the two tendencies had overlapped but there was no natural affinity between them. Jansenius was an ultramontanist at least in the sense that he believed in papal infallibility, whereas Saint-Cyran was rather a Gallican. Earlier, the papal policy had been to do everything to rouse Gallican sympathies among Augustinians (even if they occasionally employed ultramontanist arguments when convenient) and the *Unigenitus* completed this development. And it contributed to making Jansenism into a political antiroyalist movement. The pope, so to say, overdid it, and unwisely stretched the front line beyond—as it turned out—the capacities of his army; by the brutality of the condemnation he needlessly multiplied his own enemies and those of the Holy See.

The question "Who won the contest?" can thus be seen in political terms and from the perspective of the later eighteenth century. The role played by the Jansenists, or post-Jansenists, in the French Revolution has been stressed by a number of historians, starting with Michelet. There was certainly nothing republican, let alone revolutionary, in the original message of the movement. The Jansenists repeatedly swore loyalty to the monarch, even amidst persecutions; their involvement in the Fronde was negligible. They tried by all possible means not to give their enemies grounds to justify the suspicion that they were plotting against the crown. But step by step, without seeking it, they were becoming the center which attracted various sorts of antiroyalist opposition.[173] Political Jansenism had little to do with efficient grace or with the proper interpretation of Holy Communion and penance. Among the great figures of the movement, some, like Arnauld and Nicole, accepted the idea of Christian politics based on traditional principles, whereas others, more radical, like Saint-Cyran, de Barcos, and Pascal, tended to see politics as a futile exercise or a necessary evil. And so, like the *Provinciales*, which became libertine reading, Jansenism, if it won in the revolution, did so in a perverse way, against itself, as a result of a strange mutation. This was, of course, the destiny of many influential ideas in history. The original Jansenism survived, certainly, but its significance was negligible.

We may go further yet and ask "Who won?" in terms of today's Catholic Church and its standard teaching. And then the answer is: the Jesuits did. Already in the late seventeenth century and even more so after the *Unigenitus*, the normal Catholic catechesis was semi-Pelagian, and popular Protestant writers as a matter of course identified the Catholic doctrine of grace and predestination with the Jesuit theology.[174] One hardly finds nowadays defenders of the Jesuits' loathsome and sometimes sadistic conduct in the affair, but the Jesuits won; not with the moral precepts of the "laxists," of course, but with the semi-Pelagian concept of grace. Recent official documents (e.g., Pius XII's encyclicals *Mystici Corporis Christi* of 1943 and *Mediator Dei* of 1947) and popular catechisms or handbooks speak of human *cooperation* with grace, meaning it literally, as cooperation in the sense of voluntary and free assent of the will (in the Augustinian sense, cooperation, even if the word is used, is ultimately fictitious because our will, in order to assist grace, has to be infallibly propelled by this very grace). The heavenly spirit, says the pontiff, does not want to help us in our striving after Christian perfection "unless men do their part by their everyday active assiduity" ("nisi homines quotidiana actuosaque navitate suas partes agent");[175] and in the sacraments there is no contradiction between efficacity *ex opere operato* and *opus operantis*, meritorious acts. Again, there is no shortage of biblical quotations: did not the apostle beseech us, as workers together with him, not to "receive the grace of God in vain"? (2 Cor. 6:1). Did he not say that "his grace which was bestowed upon me was not in vain"? (1 Cor. 15:10). The standard message of the Catholic Church to the faithful is: God wants to help you and indeed does help you to be worthy of salvation, but you have to help him, to put forth your will and make an effort if you are to be saved. We are capable, according to this teaching, of spurning divine aid or accepting it by a free act of assent. And since God refuses his assistance to no one, ultimately our salvation depends on us. This is the semi-Pelagian doctrine (at least as far as the so-called "synergy" is concerned, not necessarily in the sense that the first step towards conversion is taken by the human will alone, without the contribution of grace). A Catholic who believes that God gives some people irresistible grace, thus electing them to glory, and refuses aid to others by his sheer will, irrespective of their own merits, is probably a rarity today. And it would be extraordinary to meet a Catholic who is convinced that innocent infants, if they die without baptism, will suffer everlasting torment in hell. In fact, even the hope that ultimately everyone will be saved does not seem to some inconsistent with Christian dogma, the condemnation of Origen notwithstanding; and the theory of apocatastasis—including even the restoration of demons—was preached, apart from Origen, by a number of fathers, like Gregory of Nyssa and Gregory of Nazianzus.[176] Even the fact that the sacrament of penance is usually referred to as the sacrament of reconciliation shows the prevailing belief in "cooperation," in the full sense of the free will acting together with divine help in meritorious acts. In spite of all the condemnations of Pelagian and semi-Pelagian teaching, and in spite of the great popularity of Augustine's writings among today's active Catholics, the cornerstone of his theology of predestination seems to have been nearly lost. The Roman Church largely adopted, following the Jesuit philosophy, a doctrine which seemed more in keeping with the modern rationalist notion of justice, and this implies, ultimately, the long tradition notwithstanding, that salvation is not offered or denied gratuitously.

One might argue that the Augustinians' fears and worries were not well grounded, as Christianity has after all survived after adopting a semi-Pelagian doctrine of salvation; neither has it been transformed into a secular philosophy, despite the intense efforts of many Catholic theologians. The powerful image of Jesus Christ is still there: a good shepherd with wide-open arms. But it is not the Christianity that the Jansenists carried in their hearts. If they were here now they might say, with infinite sadness, that "the cross has been emptied." As a result of the long anti-Jansenist campaign, Christianity did undergo a mutation in both theological and cultural terms, imperceptible at the time. This probably made the survival of the Church possible, but at a price which the seventeenth-century Augustinians would have found exorbitant.

PART
TWO◆

Pascal's Sad Religion

Pascal's Heresy

When we ask whether Pascal was a heretic, the answer is no, not in the technical sense, of course, as he had never been declared a heretic by the authorities; if we ask instead whether he professed a heretical doctrine, the answer is yes, in the sense that all Jansenists professed a heretical doctrine as defined in the constitution of Innocent X.

A rapid survey of the texts known as *Écrits sur la Grâce* shows, unsurprisingly, his full agreement with Jansenius's and Arnauld's theology of efficient grace. This is Pascal's only properly theological treatise. Although never completed, and found in the form of a disordered manuscript which posed immense editorial problems to scholars, it is clear and unambiguous in its main idea. Jean Mesnard, who, after enormous labor, provided us with the definitive text and dated it convincingly (between the autumn of 1655 and the spring of 1656, i.e., shortly before, or concurrently with, the first of the *Provincial Letters*), says that it is "one of the clues to Pascal's entire oeuvre";[1] in the crucial questions concerning the Augustinian concept of grace, the *Écrits* follow the already established Jansenist doctrine, but the exposition is concise, lucid, and less involved in the polemical context than Arnauld's works. They give a much better insight into Pascal's views than the few sentences in the *Pensées* or the first three and the last two *Provincial Letters* that are devoted to the same or related topics. On a few points, however, we find interesting and original remarks which might be of relevance in reading the *Pensées*.

According to the "abominable opinion" of the Calvinists, God created some men for damnation and others for salvation by an act of absolute will, without foreknowledge of their merits; he caused Adam's fall and he sent Jesus Christ for the redemption of those he wanted to save; to the latter he gives charity and salvation, and he abandons the damned for their entire life; and there is no distinction in God between doing and permitting. The Molinists' error, on the other hand, consists in attributing to God a conditional will to save all people: Jesus Christ gave his redemptive grace to all without exception, and it is up to the human will to make or to fail to make proper use of this gift. Thus the Molinists make human, and not divine will, the cause of salvation or damnation. The Augustinians stress instead the crucial distinction between the innocent state of man as he was created and his condition after the Fall. What the Molinists present as the permanent condition of mankind applies only to the short span of time *ante lapsum*, when God could never justly damn anybody. After the Sin he could justly damn everybody, but he saves some "by an absolute will based on entirely pure and gratuitous mercy." It was Jesus' will that his merits be salutary to these people only. The damned perish by their own misdeeds, the predestined are saved by grace; there are, among the former, those who are "called" but do not persist in virtue and die in mortal sin because God refused them the grace of perseverance, without which they cannot have an effective will to the good. How the elected are separated from the mass of failures is "God's impenetrable secret," an "inconceivable mystery." It is not true, nevertheless, that the human will is passive in the process which leads people towards their eternal destiny; the human and divine wills converge (*concourent*) in both routes but the latter is dominant, "maîtresse"; it is "the source, principle and the cause" of the former and it works infallibly. While the first man's will, supported by grace, was at the beginning indifferent to good and evil, so that he could employ his freedom in either way, all his descendants inherited a will corrupted by the enormity of his crime and this will inevitably delights in evil. It is through gratuitous divine aid that the will without fail chooses God instead.

As to the impossibility of the just to abide by the commandments, the Augustinian-Jansenist tenet is repeated: it is always possible to fulfill all the commandments if the corresponding grace is given, and it is never possible without it; some of the predestined are temporarily deprived of help and, thrown upon the resources of their will, necessarily commit sins. If some anathemas of the Council of Trent are ambiguous on this point, they have to be interpreted in terms of those that are unequivocal, and then one sees that they bear out the Augustinian view.

Whereas the Calvinists' God strikes us by his cruelty and the Pelagians' doctrine is pleasant and flattering to common sense, the orthodox teaching of the Church is free of both errors. Still, according to Pascal, it is quite conformable to common sense.

It appears that the respective heresies of the Calvinists and the Molinists differ in that: while the latter extend the innocent status of the first man onto his entire corrupted progeny, the former see no difference between human nature before and after the Fall and see God's verdicts as independent from, and preceding, original sin. The two errors are thus symmetrical, even identical, to the extent that they both fail to see the fundamental difference between the human race before and after the Fall. One should conclude, therefore—even though Pascal does not say so in so many words— that the Jansenists differ from the Calvinists insofar as the status of Adam is concerned, but agree on the subsequent condition of mankind and on efficient grace. This "dialectical" method of reducing two opposite doctrines to a single mistaken tenet was to be called "récoupage" by Bergson, who used it on various occasions, for instance in pinpointing an identical error in both strictly teleological and determinist metaphysics.

There is no point in repeating the previous remarks on the five propositions. In theological terms Pascal does not seem to add anything to Arnauld's defense of *Augustinus*. Grace is both a necessary and a sufficient condition of human good deeds and it works irresistibly; from the very beginning conversion is God's act;[2] the elect can indeed keep the commandments as long as they enjoy the support of grace; their meritorious acts are necessary, but they are free all the same, as it is by molding the will that efficient grace performs the miraculous change; we can resist God's will, but never successfully; Jesus Christ died for the elect (one should mention, however, what Pascal—inconsistently—says in the seventeenth

115

Provincial Letter: that the fourteenth *Provincial Letter* had implied, contrary to Father Annat's contention, that Jesus Christ prayed for the damned). All five heretical statements are in Pascal's exposition and they keep the meaning obviously intended by the bull. By singling out, between the elect and the damned, the category of those who arrive at faith but go to hell because they lack the gift of perseverance, Pascal does not go beyond his teachers' dogma; the Jansenists had always admitted the presence of "justes temporels," people to whom God granted a measure of grace, thus enabling them to perform some good acts, but refused further support, indispensable (and sufficient) for salvation. By stressing the two kinds of "delights" (*délectation, suavité*) by which the just and the damned are attracted—God and earthly goods respectively—Pascal is not making a separate theological point either; this is no more than another wording of the same doctrine: instead of "compelling" people to do something against their will, God changes the will itself. And the reader is puzzled, no less than in the case of other Jansenists, by the meaning of the difference between the monstrosities of the Calvinist heresy and the true Catholic teaching in the question of the "absolute will" by which God from the very beginning decided to save some and to damn the others without "prevision of merits"; to say that God arbitrarily divided his creatures into sheep and goats "after" the sin of the first couple or "after" the prevision of their offense, simply makes no sense in theological terms, considering his timelessness. The distinction between Calvinist "supralapsarian" and Jansenist "infralapsarian" doctrines is a distinction without a difference, much as the Jansenists insisted on it in order to defend themselves against the accusation of crypto-Calvinism.

But the doctrine that the just must never be certain of the uninterrupted delivery of grace in the future (nor, however, must they despair) is indeed a Catholic, and not a specifically Augustinian one, and on this point, as Pascal says, the difference with Calvinism is real. And he points out that, even though in the Church's teaching the elect are sometimes called "all" ("parce qu'ils font une totalité"; an obvious reference to Jansenius's interpretation of Paul's fateful statement that Christ shed his blood for all), they are also called "few" because they are indeed few by comparison with the mass of the rejected.

Not unlike Arnauld, Pascal quotes in his exposition Augustine, some later doctors and some councils, but not earlier fathers.

The whole is summed up in an admirably brief remark in the *Pensées* (fr. 824): "the law obliges us to [do] what it has not given us [means to do]; grace gives us [the means to do] that which it obliges us [to do]." This is an apt rephrasing of Augustine's "God crowns his own gifts."

What is perhaps new in the text under scrutiny—though quite in keeping with Jansenist theology and indeed based on Augustinian texts—is Pascal's insistence on timing in the works of grace: "all those who have faith and prayer have it by efficient grace; and all those who do not have it have not full power to have it in the future" ("le pouvoir prochain," an expression ridiculed in the *Provincial Letters* but employed seriously in the *Écrits*). "This entails that all those who persevere in praying have an efficient grace which makes them pray and persevere in praying, and all those who have this grace do pray, whereas those who do not persevere in praying are deprived of this efficient grace and of grace sufficient in future ["grâce prochainement suffisante"], and those who are deprived of this sufficient grace do not pray; thus a just man stops praying only after God deprives him of efficient grace and of the grace sufficient in future for prayer." The anti-Calvinist point of this somewhat repetitive explanation apparently is that grace is not given as a single gift, enabling the beneficiary endlessly to draw on its wealth, but is a continuous process which can, however, be stopped at any moment by God's will; there is no guarantee from one moment to another. We ought to be unceasingly vigilant and to keep in mind the sacred dimension of time.[3]

Not being a priest, and therefore having perhaps a less restricted margin of intellectual maneuver than Arnauld, Pascal could afford to be more radical in his opposition to the papal verdict; he repeats the biblical "better to obey God than man" (fr. 916). The possibility of excommunication would have been, in his case, less calamitous and less threatening.

In the discussion on the signature of the "formulaire" he took a more intransigent position than Arnauld and Nicole, who were ready to make concessions and resort to ambiguities in order to prevent their "party" from being excommunicated. Pascal argued that to sign a formula condemning the five propositions "in Jansenius's sense" amounted to condemning Augustine and Paul, and that a reservation must be made to the effect that the signatories accept the papal bull only in matters of faith. He acted as a man of ideas to whom intellectual integrity is above tactical interest, whereas to the others the protection of the "party" was of paramount importance. Apart from the religious issue, this was a typical difference between an "ideologue" and a "politician."

The Strategy of Conversion

What is the relevance of Pascal's adoption of the Jansenist theology of grace to the reading of the *Pensées*, apart from the few references to this issue and the few anti-Jesuit remarks connected with the *Provincial Letters*? Or, to put it more strongly, in what sense are the *Pensées* a Jansenist text? The answer is not obvious. One may say, to be sure, that the omnipresent message of the text is that nothing matters more, indeed nothing else matters, than eternal salvation and God. Thus phrased, there is nothing specifically Jansenist in this saying and few things can be perceived in the Gospels with such certitude; if anything is unmistakably, unalterably Christian, this is.

But it makes a difference not only how seriously we apply this obvious rule but above all how we interpret it in terms of our daily life, our secular preoccupations. And the supreme rule does not by itself provide us with a clear answer. Should we escape from the world as much as possible, avoid contact with its dirty business, and strive after sainthood in isolation? Should we devote our life to converting others? Should we engage in all sorts of ascetic exercises and painful mortifications? Should we simply avoid major sins within our strength but otherwise enjoy the earthly life? Should everything in our life, at every moment, be consciously subordinated to the great rule, so that when faced with any decision, however trivial and inconsequential, we must ask about its possible relevance to salvation and perform no acts which, no matter how seemingly innocent, do not contribute to this goal? Or has the secular life some measure of independence, such that we may do our business without bothering about eternity, if only we do not use it as a pretext for unpardonable sins?

The answer given by the Jansenists—or rather by Saint-Cyran, Nicole, and Barcos—is sharp and unambiguous: whatever we do is for God or for the devil; nothing is morally indifferent; our every act and thought has to honor the Creator; we ought to fulfil our earthly duties, of course, but only as a matter of obedience to the commandments, never for our enjoyment, for pleasure, for gain, glory, or power. And they would have shrugged off the objection that they imposed impracticable requirements: our eternal bliss is at stake.

One of the issues involved was politics. Assuming that a genuine Christian must not take part in the immoral life of the court and power intrigues, is politics his legitimate concern, at least insofar as it deals with justice on earth? Or should we rather avoid the dangerous contamination of this filthy area and accept that secular justice is unattainable anyway and the world is incorrigible, beyond remedy? Another was the place of natural reason: to what extent is its use justifiable, especially in religious matters? Both issues are clearly prominent in Pascal's thinking.

It is an easy bet to make about the *Pensées* that no other single philosophical (if that is the proper adjective) text has absorbed so much of the energy and ingenuity of scholars, editors, and commentators, even though Lafuma proved that it had been left in a much less chaotic state than had been previously supposed. It is both hell and paradise for philosophers who parasitize on the assiduity of the investigators of manuscripts. On the one hand the disorder is still great, and will remain so; the margin of uncertainty is large, the internal concatenation of thought often doubtful, and the meaning of particular "items" sometimes opaque. On the other hand this very uncertainty opens to commentators a vast field to romp on, picking various flowers in a largely arbitrary order and arranging them in an attractive-looking bouquet. One often has the impression that various ways of reading the *Pensées* depend on where we decide to start and what we consider crucial or less important; and there are numerous fragments each of which one may put in the center and around which a coherent whole can be plausibly built. This is probably unavoidable. That the text has to be read in the Jansenist context is not a matter of contention, and philosophers who reflect on it usually avoid the peril—otherwise frequent and understandable—of dealing with it as a collection of ingenious aphorisms. Because of their popularity, there is even something embarrassing in quoting the *Pensées*: so much of it has been trivialized and worn out by overuse. One could even make a list of sentences that have become clichés as a result of this overwork. They are, at a guess (and in that order, setting the Wager aside):

"The heart has its reasons which Reason does not know." (fr. 423)

"If the nose of Cleopatra had been shorter, the entire face of the earth would have been different." (fr. 413)

"Man is only a reed, the weakest in nature, but he is a thinking reed." (fr. 200)

"What is man in infinity?" (fr. 199)

"The eternal silence of those infinite spaces frightens me." (fr. 201)

"The 'I' is hateful." (fr. 597)

For all that they grew on Jansenist soil, the *Pensées* obviously owe their significance and perennial freshness to the fact that they were the fruit of the intense meditation of a great independent mind and were not a party work, unlike Arnauld's *Fréquent Communion*, Nicole's *Imaginaires*, or, for that matter, the *Provincial Letters*. This is self-evident but perhaps worth mentioning as a point against artificial attempts to reduce the *Pensées* entirely to their Jansenist meaning. Apart from a handful of historians no one really any longer reads Jansenius, Saint-Cyran, Nicole, or Arnauld (except for the objections to the Meditations; but there the interest is in Descartes); even the Port-Royal Logic is reserved for a tiny bunch of people specializing in the intellectual history of the seventeenth century. And we read in the latter work (Second *Discours*): "there is no greater flaw in a book than the fact that it is not read."

The *Pensées* were meant to be an apology for Christian religion, that is, like all apologetical works, they attempted to reach and convince skeptics, doubters, the incredulous, rationalists or half-rationalists, those who hesitated or—and especially—were indifferent, and not pious souls blissfully immured in their faith. They were certainly not an effort on the part of the author to convince himself; there is not the slightest reason to doubt Pascal's unshakable faith, not only after but also before November 1654, the date of the "second conversion." (The expression "certitude, certitude" in the *Mémorial* (fr. 913) might suggest doubt: did he lack certitude before? But one should not read too much into this word.)[4] All the parts of the text have to be read as building blocks of an apology, not as a Jansenist pamphlet, and they are intelligible as such. At least two general characteristics of the text obviously resulted from its meaning as an apology.

First, to be effective, a defense of religion must examine and recognize the state of mind of the people whom it is supposed to convince. The author has to step into the shoes of his addressee, to take, at least provisionally, his standpoint, his interest. It is ineffective if it simply provides the reader with a number of time-honored, rational or spuriously rational arguments—as most apologies of this period did—without noticing the changes that had occurred in the mentality of the educated classes, without realizing that those changes made people intellectually immune to this kind of persuasion, but at best giving self-confident believers a guide, a collection of recipes to use when they are challenged in a discussion. Pascal sarcastically lets a Jesuit father say in the sixth *Provincial Letter*: "People today are so corrupted that, being unable to make them come to us, we had to go to them." The irony might not have been out of place considering the very generous interpretation some Jesuits used to give this prescription (to accompany sinners in order to convert them)[5] but in the fundamental sense he was following the same rule; one has to understand the mind of a reader (a libertine or an incredulous), make him understand his own situation, disclose to him his own soul and let the Christian truths hook on to what he really, if perhaps unconsciously, is, rather than simply repeating how he ought to conform to the Christian model.

Second, an apology, to be effective, has to be rational when addressed to people who boast of being rationally and critically thinking creatures. "Rational" does not mean "rationalist," that is, implying a well-defined epistemological doctrine. Pascal made little account of philosophy; this is clear from the section on philosophy in the *Pensées* (frs. 140–46) and other remarks. Philosophy, to

him, was above all, Aquinas and Descartes.[6] And if he had to attack
rationally the mind of a skeptic he would have done better to dis-
pense with Thomist and Cartesian proofs of God's existence and of
immortality: the skeptic was not prepared to swallow them. But he
might conceivably have been ready to listen to other arguments,
not "metaphysical" but rational all the same, i.e., conforming to the
"bon sens," appealing to normal human intuition (or "heart"). Pascal's was not a romantic "sentimental" religion, relying on some
undefinable and vague feeling by which nobody, except for the already converted, could be converted ("you have such feelings about
God? All right, and I do not have them and that is that"). He did
not, needless to say, "escape" into irrationalism (or irrationality),
as was frequently claimed earlier on, albeit less so now.[7] He both
acted and thought rationally by not only pointing out the limits of
reason but trying to prove why this and not that should be believed
in the realm that is beyond reason. Voltaire, of all people, even objected that Pascal made a philosophy of Christianity.[8]

A Jansenist embarking upon missionary work, pastoral or literary, falls naturally into a theological quandary: however zealous
he might be, he knows that really to convert a sinner is exclusively
God's business, rather than his. Genuine faith belongs to the supernatural order and can never be produced by human effort, either by
a priest or by the convert-to-be. So what is this effort for? The Jansenists, and the Calvinists, for that matter, did not bother about
these kinds of objections. We ought to do our duty whatever God's
hidden plans, of which we know nothing; man ought to plough his
acres and must not lie idly by on the pretext that God can do everything. This might not be an exact analogy, because the ploughman
knows that he is capable of performing the job himself, whereas a
Jansenist moralist or missionary knows that only God, and not he
himself, can do it. But the simplest answer is: God's ways of converting sinners are various, and it is normal, rather than exceptional, that he should employ other people as his tools. I can never
be sure that I will be effective working as an instrument, but I must
do my duty nevertheless; otherwise why would Jesus have sent his
disciples to preach his truth to heathens?[9]

We know the plan of the Pascalian Apology from the long
lecture he once gave to his friends of Port-Royal in 1658 and of
which we have a résumé, written over eight years later, by Filleau

de la Chaise to whom a participant of this meeting confided his memories. This text, about sixty pages long and published for the first time in 1672, is considered credible by scholars, even though it is a secondhand record and cannot be used as a literal reproduction of Pascal's speech.[10] And it certainly contradicts nothing we know from the authentic writings.

The clue to this lecture is Pascal's belief that the "ordinary proofs" of Christian truth, taken from God's works, are ill-adapted to the "natural state of the human heart" and that the human mind is ill-equipped for metaphysical reasoning, while "moral and historical proofs as well as some sentiments from nature and experience are within their grasp." There are indeed many certainties that are not acquired by a "geometrical way" but that it would be foolish to doubt, for example, that there is a city of Rome, that Mohammed existed, and that there was a big fire in London. Historical proofs taken from the Bible are of this sort: prophecies and miracles. Except for divine inspiration there is no way to explain Moses,' Isaiah's, or other prophets' exact knowledge of events that would happen centuries later, as there is no natural method of such predictions. And it is inconceivable that this magnificent law given to the Jews could be a human invention, the work of an impostor; "let them [the critics] make us see by what chance this law invented by a man happens to be, at the same time, the only one worthy of God, the only one that is contrary to the dispositions of nature and the only one that has always existed?"[11]

The very greatness of Christian teaching points unmistakably to its divine origins. "If there is no God, it is unthinkable that an idea so sublime as that of the Christian religion should have been born in the mind of man and that he should have shaped his life accordingly."[12]

So far, Pascal's arguments are mainly of a historical nature. If they appeal to the "heart" this is not primarily in the sense that the sublimity of the Christian teaching fills us with a feeling of enchantment (although this is true, too), but in that it conforms to the intuition we normally rely upon in historical thinking: it is simply impossible in terms of common sense, to *explain* the prophecies without taking account of divine aid, or to *imagine* that human nature should have been able to create a law which is opposed to the inclinations of this very nature. And so, we take the *facts* as a starting point and look for an explanation. Or so it seems. We know why this reasoning is not "geometrical," but it is not clear why, then, the traditional arguments for God's existence, which are supposed to start with facts as well (movement, causality, final order, contingency of finite things, gradations of perfection), are unreliable. Probably (Pascal doesn't exactly say so but there is strong circumstantial evidence for this interpretation) not because they are necessarily unsound logically, but because they do not appeal to the "heart" in another sense: they leave us cold, so to say, whereas historical arguments and meditation on the moral greatness of Christian teaching, while also good enough in explaining things, give people a feeling of gratitude, of love, of awe. Even things that belong properly to the mind and about which there is more than enough light to convince people, do not convince them without the acts of the "heart"; if the heart resists, the mind does not surrender either; and "God did not wish us to come to know him in the same way as one arrives at geometrical truths in which the heart plays no role, or that good men should have no advantage over wicked ones in this investigation."[13]

The second category of facts referred to in the lecture as opening the path to God is far more prominent in the *Pensées*. These are the facts we come across when we turn our attention, not to stars and plants, not even to prophecies and miracles, but to ourselves, to our spiritual constitution. They are more important insofar as our unwillingness to absorb and accept the truth of Christianity comes chiefly not from our intellectual ineptitude or from the intrinsic logical trouble we face when we try to weigh the proofs—any proofs, metaphysical or historical—but from the passions that dominate us and make us resist the divine. Pascal "wanted to recall men to their hearts, that they should start by getting to know themselves."[14] Everyone will inevitably "be terrified by what he has discovered in himself and will see himself as a monstrous collection of incongruous parts"; then he will not be able to doubt that "a nature so full of contradictions [*contrariétés*], both double and unique, as he feels, could be a simple effect of chance, or have come as it is from the hands of its author."[15] This leads us to a recognition that mankind must have fallen from a much higher position, of which the traces are still visible in it, mixed up with a mass of corruption, and this bears out the biblical story of the crime our

ancestors committed by trying to deny their dependence on God
and to become his equal. As a result "[Adam's] mind was clouded
and God hid himself from him in an impenetrable night." A slave of
sin, "he retained from the light and knowledge he had had only an
impotent desire for knowledge that was there to torment him";
"eventually he became this incomprehensible monster one calls
man and, by spreading his corruption to everything issuing from
him, he populated the universe with miserable blind criminals like
himself."[16]

God, as we see from Holy Scripture, wants us to submit our
will entirely and uninterruptedly to him, to do nothing of which he
is not the end, and to love him. "Because fear, admiration, even adoration, when they are severed from love, are no more than dead
feelings."[17] The confusion of human affairs, the persistent tri-
umphs of wickedness, "this monstrous mixture of the poor and the
rich, the healthy and the sick, the tyrant and the oppressed"—all
this has made philosophers doubt providence. "God wants things
to remain in obscurity, letting people go their way, letting them follow the desires of their hearts and willing to disclose Himself only
to a small number of those whom He himself shall make worthy
and capable of true virtue."[18] We see that we are helpless in resisting our corruption by our own forces and "that we ought to ask
God for help which He will not refuse."[19]

As to the transmission of the original sin being unjust and incomprehensible, it is enough to say that "what [God] does cannot
be unjust because His will is the unique rule of good and evil and
the point is not to investigate what a thing is in itself but only
whether those who speak in God's name deserve credence."[20] God
could have created all people in glory but he simply did not wish it.
"It is up to us to take what it has pleased Him to give us; the more so
because, having deserved nothing but His wrath, the damned
should not complain about the conditions of their grace."[21] Once
again: God owes us nothing.

Filleau de la Chaise, in his own commentary, observes with
sadness that in spite of the unique force of the *Pensées* in overcom-
ing human obduracy of heart, very few people will benefit from its
reading, and that Pascal's work is only for good Christians, as the
majority devote their life to their business, to pleasure, vanity, or to
the knowledge and study of nature.[22] Pascal himself, however, did

not say this; while he had no doubt that the elect made up only a tiny minority of the human race, the arguments of his apology seem rather to imply that they might cure at least some people of their self-inflicted blindness.

The *Discours*, although not coming directly from Pascal's pen, is important insofar as it provides us with the best guide to the bulk of the *Pensées* and clarifies some of the cryptic notes which (as we are told by his nephew Etienne Perier, the author of the *Préface de Port-Royal*) he wrote for himself in order not to forget them in composing the work; this work, as he often used to say, required ten years of healthy life to be completed.[23]

Our Death, Our Body, Our Self-Deception

The absolute sovereignty of God and the utter corruption of man are two strictly interconnected tenets that make up the core of Jansenist theology. God's sovereignty is opposed to the "legalistic" concept, to the idea of a contract on which divine-human relationships are based (after the Fall); this latter belief, Augustinians claimed, was characteristic of Judaic and Jesuit doctrines. Pascal shared this theology, of course, and extended it to the very definition of sin. Only once did he say, but did it unambiguously (in a letter to Charlotte Roannez of autumn 1656); "the reason why sins are sins is only that they are contrary to the will of God."[24] This clearly suggests that the only source of distinction between good and evil is divine positive legislation (or God's *voluntas simplex*, as the scholastics used to call it), rather than the intrinsic good or evil of what we do. God prohibits some acts not because they are evil; they become evil by the fact that God prohibits them; otherwise it might seem that he is not sovereign any more and depends on rules he has not set up. Christian humanists could not swallow this definition—which the initiators of the Reformation took up from the later medieval nominalists—since it seemed to portray God as a tyrant who demands moral recognition for his laws apart from their content, which, according to our "human logic," could be opposite to what it actually is (God "could" have ordered that homicide and incest be praiseworthy and almsgiving sinful, etc.). One could probably counter the humanist argument in theological terms by invoking the identity of essence and existence in God (we may not legitimately use a reasoning which implies "before" and "after" in God or makes the distinction between his essence and his acts), but if we cling to conceptual categories that are accessible to our limited intellect, the choice is unavoidable: either God is sovereign and then only his verdicts make sins sinful, or he simply tells us what is sinful *because* it is sinful in itself, in which case he is not sovereign.

God's sovereignty and the corruption of human nature are linked in various ways. God's will is the only measure of justice: were it not, we would produce the rules of justice conformably to our wishes and whims and it is certain in advance that justice thus concocted would opt for evil because that is what we notoriously, inescapably, time and again do without grace.

And it is clear that we must not ask *why* the elect are elected by God and why there are so few of them. Even if only one were elected this would testify to God's infinite mercy. And we must never complain about his mercy being insufficient and unevenly distributed.

Our corruption explains why God is hidden, and his sovereignty explains why he is not absolutely hidden; it explains why our reason is helpless beyond certain limits and why it is nonetheless reliable within limits that are assigned to it: the Pascalian theme par excellence.

Virtually everything in human life becomes understandable within the framework of these two "facts." If God acted only according to the rules of justice and we were thrown upon our corrupt nature, nobody would be saved. Therefore it is of crucial importance that by doing this or that God *makes* this or that just, instead of his orders being subordinated to abstract standards of justice. This explains the entire history of redemption.

Is he the God of love? The question is not nonsensical. When Pascal speaks of love and charity, it is normally in the sense of our duty to love God; when he speaks of God's dealing with our affairs, it is in terms of mercy rather than love. The two are not the same. Mercy is the *royal* privilege, and Pascal's work itself implies that the object of mercy *does not deserve* it by justice. Love is what a mother or a father feels towards their children, lovers towards each other, friends towards each other; it makes no sense to ask whether or not someone deserves someone else's love. The Jansenists' God shows royal mercy, rather than fatherly, let alone motherly, love; his mercy is exactly like the act of a king who spares the life of a criminal *justly* sentenced to death.

In the *Mystery of Jesus*, which is half-meditation, half-prayer (and does not belong to the *Apology*), the Savior indeed says "I love you more warmly than you loved your filth" (fr. 919). But this is a rarity. And it is easy to see why God's love toward men is not a Jansenist topic. It poses an awkward theological problem. For who is the loved one? Certainly not everybody, since the overwhelming majority is condemned to eternal fire by justice and Jesus did not die for them; and, by the same standard of justice, the elect no more deserve their luck than the rejected. Highly selective love is natural in human affairs—one deserves something by justice but nobody, strictly speaking, deserves love; but how may we attribute to God the same emotionally inspired fastidiousness? Mystics are often overpowered by an intense sensation of ubiquitous love; they feel that the world, for all its horrors, *is* love. But not the Jansenists, not anybody who preaches double predestination.

That the topic of human corruption pervades the *Pensées* (as well as the *Écrits sur la Grâce*) there is no need to prove. As has been mentioned, the Jansenist belief in the eternal damnation of unbaptized babies suggests that this topic outranks even that of the sovereignty of God. And one perceives in the *Pensées* a kind of *odium corporis*, a hatred of the body. According to the testimony of his sister Gilberte, Pascal could not suffer her hugging her children, as he thought this habit harmed them; he was angered when she said, for instance, that she had seen a beautiful woman: he considered such expressions harmful when heard by servants and young people.[25] We should, he thought, love death, because it detaches the soul from the "body impure." There is in Pascal a suggestion that the human body is not properly human: "what is natural in animals we call misery in man" (fr. 117). To be sure, the fact that our nature is bestial reveals to us that we have fallen from a better nature; but in our present state it is clear that our body, far from harmoniously and Thomistically coexisting with the soul, is a curse.[26]

Certainly, the abomination of everything bodily might have been, in Pascal's case, a simple psychological reaction: he was not on friendly terms with his own body, which tormented him, as we know, most of his life; since the age of eighteen he lived not a single day without pain, according to the same testimony.[27] But it was a typically Jansenist, ideological, semi-gnostic detestation as well. This is in keeping with the general and fundamental commandment that we ought not only to love God above everything but to love only God; our love or attachment or tenderness towards other people should be indirect, by reference to God. To Pascal—still in Gilberte's words—"tenderness cannot be perfect unless reason is enlightened by faith and unless it makes us act by the rules of charity. Therefore he did not make a big difference between tenderness and charity, nor between charity, and friendship. . . . So did he conceive of charity and this is why it worked in him without attachment or amusement, and since charity could not have any other end but God, it must attach itself to God only and must not stop at anything that is amusing"; consequently Pascal wanted nobody to be attached to him.[28] The coolness towards others and the loathing of everything profane, however characterologically explicable, are clearly doctrinal. Even "our prayers and our virtues are abominable before God if they are not the prayers and virtues of Jesus Christ" (fr. 948). "We make an idol even of truth, because truth apart from charity is not God, but his image and idol, which we should not love or adore . . . " (fr. 926).

Our nature is not only corrupted by sin, it is corrupted irredeemably; to yearn after a noncorrupted world would amount to shedding whatever is natural rather than trying to heal and to improve it.

But how to convince the incredulous of this picture of the world if they indulge in all sorts of natural pleasures, surrender to carnal passions, and delight in the filth of mundane amusements? Pascal's crucial and most persuasive message to them is: *You will die!* Not a very enlightening or original piece of news, it might seem. But Pascal knew what he was talking about. Everyone is aware that we are all mortal. But not everyone really believes in this, in the sense of living constantly in the shadow of his own inevitable and imminent end. That everyone is mortal is a natural fact, but the insight "I shall die" is not natural; Pascal's remarks on death are easily associated with Heidegger's "Sein—zum—Tode" as a fundamental characteristic of human existence, with his insistence on death as an irreducibly private matter: my death is not a particular case of a universal phenomenon, it is exclusively my business. Heidegger does not mention Pascal on this occasion, he only mentions Tolstoy's story about the death of Ivan Ilyich, where the same insight is depicted: the hero remembered from his school days the syllogism "all men are mortal, Socrates is a man, therefore Socrates is mortal," and he suddenly, for the first time, on his deathbed, realizes that it was he who was meant, not an abstract "man" or Socrates. This is exactly what Pascal tries to make his reader aware of. "Fear death when there is no danger, and not in danger, because one should be man" (fr. 716). "We are content in the society of people like ourselves, miserable like ourselves, impotent like ourselves; they won't help us; we shall die alone. We should thus behave as though we were alone" (fr. 151). "It is easier to bear death without thinking of it than to think of death without danger" (fr. 138).

The celebrated fragment 427 includes virtually the entire message: "the immortality of the soul is something that matters so much and concerns us so profoundly, that we would have to have lost all feeling to live in indifference to it. All our actions and thoughts must take such different paths, depending on whether or not there is hope of eternal blessings, that it is impossible to make sensible decisions without regulating them in light of this point, which ought to be our ultimate goal." Pascal admits that it irritates him to see people monstrously negligent of this supreme worry on the pretext that they do not find enough light in themselves and fail to look for light elsewhere whilst they know that death is the only certain thing in life (cf. fr. 164).[29]

Thus we have a picture both of Pascal's readers and of his tactics in assaulting their minds. Although he had no doubts about the reality of eternal life as a matter of faith, he admitted that he was unable to convey the same certainty to others as a matter of natural light. He did not want to provide them with the satisfaction of certainty, as this was simply unfeasible; on the contrary , he tried to stalk them, so to say, and to awake the feeling of uncertainty and of shame in the mind of a potential convert; "how can you be so stupid as to avoid the only question that really matters—death and immortality?"

Pascal wants to change the moral attitude, "the heart," not to improve intellectual skills. The vanity of all destructible goods is his frequent theme. As we read in the early essay *On the Conversion of a Sinner* (dated 1653 by Lafuma), a soul inspired by God "sees all perishable things as perishing or as having perished already; and it is frightened at the sight of the sure annihilation of everything it loves; it sees that every moment tears it away from the enjoyment of its goods and that things dearest to it run out. . . . It then begins to see as nothing everything that must go back into nothing—sky, earth, its mind, its body, its parents, friends, enemies, possessions, poverty, disgrace, prosperity, honour, ignominy, respect, contempt, authority, privations, health, sickness, and life itself."[30] He was speaking to people who simply preferred to avoid the question while running to the abyss with their eyes closed, and he wanted to shake or to corner them by compelling them brutally to face the question.

But what about people who do not blind themselves—or so they think—but are unswervingly convinced that there is no afterlife or God? They would be impervious to his arguments because they know that there is nothing to search for; there is one life, however short, and earthly pleasures, however volatile. Pascal makes the distinction between those who serve God after finding him (and who are "reasonable and happy"), those who search but have failed to find him ("reasonable and unhappy"), and those—"foolish and unhappy"—who live without this search (fr. 160). Perhaps he assumed that die-hard unbelievers, unshakable in their irreligion, did not really exist, no matter how many displayed their staunch materialism or naturalism in libertine literature; perhaps he believed that a tiny spark of the divine, a feeble spot of sensitivity to the "question" of God and immortality, had remained even in their corrupt hearts. He did not say this in so many words, but it was in keeping with his belief that this sensitivity or some vestiges of the glorious origin of our race make us human in the most elementary sense, and that it is our passions, not intellectual considerations, that put obstacles on our path to God.

And so, apart from true Christians satisfied in their faith—presumably a tiny minority of mankind—everybody is unhappy. After "you will die," this is the second part of the same message: you are miserable, don't pretend otherwise. "Let us imagine a number of people in chains, all of them sentenced to death, some of them slaughtered every day before the eyes of the others, the remaining ones seeing their own fate in that of their neighbors, looking at each other in pain and despair, waiting their turn. This is the image of the human condition" (fr. 434).

Whatever the reasons for our misery, listed in many fragments of the *Pensées*—the certitude of death, our general corruption, the obscurity of the world around us, all sorts of suffering and injustice—this is certain: "all people want to be happy, without exception . . . this is the motive of all the actions of all people, including those who are going to hang themselves. And yet for so many years nobody without faith has ever attained this goal, at which all people incessantly aim" (fr. 148).

This message—"you are miserable"—more than anything else irritated great writers of the French Enlightenment, Voltaire above all. We are not all as miserable as this "sublime misanthrope" would have it; Pascal "writes against human nature more or less as he wrote against the Jesuits."[31] "Why make us horrified with our existence?" The world is not a prison, human beings are happier than any other creatures and, instead of complaining of not being Gods, we should be thankful to God for not being worse than we are; of course we are imperfect and limited, but this is not a reason to be driven to despair. "Nature does not make us unhappy all the time. Pascal always speaks like a sick man who wants the entire world to suffer."[32]

In other eighteenth-century writers—Diderot, Condorcet —we find a similar abhorrence of Pascalian topics; the belief in the utter corruption of the human race, the exhortations to despair and self-hatred, display the sick mind of a genius. Voltaire seems to be particularly outraged, but also fascinated, by the *Pensées*, as one may guess from the frequency with which he returns to Pascalian "absurdities" in his later writings.[33]

The conflict was not soluble by rational arguments. The mind of Lumières was governed by self-confident common sense: why should we believe that we are permanently miserable? That people are sometimes unhappy and sometimes happy is trivially true; they suffer, but they delight in the blessings of life as well. But Pascal's point was not to deny the obvious. It was rather: if you are not miserable, this is bad faith, you only imagine yourself to be happy. But isn't happiness a feeling, a state of mind, a "subjective" phenomenon and isn't it silly to say to someone "you only *seem* to feel what you feel?"

On this crucial point Pascal was modern, like his contemporary La Rochefoucauld. He was not the first to reflect on human self-deception; the topic is to be found in ancient Latin literature and, of course, in Montaigne. Unlike Montaigne and La Rochefoucauld Pascal unmasks our skill in self-cheating for specifically Christian purposes. He seems to repeat St. John's warning: "Because thou say'st, I am rich, and increased with goods, and have need of nothing; and knowest not that thou art wretched, and miserable, and poor, and blind, and naked" (Rev. 3:17). The point is not simply that we are capable of making ourselves unaware of our own motives, of concealing from ourselves what we are really after, and thus of being nobler and better in our own eyes than we are; it is rather that we doggedly refuse to face our misery because to face it would compel us to search for a remedy, and the only remedy is offered by Christianity; and to admit this amounts to admitting that we ought to tame our natural passions and give up the pleasures of life: not an easy decision. The goal is not to show us that we tend to embellish our image for our own comfort as well as for the eyes of others, but to make us realize that, whatever we might think, we are really unhappy, and only pretend not to feel our pain. The ultimate goal was Jansenist, no doubt, but there is nothing specifically Jansenist in the tactic; the message "you are unhappy" did not belong to the normal Jansenist method of persuasion. If the goal is set aside, the tactic seems rather Nietzschean or even Freudian; but the goal cannot be set aside, of course, for it gives meaning to the method.

Once we realize our misery, we come to see that we spend most of our time seeking an illusory escape from reality into all sorts of "divertissements." This, as any reader knows, is a recurrent theme and a pillar of the Apology. "Unable to cure death, misery, ignorance, they decided, in order to make themselves happy, not to think about it" (fr. 133, cf. 134). And this self-imposed non-thinking fills our life: "Without investigating all particular occupations, it is enough to encompass them under [the heading] 'divertissements'" (fr. 478). "This is the only comfort we have in our misery, and yet it is the greatest of our miseries; for . . . it brings us imperceptibly to our death" (fr. 414). The long fragment (136) on the subject purports to reveal that the essence of our life consists in escaping from the present in order not to have a moment for concentrating on ourselves; the action of hunting is more important than the catch, the action of gambling more than the prize: the point is only that I must not be left with myself, otherwise I might look at my condition as it really is, and be frightened. In a moment of ennui we are overwhelmed with an unbearable sadness without knowing its causes; if we knew them we might become aware of where the medicine is; but we prefer to evade them, to decamp into the future. Kings employ an entire army of people whose only job is to keep them diverted.

When Pascal speaks of "divertissement" in the more specific sense of entertainment (fr. 764), he insists, not unlike Nicole, on the terrible dangers of the theater: the dramatists depict passions, earthly love above all, in such a way that they seem both attractive and innocent, and the viewer wishes to imitate the heroes, unaware of being caught in a trap. This point however is less important; it deals only with the immorality of spectacles. "Divertissement" as a "metaphysical" rather than moralistic phenomenon, as a fundamental manner of living, is close to the original sense: diversion, detour, turning away; we flee into the irreality of mundane amusements of all sorts—including war with its perils—in order not to face death and the dilemma it compels us to think about. The dangers of entertainment are a Jansenist topic, "divertissement" as a mode of existence is not.

We should understand that our entire life is nothing but diversion unless it is searching for God and delighting in him. Pascal naturally takes his examples from the life of the upper or rather leisure classes: hunting, playing, dancing, going to war, chatting in drawing-rooms, and so on. These occupations, in his view, are simply useless apart from being instruments of self-blinding. Would he say that sowing seed, making clothes, and in general performing tasks that are necessary to life, is no more than seeking refuge from reality? Are peasants and artisans victims of the same void which surrounds the life of idle nobles? It would be in accordance with his attitude to say that anything we do—useful or not, necessary or otherwise—is at the service of the devil if it is not done for God's sake; if it is not, in people's minds, an act of obedience to the divine commandments and of praising the Lord. Any other goal—not only pleasure or gain but the sheer necessity of sustaining one's own life—is illicit if it is the goal in itself. Pascal does not say this quite explicitly; it is no more than a conclusion from general principles he shared with his fellow Augustinians. But the question illuminates what is in any case obvious: Pascal was preoccupied with his peers, his fellows from the privileged classes. Not that he despised peasants or artisans, of course; but the poor deserved attention mainly insofar as almsgiving is our religious duty. Did he believe that the toiling people were naturally good Christians by Jansenist standards and that, when they were mowing rye or shearing sheep, they directed their thoughts to God, instead of just bothering about their own survival? Perhaps this kind of question did not cross his mind; when he was thinking and writing about salvation, he meant the salvation of people from his own milieu, perhaps the most endangered in this respect. But even if a soldier or a laborer complains about his toil, just try giving him no work (fr. 415): a hint that even a soldier or a laborer uses his work as a "divertissement."

He tried to shake their faked security. Insecurity, no doubt, is an inalienable part of the human condition, but in some epochs in history it is felt more strongly than in others. In the era of religious wars, social upheavals, the Fronde, religious uncertainty, the feeling of insecurity affected everybody, from the monarch to his humblest subjects. Pascal's task was to show his readers that all attempts to relieve their anguish by amusements or quotidian chores are futile and that there is no cure except God.

Spotting God in the Lifeless Universe

But how to find the great hidden Healer? To find him, that is, in the post-Cartesian world? Whatever Descartes himself might have thought, his readers, whether followers or critics, whether Catholics or Protestants, soon, albeit not necessarily at once, had to notice that to give him full credence amounted to giving up the normal mentality of the Christian flock, the habit of seeing providential signs in whatever happened, of perceiving the mysterious divine hand—benevolent, punishing or warning—behind all natural and human events—rain or drought, birth or death; the habit of seeing the world as a continuous series of miracles. This was an archaic mentality and it survived undistorted despite the conclusion reached by medieval thinkers, above all by Aquinas, that God rules the universe through the intermediary of natural secondary causes. But Descartes—and this was striking and frightening—left the world soulless and godless. God set up by decree a few simple mechanical laws that explain everything in the world of matter, particularly in living matter; life was no longer a separate realm, and what we call living organisms are no more than particular aggregates of material bodies moved by the same laws that govern the motion of stars, winds, or falling rocks. Human death is a purely physical deregulation of the mechanisms that keep the body functioning; the immaterial soul leaves the body as a result of death, not the other way round. Apart from the philosophically established truth that God created the world and sustains it, he is not perceivable in the world. This was perhaps the mightiest blow inflicted by Descartes to both the standard mentality and standard Christian philosophy: there is no way that leads logically from nature to its maker, no possibility of experiencing directly the divine finger in natural events.

Even if Descartes did not deny providence, his philosophy did. Right or wrong, the proofs of God's existence in the *Meditations*, in the reply to the *Second Objections*, and in the *Principles*, not only fail to provide us with clues about how God rules the world (apart from the laws of physics) but suggest that those laws are all that he left us with. Again: Descartes might not have denied miracles, but his philosophy did. One could, as Malebranche and others did, concoct a metaphysic that, by doing away with natural causality altogether, asserted simply that whatever happens is God's direct act (although God follows regularities he himself established) and thus every natural event is, as it were, a miracle. But the idea of a miracle makes sense only if a miracle is contrasted with the effect of natural causes; if everything is a miracle, nothing is. Yet this attempt to reforge Cartesianism into a pillar of orthodoxy and piety has remained an oddity in the annals of philosophy, and Descartes proved to be unassimilable within Christianity; this is something a number of great Christian thinkers have known all along, from Bossuet, to whom what mattered was mainly Descartes' notorious contempt for history, tradition, antiquity, and authority, to twentieth-century Thomists such as Gilson and Maritain. Pascal knew this too, of course. His often quoted remark, noted by his niece, that he "could not forgive Descartes because he would have preferred to do without God, but eventually let Him give the world a flick of his finger to set it in movement, after which he didn't need God anymore" (fr. 1001), might be "technically" not quite correct but it grasps the fundamental meaning of Cartesian thought. He perceived Descartes as a herald of deism, and deism, consisting of "the adoration of God as great, powerful and eternal," is "almost as remote from Christian religion as atheism" (fr. 449).

Without endorsing the specific Cartesian tenets concerning matter and void, which he refuted by his famous experiment, Pascal nevertheless absorbed the image of a material universe that is terrifyingly infinite, homogeneous, and without privileged points or spheres, a universe that seems indifferent to our existence and instils in us an overwhelming feeling of homelessness. "When I consider the short duration of my life, absorbed by eternity before and after—*memoria hospitis unius diei praetereuntis*—the little space I fill, and which I see swallowed up in the infinite vastness of spaces that I do not know and that do not know me, I am frightened and astonished by seeing myself here rather than there, as there is no reason why I should be here rather than there, or now rather than then. Who put me here? By whose order and guidance were this place and this time assigned to me?" (fr. 68).

This might seem a strange confession. Pascal knew well "by whose order" he was placed there and then. Was it a moment of doubt, even of despair? Or perhaps, as has been argued, a rhetorical device, words to be put in the mouth of a would-be convert in order to be refuted? This is not certain. There is similar questioning elsewhere (frs. 194, 198, 199) about man lost in the "mute universe," thrown upon his own resources without light, on a "deserted and horrifying island," not knowing why he is there in the infinite span of time and space. But another fragment, when again he observes, "I feel that I might not have existed at all," concludes with the happy ending: "I am not eternal and infinite but I see that there is in nature a necessary, eternal, and infinite being" (fr. 165).

What we read in numerous remarks about the dread-inspiring randomness of existence in the Cartesian world neither displays a momentary oblivion of God nor is it the trick of an apologist. It is the expression of a genuine experience; while it might be used for apologetic purposes, it is not in itself a philosophical or theological assertion. We do not need to assume that Pascal was oblivious of God in moments of desperation. A man who totters on the brink of a precipice cannot be free of ("animal") fear even if he believes in providence;[34] and the specifically human (as Pascal would have it) fear—in the face of death as a necessity of contingent existence, in the face of the mute and deaf universe—this fear from which we cowardly attempt to run away into mindless, intoxicating amusements, is not abrogated by belief in God either. Perhaps in the completed text of the *Apology* the remarks just quoted would have been inserted in a dialogue as a libertine's words. But this was not how libertines expressed their feelings. It was Pascal who taught them how they *ought to* feel if they were lucid, and he knew this because he himself had experienced this insight.

Whether or not the conversion of November 1654 may be properly called a mystical experience, Pascal was not a mystic.[35] Certainly he did not think that the world had been abandoned by God. But he was not a mystic in the sense of a man whose immersion into the divine reaches such a depth that he really achieves total or nearly total indifference to the world, whom God shelters uninterruptedly from fear, who sees death as moving from one house to another and doesn't care about "infinite spaces." While he believed that "all things are veils that cover God" and that "Christians ought to recognize him in everything,"[36] he painfully experienced the absence of God in nature.

According to his own criteria Pascal should have been "reasonable and happy," having found God. He was more than reasonable, he was a genius; but the last thing that would occur to any reader of the *Pensées* is that they were composed by a serene, contented man, reconciled with a God-controlled world. Was he—to use a somewhat absurd description—theoretically happy, that is, believing in his happiness but not experiencing it? He who has found God is happy, he said, but he also said that nobody is.

All the same, he wanted to convince the incredulous. To convince them—of what? Not that they should accept the statement "God exists" as true. This can be accepted by a deist, who has no faith in the real sense. And one cannot be "convinced" into faith. In the essay on the "Art de Persuader" he explicitly sets aside the "divine truths" to which this art is inapplicable, "as they are infinitely above nature; God alone can put them into the soul in a way that pleases him." He wanted them to reach the heart first and from there the mind; indeed, "the saints say, when they talk about divine things, that one should love them in order to know them and that one enters truth only by charity." "God sheds his light on minds only after quelling the rebellion of the will."[37]

We are back in the same immobilizing Augustinian quandary: since no one save God can crush the refractoriness of our corrupted will, what is the point of converting other people or writing an apology? But, as we have mentioned, the inconsistency might be overcome by saying that we do our duty relying on God's will, who alone can make our efforts efficient if he so wishes.

To say that knowledge of God by natural light is in itself useless does not necessarily mean that it is impossible. The reasons based on the order of nature are the most unreliable. "Do you yourself not say that the sky and birds prove God? No. Does not your religion say so? No. Even though it is true in a sense for some souls to which God gave this light, it is nonetheless false for most people" (fr. 3). "It is remarkable that no canonic author has ever used nature to prove God. They all strive to make people believe in him. David, Solomon, etc. never said 'there is no void, therefore there is God'" (fr. 463). The "metaphysical proofs" are no better (fr. 190).

The words "even though it is true," etc., are both Cartesian and Augustinian. They do not suggest, absurdly, that for some people there is a logically sound way from the sky and the birds to God, whereas it is closed to others. There is no logically sound way. But a believer perceives God everywhere. It is Cartesian to say that there is no reliable reasoning from the sky and birds; it is Augustinian to say that once you have faith you see God in the sky and birds. Since it is a matter of faith, the sky and birds are useless in convincing the skeptics and unbelievers; they won't be convinced, and rightly so.

Obviously faith is God's gift and not a result of human reasoning (fr. 7, 588). So what benefit may we have from a natural knowledge of God, if it is possible?

Pascal repeats the traditional doctrine: faith is above but not against the testimony of the senses (fr. 185). Religion is not contrary to reason; we should begin by showing that it is not, and then make religion "aimable," because people fear that it might be true (fr. 12).

On this point, however, there is an ambiguity in his blueprint for conversion. The Christian religion is necessarily opposed "to nature, to common sense, to our pleasures" (fr. 284). This is to Pascal a strong argument in favor of Christianity: a religion so contrary to nature would not arise, or survive, were it not supported by divine force, were its source not in a supernatural order. But is not reason a part of our nature, and is it not corrupted like all its parts?

Yes, reason is corrupted insofar as it naturally yields to the passions (fr. 530): more often than not we prefer to believe in things that are pleasant and flatter our natural instincts. This does not mean, however, that it is simply impossible to follow—not "common sense," which is no more than widespread opinion, but rather "le bon sens," the ability to distinguish truth from falsity; this ability is not quite extinguished. "If man had always been corrupted he would have no idea of truth or beatitude" (fr. 131).

The real difficulty is less the sheer existence of God than those specifically Christian dogmas, especially original sin and redemption, which are the core of Augustinian religiosity. Original sin is indeed madness ("folie") in human eyes, it is even contrary to reason (fr. 695). Pascal seems, at first glance, to contradict himself: religion is "above, not contrary to" reason, and then "contrary to" it, after all. But the contradiction is less corrosive to his apology than it appears. The doctrine of original sin is indeed foolish, as it contradicts the norms of human "miserable justice." But it has, or seems to have, a kind of explanatory power: it is only through it that we can understand the human condition: "this mystery, the most remote from our knowledge, which is the transmission of sin, is a thing without which we can have no knowledge about ourselves . . . nothing shocks our reason more than saying that the sin of the first man made guilty those who are so far away from this source that they seem incapable of having taken part in it . . . but without this mystery, the most unintelligible of all, we are unintelligible to ourselves" (fr. 131).

Could we then see the story of original sin as a sort of empirical hypothesis, explaining the facts of life? Not quite. Pascal never suggests that we could, by collecting "facts" and relying on our own intellectual ingenuity, invent such an explanatory device. This is not empirical (let alone "geometrical") reason. The story had to be revealed to us by God; but once we know it from his word, we realize that all the absurdities of human destiny, all the miseries and "contradictions" of the human soul, our corruption and despair, the very weakness of our intellect, our elaborate methods of self-deception, all this mass of woe, deprivation, and sickness, become understandable. In this sense the tale is "rational," even though it requires a mind illuminated by God and could not have been contrived by this mind itself.

But then, can we make the fact of revelation "rational" in its turn? Can the natural light alone show us the reliability of revelation? If so, one might argue that, *faith* being supernatural, *religion* is rationally trustworthy.

Religion is not certain. Pascal says this clearly, and adds that it is reasonable to venture into various uncertain endeavors: sea voyages, battles (fr. 577). This idea is, of course, developed in detail in the Wager. That religion is uncertain does not mean that a man of faith is uncertain about his own beliefs, but rather that it is uncertain as a practical task, that if we decide to bet on God on rational grounds, the outcome is uncertain.

Religion is uncertain but it is trustworthy even apart from the infusion of faith. There are in particular two grounds we can rely upon: prophecies and miracles. The Old Testament prophecies and miracles had always been, of course, standard parts of Christian apologetic, and for our purpose there is no need to venture into exegetic work or to analyze Pascal's excerpts from Jeremiah, Daniel, and Isaiah. In terms of the Pascalian tactic of persuasion the interesting question is: to what extent can such arguments, in his view, be compelling to the mind of an unbeliever? Is there a way to let him see that, relying on his natural light alone, he cannot reasonably reject those signs of God's presence in the world? Does one have to live in faith before accepting that a prophecy is indeed a prophecy and a miracle is a miracle—in which case persuasion would apparently be in vain—or are those divine interventions so irrefutably clear that no one, including obstinate unbelievers, can in good faith shrug off those proofs, and one would be foolish to deny them? (Like nearly all his contemporaries, Pascal treated the Bible as a single block, a continuous God-inspired text of which all the parts and all the sentences are immutably true, severally and jointly.)

Pascal's answers might be ambiguous but the fact that he confronted these issues, at least implicitly, displays a modern mind. He knew, it seems, that it was not enough to tell people: "read Isaiah and tell me how it was possible that Jesus' coming, birth, and life, could be predicted by natural means alone centuries before the event? And how can you deny the miracles seen and reported by so many trustworthy witnesses?" etc. Both prophecies and miracles are good proofs; indeed, "the greatest of proofs of Jesus Christ are prophecies" (fr. 335); but more is needed to let skeptics see the light. This "more" is Pascalian.

Prophecies seemed to be obvious, but the same Jewish people ("peuple charnel") who had carried them from one generation to another for millennia failed to see that they had been fulfilled. "It is remarkable to have made Jews great lovers of things predicted and great enemies of their fulfilment" (fr. 273). Remarkable, but understandable in terms of what is the dominant theme of the *Pensées*: the hidden God. God discloses himself in part and conceals himself in part, and this is just. The prophecies, conforming to the same order of things, both enlighten and blind: they are understood unhesitatingly by those who are pure of heart and they portend doom to obdurate sinners. This is indeed both a Jansenist and a Calvinist principle: "there is enough clarity to enlighten the elect and enough obscurity to humiliate them. There is enough obscurity to blind the reproved and enough clarity to condemn and leave them without excuse" (fr. 236). Calvin said the same: however little natural light can instruct us about God, it is just sufficient for the damnation of the damned. That this is so Scripture itself proves to Pascal: "prophecies should be unintelligible to the impious [Dan. 12, Hosea Ult. 10] but intelligible to those who are well instructed" (fr. 487).

No doubt there are many similar warnings in the Scriptures to the effect that God's children listen to, and understand, his words, but others do not.

This leads us back to the same perplexing question: natural light is sufficient to believe in God, but in order to see this you have first to be elected, and to believe. Is there a way out of this apparent circle? Pascal found a solution in the Wager.

Sometimes the prophecies—or other parts of the Scriptures —seem to be false or to contradict each other. But then we can always explain the riddle by pointing out the double sense of the text, literal and figurative. This, too, is of course a traditional device. "When the words of God which are truthful are false literally, they are true spiritually. *Sede a dextris meis*: this is false literally, therefore it is true spiritually" (fr. 272). Sometimes even contradictions display the greatness of Holy Writ; if there is a discrepancy between the genealogies recorded in the Gospels of Matthew and Luke, this proves that this "was not done by arrangement [*de concert*]" (fr. 236). God often speaks in terms of earthly goods when spiritual goods were meant. The Jews proved to be unworthy, therefore God did not want to disclose things to them; but since he wanted those things to be disclosed nonetheless, he clouded them in figures, so that those who love things that are used as figures (i.e., earthly goods) stop at them, whereas those who love real (spiritual) sense could see it. When David predicts that the Messiah will liberate his people from its enemies, one might think that the Egyptians are meant, in which case the prophecy would not be fulfilled; but in truth he had in mind real enemies, that is, the iniquities of the Israelites. Daniel likewise, speaking of the liberation of the people from bondage by their enemies, was in reality speaking of sins (fr. 269). Indeed, as we read elsewhere, it would be unworthy of God to promise temporal goods, and the prophets, when they used such language, pointed out that, since their words were obscure, obviously another meaning was intended. If the spiritual sense had been overtly stated, people would not have loved it; and if they had loved those spiritual promises, their testimony would not have been credible, because they loved them (fr. 501). This dialectic might be somewhat difficult to absorb but it fits perfectly in Pascal's *discourse*: whatever the Scriptures say is by definition true, therefore it we find something incredible in them the real meaning must be different from the ostensible one. But then the reader, in order to understand God's word, has to know in advance that this is verily God's word; he has to "believe in order to understand." Obscurity in revelation is a part of God's wise tactics of concealing himself, albeit not entirely. Pascal even says, somewhat cryptically, "do you think that the prophecies quoted in the Gospels are reported in order to make you believe? No, it is to distance you from belief" (fr. 763). Perhaps he had in mind verses such as John 19:36: "these things were done that the Scripture be fulfilled," which might suggest that some acts were performed deliberately in order to make the prophecies come true and thus they cast doubt on the veracity of the prophets. We may guess that God let such things be inserted in the revealed word in order to confound the incredulous, as in other, purposefully misleading, fragments of his message. This "hermeneutics" certainly makes God's truthfulness safe forever, always bearing in mind that this truth is manifested through faith.

An analogous interpretation applied to miracles. They are not for converting people but for condemning them (fr. 379). This clearly suggests what was said about prophecies: miracles are good enough to deprive the unbelievers of an excuse but not good enough to convert them. Like prophecies, miracles and other proofs are not "absolutely convincing," but "one cannot say that to believe them is to be unreasonable. They have enough light to enlighten some and enough obscurity to blind others. It is not reason that might induce people not to follow what is obvious in them, therefore it must be concupiscence and viciousness of heart." They show that "those who follow [these obvious signs] do so by grace and not by reason, and those who run away [from them] do so by concupiscence and not by reason" (fr. 835).

This is the essence of the Pascalian view on miracles as instruments of conversion. If we argue that they are unconvincing, this is proof only of our obduracy in immorality; were our hearts pure, we would perceive their irresistible force. To be sure, "one should judge the doctrine by the miracles and the miracles by the doctrine" (fr. 840, cf.832), but this seems to be a rule for distinguishing genuine miracles from fakes, especially from devilish artifices. Doctrine is borne out by miracles, but in order to admit this circular confirmation one must first be converted. Miracles are powerful; indeed, it would not be a sin not to believe Jesus without them (fr. 184). Even the fact that there are many false miracles is to Pascal proof that there are genuine ones: "people could not possibly imagine so many false religions if there were no true religion" (fr. 734). That the Pharisees failed to believe Jesus despite his miracles can be explained only by "supernatural obduracy," not unlike in the memorable case of the Pharaoh (fr. 840). Does this imply that any refusal to give credence to miracles is "supernatural"? Not necessarily. Being corrupted, we prefer to dismiss miracles because we prefer to believe that Christianity is not true, otherwise we would have to abandon our earthly delights. But the corruption is ours, not God-induced. The cases of supernatural corruption, presumably exceptional, do not seem to bother Pascal, much as they might be disturbing to those who rely on God's benevolence.

There is nothing illogical in Pascal's contention that some factual grounds for accepting the Christian truth are convincing or even compelling to the faithful but not to others. This does not imply that there are two kinds of logic—one for believers and another for unbelievers. In religious matters reasoning is not *in itself* irrefutable, unlike geometrical proofs, where to reject it would be a symptom of foolishness. Pascal repeatedly made the distinction between mathematical reasoning and the way in which we accept a religious truth. This is explained by what is perhaps the most celebrated category of his Apology, the concept of the heart.

Good Reason, Bad Reason, Heart

As has been mentioned, the heart, at least in its primary sense, that related to the acquisition of religious truths, is not a sentimental attitude or an emotion. It is a faculty of *intellectual* intuition whereby we accept truths unattainable either by mathematical reasoning or by the testimony of sense experience. In the essay *De l'Esprit géométrique* the word "heart" does not appear, but fragment 110 of the *Pensées* clearly confirms that the notion is applicable even in the context of geometrical investigation. This essay is immensely rich, and only one crucial point needs to be recalled here. In geometry, "almost the only human science that produces infallible [demonstrations]," it is impossible to define primitive concepts and to prove initial principles; the infinite regress which ensues is out of our grasp. Geometry "defines none of these things, such as space, time, movement, number, equality, or the like, of which there are very many, because these terms designate the things they signify so naturally to people who understand the language that any clarification one could make would bring more obscurity than instruction."[38] This applies to other common notions like "man" or "being" (to try to define the latter would result in an absurd circularity because one would have to say "being *is*" . . .). The objects and the axioms of geometry are of "extreme natural clarity." We can even prove statements which we are not really capable of understanding, like the infinite divisibility of space and time, or, for that matter, anything that involves the idea of infinity, and we do this by reflecting on the statement that denies the one under scrutiny and perceiving its absurdity (like the finitude of space or the concept of its indivisible units; this is a Cartesian remark, except that, to Descartes, while we are unable to "understand" infinity, we can "conceive" it).

All these undemonstrable truths are, however, according to fragment 110, known by the faculty of the "heart." The heart or the instinct infallibly knows the "first principles"—space, time, movement, number—without the help of reasoning. The heart knows that there are three dimensions of space and that the numbers are infinitely many. And there are other, nonmathematical certainties: "we know that we do not dream" (so much for Descartes). Our impotence to prove such principles "can only humiliate reason."

How does this apply to religious truths? The fragment explains: "therefore those to whom God gave religion by the feeling of their hearts are blessed and legitimately convinced, but to those who do not have it we can give it only by reasoning and wait until God gives it to them by the feeling of their hearts, without which faith is only human and useless for salvation."

There is a perplexing ambiguity in this distinction. It appears that to know God by "feeling in one's heart" is the same as having faith in the proper sense, that is, receiving the supernatural gift of grace. On the other hand the "heart" is an intuition whereby obvious and nonreligious mathematical axioms are absorbed, for the understanding and acceptance of which no grace is required.

Since it is hard to imagine that Pascal, even in the notes he wrote for himself for further elaboration, could be sloppy about or forget the fundamental distinction between genuine faith and natural knowledge, we must suppose that the word "heart," thus used for two disconnected purposes, is implicitly defined only by negation: it is an intuition by which even things that cannot be proved either by infallible mathematical deduction or by the testimony of the senses are nevertheless *known*, either with unshakeable certitude (like the truths of faith for the God-enlightened) or, to use Descartes' idiom, with a "moral assurance"; the latter category would embrace both the proposition that "we do not dream" and unprovable but self-evident axioms of the kind, "if A = B and B = C, then A = C."

There is nothing logically unsound in such a negatively defined notion. And it might include even the knowledge of God by natural light to the extent that such knowledge, albeit "useless for salvation," is nonetheless accessible. When Pascal insists that "it is the heart that feels God, not reason. That is what faith is. God is sensible to the heart, not to reason" (fr. 424), he has real faith in mind; but this is less obvious when he says, "the heart loves the universal being naturally and it loves itself naturally, whichever it devotes itself to, and it hardens against the one or the other according to its choice" (fr. 423). It appears that we believe in God and love him (ultimately, that is the same) naturally. But then the very presence of atheists would be incomprehensible. There is a Pascalian answer to this objection, always the same. Whether we love God or ourselves (mutually exclusive options) is a matter of will, not of reason. "The will is one of the main organs of belief, not because it produces belief but because things are true or false according to the angle from which one looks at them" (fr. 539). It is our will that directs our mind towards this or that, depending on the pleasure we find in either. Therefore conversion is a matter of healing the will, not of mending the intellect. Atheists, who have no faith, do not lack this "natural feeling," but they do not want to discover it in their hearts because their will and the attraction of temporal pleasures conceal it from them. Probably they are guilty for their incredulity and can never seek an intellectualist refuge: "if only I had proofs . . . ."

Nevertheless it is true that this "natural feeling," whether related to geometrical axioms, to commonsense belief, or to religious matters, is never absolutely reliable, a fact the skeptics do not fail to exploit; the "force of Pyrrhonism" consists in the fact that "we have no certainty of the truth of those principles, apart from faith and revelation, except that we feel them naturally in ourselves, Now, this natural feeling is not a convincing proof of their truth, because, having no certainty, apart from faith, about whether man was created by a good God, by a wicked demon, or by chance, it is doubtful whether those principles given to us are true or false or dubious, according to our origin" (fr. 131).

This remark, obviously inspired by a reading of the *Meditations*, not of Montaigne (and references to Descartes are much more numerous in the *Pensées* than the three cases where his name actually appears, somewhat enigmatically), seems to confirm the incurable uncertainty of *all* natural knowledge unless it is supported by certainty about God. It suggests that as long as the Cartesian hypothesis of the "malicious genius" has not been illuminated —and only faith can disprove it absolutely—even geometrical axioms, not to speak of the belief that we are not dreaming in our waking state, are in the shadow of legitimate doubt. Descartes was perhaps not quite consistent about mathematical truths; we are not ultimately sure whether we can have "metaphysical certitude" without relying on God's veracity; the cogito is beyond the reach of the possible mischievous demon, to be sure, but this is not Pascal's theme. Otherwise everything seems precarious in our knowledge; but Pascal does not say that once God's existence is known to us, those "secular" certainties are thereby established. He admits that the Pyrrhonists have good arguments but he does not believe that they can ever be perfectly consistent. In fact, one need not necessarily to appeal to God to confound their extravagances: "Nature" does this, and lets us rely on the soundness of "bon sens." He says once that man owes to God the acceptance of the religion he gave him, and what God owes to man is not to lead him into error (fr. 840). This seems to contradict the implicit principle of Jansenism that God owes us nothing. The context—miracles—may dispel this contradiction. God would indeed deceive us if he gave us no means to distinguish between true and false miracles: the "error" in question concerns religious truths, not any kind of knowledge. Otherwise we would never err, or at least we would have at our disposal criteria by which in all matters truth could be infallibly distinguished from falsity; that we have no such criteria is self-evident to Pascal. We can commit errors in religious matters as well, of course, and even in understanding the revealed Word we can easily be mistaken. Of such mistakes we are guilty. Since it is always a valid principle that only the faithful have a proper understanding of faith and revelation, and that gratuitously given faith enables them to perceive miracles as miracles and to understand a prophecy as a prophecy, Pascal's claim that God "owes" it to us not to lead us into error can refer only to the elect; in other words, God does not deceive the faithful about the content of faith. In the realm of natural knowledge the light is dimmed and there is no certainty; God is hidden.[39]

While the expression "Deus absconditus" comes from revelation, its Pascalian use displays, as had been said, a sad resignation in the face of the post-Cartesian universe: birds or sky no longer give testimony of God's omnipresence. Pascal's almost obsessive preoccupation with God's absence is well understandable; that is what religion is ultimately about, apart from the infusion of grace. This alarming "fact" urgently needed an explanation and it was provided by the Augustinian concept of original sin. Since we deserve nothing but God's wrath, it is natural that we do not deserve to see his face clearly. Given human corruption it would be *unjust* if he manifested himself unveiled before our eyes as he will on the day of reckoning; but it would also be unjust if he were so hidden that even those who seek him sincerely and to whom his mercy was offered could not recognize him (fr. 149). Perfect clarity would help the mind and harm the will (fr. 234). We must not complain; if you claim that you are worthy of God's manifest revelation, you prove that you are unworthy, for you are presumptuous; if you say you are unworthy, you confirm the truth: you are unworthy (fr. XIV). You cannot win.

Thus the salutary remedy for the horror of the "mute universe" has been found. God's concealment confirms the truth of Christianity, because no other religion says that God is hidden. To be sure, to complete the picture of the degraded human condition, it was not enough to read the Book of Genesis; a peculiar Augustinian interpretation of hereditary guilt was also necessary. But it fitted perfectly in the Pascalian explanation. This was how Descartes and Augustine were blended into a coherent alloy.

To "seek God sincerely" is to find him. But we know that faith precedes understanding, therefore even to seek God sincerely would seem to require irresistible grace. No good exit from the tormenting circle.

And faith, it appears, does not produce an *intellectual* understanding of God or of any other religious truth. The elect trust

God, and indeed, feel his presence, but they do not master divine things in intellectual terms; otherwise they would be capable of convincing the unbelievers by natural light. "It is incomprehensible that God should exist and incomprehensible that he should not, that the soul should be with the body, and that we should not have a soul, that the world should have been created and that it should not, etc., that there should be original sin and that there should not" (fr. 809).

That is a philosopher who speaks, and speaks with a note of despair. The explanation of the mind-body union, either in Thomist categories (rational soul as the form of the body) or in Cartesian manner (the impossibility of causal contact between the two substances) does not help. And God is incomprehensible by definition.

Pascal's "christocentric" religiosity is a part of his radical separation of faith from knowledge. This is what links his fragments on Jesus with his consistent emphasis on the impossibility of converting Christianity into a philosophy. "We do not know God except through Jesus Christ. Without this mediator all communication with God is taken from us. It is through Jesus Christ that we know God. All those who have claimed to know God and to prove his existence without Jesus Christ had nothing but ineffective proofs. . . . Through Jesus Christ and in him one can prove God's existence and teach both morality and doctrine. Jesus Christ is thus the true God of men" (fr. 189). "It is not only impossible, but useless, to know God without Jesus Christ . . ." (fr. 191). "To know God without knowing our own misery produces pride. To know one's own misery without God produces despair. The knowledge of Jesus Christ is in the middle because we find in it both God and our misery" (fr. 192). In other words, the faith of philosophers is not faith at all; their proofs of God's existence are futile. Pascal speaks of historical proofs concerning Jesus; but did he believe that not only his life, deeds, and words were historically proven but the dogma of the Incarnation as well? And would this imply that "normal" historical knowledge can lead to genuine faith? Certainly not, since in the act of faith, knowledge and charity are one, and no knowledge, however extensive and however theological in content, can produce faith. Only faith can "give" us Jesus in the Christian sense, not philosophical or theological inquiry. "God of Abraham,

God of Isaac, God of Jacob, not of philosophers and scholars"—as we read in the "classic" formula of the *Mémorial* (fr. 913). It is futile to try to transmute Paul's Epistle to the Romans into a philosophical treatise. Besides, as we know, proofs based on miracles and prophecies are good enough but only the elect can perceive their truth. This is important, otherwise we would think that the godless and the unfaithful can have the same knowledge of God and Jesus as true Christians. Christianity is about salvation and the healing of our corruption; the only Christian knowledge worthy of the name is a knowledge that saves, therefore it cannot be a purely intellectual act of assertion, whether in metaphysical or historical matters.

In what sense, then, is human reason "autonomous" (a word often used in the description of the *Pensées*)? This word requires some *distinguos*.

We find a lucid and precise concept of scientific reason in Pascal's polemics of 1647 with Father Noël about *Expériences nouvelles touchant le vide*; the latter tried to question the results of Pascal's experiments that disproved the traditional belief in the *horror vacui*.[40] Before refuting the peripatetic philosopher's argument against the void, Pascal states the general rules for affirming or denying a proposition. We must not, he says, make a peremptory judgment unless the proposition under scrutiny "appears so clearly and distinctly by itself to our senses or reason . . . that the mind has no means of doubting its certainty"—in which case we are dealing with principles or axioms—or is inferred infallibly from such principles. Other propositions are left undecided (the mysteries of faith are excluded from this consideration). If a hypothesis is such that its negation results in a patent absurdity, it is thereby recognized as true; if its affirmation leads to a patent absurdity, it is thereby refuted; if neither occurs, the hypothesis is doubtful. But the main point of the letter is that, while in order to ascertain the truth of a hypothesis, it is not enough that known phenomena are consistent with or deducible from it, whereas it is disproved if it yields a conclusion that is contrary to even a single phenomenon.

This is a modern scientist speaking; one might say, anachronistically, that he suggests a Popperian rule of empiricism: we cannot be satisfied with an explanation that can give an account of new experiences because the explanation may still be empirically empty and fit into the experimental data only because of its emptiness, because there is no way of falsifying it (as was the case, in Popper's view, with psychoanalysis or historical materialism and, according to Pascal, with the theory which rejects the void; on this point the target of his strictures is both Cartesian and Aristotelian physics). This applies to invisible matter, which has no empirical properties and is supposed, according to the adversary, to fill the universe. Since its existence cannot be proved, there is reason to deny it, whereas it is illicit to believe in it for no better reason than that one cannot prove that it does not exist. An example of the emptiness of Aristotelian categories is given in the (almost untranslatable) definition of light provided by the Jesuit polemicist: "la lumière est un mouvement luminaire de rayons composés de corps lucides, c'est à dire lumineux." This sounds most distinctly like a learned explanation by a physician from Molière or a scientist's self-parody.

The Pascalian rules of scientific procedure are obviously relevant to his theology, indeed they provide us with a clue to the relationship between a scientist and a believer, and they explain why he was not and could not consistently be a Thomist, but rather was an Augustinian.

Indeed, the fact that empirical phenomena are consistent with a hypothesis does not make this hypothesis credible or even meaningful. The presence of God and his all-encompassing providence is this kind of hypothesis; whatever happens can be "explained" by divine orders and plans, but this is why God's existence is empirically empty (no "birds and sky") and explains nothing in terms of scientific rules. Briefly, God is not an empirical hypothesis, and Pascal knew that.

This then is the first rule: whatever is not scientifically testable (or rationally self-evident, like axioms) is scientifically empty. And the second rule is: whatever is testable is to be accepted or rejected according to the results of the test, and not on any other grounds. Conformably to the first rule, religious truths, in particular the very existence of God, are empirically empty and cannot be ascertained on the basis of empirical evidence. Conformably to the second rule, no scientific truth can be put in doubt by the verdict of a religious dogma; only scientifically valid tests can disprove it.

Both rules are confirmed by the often quoted fragments of the eighteenth *Provincial Letter*: our eyes are the proper judges of facts, our reason of natural things, faith of revealed supernatural matters; these three principles of our knowledge have, each of them, separate objects. "We have to believe the senses in factual matters, our reason when a nonrevealed truth is at stake, the Scriptures and the decisions of the Church in the realm of the supernatural."[41] Whenever the Scriptures seem to assert something that is demonstrably false, we have to look for another interpretation, considering the revealed word to be true as a matter of faith. This is consistent, Pascal says, with the teaching of Aquinas, who tries to explain why the Book of Genesis seems to claim that the moon is greater than all the stars: we should not cling to the literal sense of the biblical context but find another one.

Scripture, of course, is safe: it can never say something that is false according to the natural light, and in case of an apparent conflict it is Scripture's ostensible meaning that has to be differently explained (for instance, the dimension of lunar light in our sight, not the actual size of the moon, etc.). Reason and the senses are safe, too; no ecclesiastical decrees can invalidate their testimony. The monks of Ratisbone, Pascal says, obtained a decree from Leo IX to the effect that the body of St. Dionysius had been taken to their monastery; but this is plainly false and no pope can alter the fact, nor did the verdict of the pope Zacharius annihilate the antipodes.

The real problem of Pascal's time was not, of course, the antipodes or the location of Saint Dionysius' relics but the Galileo affair. And on this point his famous remark is, or seems to be, unambiguous: "in vain did you [the Jesuits] obtain Rome's decree against Galileo condemning his view on the movement of the earth. This will not prove that the earth rests; and, if one had persistent observations proving that it is the earth that revolves, all men together would not hinder it from revolving and themselves from revolving with it."[42]

The rule that human reason, properly working and observing its own code, cannot clash with the content of revelation was stated by Aquinas; he was by no means an advocate of the extravagant "double truths" theory held by some Averroists. And Pascal, like other Jansenists, could cite him when it was suitable. But Aquinas's philosophy did not imply that the reason why revelation and natural light (or faith and intellect) cannot conflict was that they simply had separate objects. On two points Pascal differed from him. The first is less important. According to Thomas, if an apparent contradiction appears between the divine word and the result of intellectual investigations, it is the former that gets the upper hand, and one must assume that the intellect committed errors in terms of its own regulations. Certainly, with his general rationalist preferences, Aquinas did on various occasions explain the meaning of Scripture in a way that would remove noticeable collisions, but his main prescription was that one must keep the revelation intact and discover how reason went wrong. Pascal, on the other hand, thought that in such cases we should manipulate the sense of the revelation to make it agree with the verdict of natural light, provided that the latter has operated properly.

But the major line of difference was this. In Thomist terms revelation and reason have no quite separate areas, they overlap. Along with items that obviously can be known from revelation only (in particular, the Incarnation and the Trinity), there are crucially important truths which God wanted to reveal to us but which can be known with certainty by natural light alone; among them are not only the very existence of God and eternal life but a great number of specific elements of natural theology, in fact most (albeit not everything) of what we are taught in the 453 chapters of *Contra Gentiles*.[43] A separation in the sense that natural knowledge is impotent in proving fundamental tenets of faith is entirely alien to Thomas. His is a philosophy of a cosy world in which all things coexist in a perfect harmony: heaven and earth, faith and knowledge, soul and body, temporal and eternal goods, church and state, holy history and secular history. There is, of course, a clear hierarchy of values and it is assumed that all temporal goods ultimately have to serve God and salvation; but our earthly life, our body, our social bonds, while not creating absolute values, do not deserve scorn, let alone condemnation.

If divine approval of everything created is taken literally, there is no dramatic split between the two worlds of which we are necessarily denizens. But in Pascal's world we are painfully torn asunder between them; call this attitude "baroque" or "gnostic temptation" or "vision tragique." None of the Jansenists, not even Barcos, expressed this incurable discord in similar terms.[44] This is the most general reason why the comforting philosophy of Aquinas was so incompatible with the way Pascal saw and experienced the world.

This might seem out of keeping with the specific case of the faith-versus-reason debate: truths acquired by faith and by natural reason do not clash with each other, and this is now commonly admitted by commentators. But this is not the end of the story. Faith and reason do not contradict each other *in content*, to be sure, and on this point the *Pensées* do not depart from the letter to Noël or from the *Provincial Letters*. Section XIII of the *Pensées* says virtually everything on the subject: "One ought to doubt when it is right to do so, to assert when it is right, and to submit when it is right. Whoever fails to do this does not understand the force of reason. There are people who do not observe these three principles, either asserting everything as proved, since they are ignorant of proof, or doubting everything, since they do not know when they should submit, or submitting in all matters, since they do not know where to judge. Pyrrhonist, mathematician, Christian: doubt, affirmation, submission" (fr. 170). "Nothing is so consistent with reason as this disavowal of reason" (fr. 182). "The last step of reason is to admit that there are infinitely many things which are above it" (fr. 188). But reason has an imperative power (fr. 768).

On the compelling force of "geometrical" reason and its limits there is nothing in the *Pensées* to contradict earlier writings: while "first principles" cannot be proved and must be accepted by the "heart" as self-evident, they are good enough to be thus accepted; the impossibility of proving them humilitates reason and reveals its limits, but this does not imply that within those limits reason cannot arrive at humanly accessible certainty or that we are entitled to doubt everything, let alone admit that any proposition is as good as its negation. While it is true that our reasoning yields to "sentiment," that reason is pliable in all directions (fr. 530), and that it is a sure loser in a conflict with passions and amour-propre, this does not mean that there are no rules at all; if two people disagree about the lapse of time since something happened and I have a watch, I don't care what they say; I am not making a judgment according to my whims precisely because I have a watch (fr. 534).

In other words: we have instruments with which to pass judgment in matters pertaining to the competence of reason. Scholastic reason is unworthy of trust because it tries to go beyond its capacities. As a man whose mind was trained in mathematics and physics, Pascal simply could not believe the Thomists' arguments because they were obviously defective in terms of the procedures that science employed. Their dismissal does not in itself logically imply that no other arguments are possible but this conclusion was at least very strongly suggested if additional considerations are taken into account. Scholastic and Cartesian arguments for God's existence, God's attributes, and the immortality of the soul were all that was available; none were compelling, convincing, or even plausible according to standards stated by Pascal; and if one looked more closely at those standards, it became clear that it was hopeless to search for other arguments that would meet the requirements of scientific reason (the ontological proof is not mentioned but one may safely assume that it would appear dubious to the mind of a mathematician, not to speak of its futility in terms of religious benefits).

Scientific reason is considerably limited even in natural matters, and in matters pertaining to our salvation it is totally fruitless apart from its possible negative capacity: the ability to see its own limitations. Within its legitimate scope of activity it needs to obey its own precepts and nothing else, especially not papal pronouncements when they clearly go beyond the authority of the Church in matters of Christian doctrine and morality.

Recognizing how little value rational arguments have in religious issues does not lead directly to being an Augustinian; one could simply stop bothering about these issues and become a libertine in a stronger or weaker sense of the word. But for a scientist who cannot swallow scholastic rationality and is a Christian who takes his Christianity very seriously (unlike those scientists who kept their watered-down Christianity only in the form of a few nonconfessional tenets—the existence of God, divine providence, immortality) there was, apart from the Augustinian tradition, hardly any option available in terms of a consistent, all-embracing interpretation of the entire body of Christianity. Deism, virtually (or totally) noncommittal, was not such an option, of course. Pascal's option resulted naturally from biographical accidents—his milieu, his father's influence, the meeting with Saint-Cyranian preachers, etc.—but it converged, and was perfectly consistent, with the mental disposition of a scientist to whom religious matters lay "on the other side" of the mind and the heart. He did not actually say, like Jansenius, that for knowledge of God memory, not intellect, is the proper organ, but he certainly would have approved this assessment. Christianity is not metaphysics. We are initiated into it by studying history—sacred history, to be sure—and not by exercising our logical skills. In the preface to the *Traité du vide*, authority, sense experience, and reason are distinguished in the same way as in the *Pensées*. Continuous and collectively achieved progress in science is stressed (the remark about antiquity being the childhood of mankind rather than its old age, a source of special wisdom, is well in the spirit of both Bacon and Descartes) but this is not denied in the *Apology* ("all the sciences are infinite in the scope of their research; for who would doubt that geometry, for instance, has an infinity of infinities of propositions to set forth?" [fr. 199]).

In terms of the separation of faith from natural light there is thus no break between the *Pensées* and Pascal's earlier writings.

What is characteristic of the period of the *Pensées* is not a denial of the legitimate authority of scientific reason within its limits, but rather a repeatedly stated mistrust of science in moral terms: confronted with what really matters in life, our salvation, science simply brings little profit. The most concise description of the human condition is, after all: "between us and hell or heaven there is only life between the two, and this is the most fragile thing in the world" (fr. 152). In this short journey towards an eternity of beatitude or of agony, curiosity directed to nature and mathematical objects is at best indifferent. "The vanity of science. Knowledge of external things will not console me, in times of affliction, for ignorance of morals, but knowledge of morals will always console me for ignorance of natural science" (fr. 23). "Once I started studying man, I saw that these abstract sciences are not proper to man and that by plunging into them I went further astray from my destiny than did others by being ignorant of them" (fr. 687). Or, as Pascal put it in his famous letter to Fermat of 10 August 1660: "To speak frankly, I consider mathematics the highest employment of the mind; at the same time I know that it is so useless that there is, in my view, little difference between a mathematician and a skilful artisan. I call it the most beautiful craft [métier] in the world but it is, after all, no more than a craft."[45]

If there is anything surprising in such a remark coming from the pen of an Augustinian, it is only that it was not phrased more strongly: the study of nature from disinterested curiosity has always been sinful in the Augustinian tradition. This is, no doubt, an incontestable consequence of the general rule which opposes "the world" and the Church to each other as implacable foes; whatever we do that is not for God is captured by Satan, and there is nothing in between. But then Pascal was not converted to Augustinian piety in the process of writing the *Pensées*, as his earlier texts testify. In his short essay known under the title *A Comparison of Early Christians with Those of Today*,[46] the hostile separation of Christianity from mundane life is stated unambiguously: "one saw then [in early Christianity] the world and the Church as two opposites, two irreconcilable enemies one of which uninterruptedly persecutes the other, and of which the seemingly weaker would one day triumph over the stronger, so that people deserted one of these opposite parties to join the other. They renounced the precepts of the one to espouse the precepts of the other; they rejected the opinions [sentiments] of the one to adopt the opinions of the other." And that was the perfect Christianity, which one could join only after arduous preparation, instead of being baptized just after birth (even though there are "very important reasons" why babies are baptized). To be a Christian, one had to forsake the world and be totally devoted to the Church, whereas today the Church is polluted by people who carry the spirit of ambition, revenge, impurity, and concupiscence. "All virtues, martyrdom, austerities, and good works are useless [when practiced] beyond the Church and without communion with the head of the Church, who is the pope," we read in a letter to Roannez of November 1656.[47]

Pascal never condemned outright the practice of science; he degraded it—against his inclination, no doubt—to a worldly amusement. And he never surrendered it to papal decrees ("the pope hates and fears scholars who are not bound to him by vows," [fr. 677]). Gilberte's claim that her brother abandoned scientific work entirely after his first conversion, and composed his major treatise on cycloids (of 1658) only by accident, when he was tormented by a great pain which prevented him from sleeping, did not withstand examination by Pascal scholars.[48] There might have been a tension between his disparaging remarks and the continuing, if enfeebled, interest of a genius in scientific matters, but this does not make his opinion any less credible and genuine. In accordance with Jansenist piety he wanted to be a Christian and nothing else, and logically this entailed not being a scientist (the exercise of science being, after all, a part of "the world"), not even being an "hônnete homme," that is, a polished, polite member of the educated upper classes, pleasantly conversing with his peers, moderate in his opinions, avoiding obduracy and strong partisan spirit.[49] And yet Pascal was both a scientist—somewhat vain and eager to assert his claims to priority—and an "hônnete homme," apart from being a Christian. If he experienced discomfort as a result of combining these roles—Jesus Christ was not a scientist or an hônnete homme, nor was St. Paul—this was not only a personal psychological problem. This discomfort is an aspect of the *Pensées*. But it is only one aspect, and not a major one, considering the main purpose of the Apology.

And the main purpose, needless to say, was not to show that Christianity is not "contrary to reason," but only "above" it; and also to show that it is because Christianity goes against our instincts that people tend to reject it. In this respect Pascal was obviously much more skeptical than the men of the schools, and he knew perfectly well that attempts to "rationalize" Christianity, to make it, at least to a large extent, a product of the unprejudiced secular intellect, were not only hopeless in terms of the capacities of this intellect, but in a sense sacrilegious, as they would deprive religion of its mystery and make void the gift of faith; such an endeavor, even if successful, would be worthless, because faith, which is necessarily coupled with love, can never spring from reason, however powerful. Pascal believed that Christianity, being contrary to human nature, is not unreasonable, but this belief boils down to two points. In the negative, defensive sense, it means that we can always, by skilful exegesis, remove the seeming contradiction between the text of revelation and natural reason by making clear that the former, being infallible by definition, has a meaning different from its ostensible one. In the positive and intellectually more fragile sense we can show that once we know from the divine word the crucial facts of man's destiny—the history of the Fall and of redemption—we can understand all the things that would otherwise seem depressingly unintelligible and revoltingly absurd: all forms of human misery, suffering, the very frailty of reason, the futility of our aspirations, struggles, persecutions, and poverty. No application of reason can make Christianity "rational"; indeed, to go beyond this would amount to an attempt to covert Christianity into a philosophy, that is, to build a new tower of Babel.

Gambling for Faith: The Discontinuity of the Universe

Pascal's main purpose is not to make "our religion" intellectually respectable but to make it *aimable*, lovable, desirable. This was to him the only way to proceed, as people naturally direct their steps to what they find attractive. "One would never abandon worldly pleasures in order to embrace the cross of Jesus Christ if one did not find more delight [*douceur*] in being despised, poor, destitute, and pushed away by people than in the joys of sin."[50]

But he wanted to show the delight not of Christianity *tout court* but of its Augustinian variant, the austere piety which included the theology of predestination in the Jansenist sense. Nicole says that he himself tried to rid the Augustinian doctrine of grace of a certain appearance of harshness which repels many people, without however altering or weakening anything in its content; Pascal shared this view and encouraged him to proceed. "While he [Pascal] was most rigid and inflexible in matters concerning efficient grace, he said that if he had to deal with the subject, he hoped to succeed in making this doctrine so plausible and stripping it so much of a certain harsh (*farouche*) appearance that it would suit the taste of any cast of mind."[51]

Did the *Pensées* succeed in softening the Augustinian theology of grace without making any doctrinal concessions? Hardly; and if they did, then it was by omission. They repeatedly stress that human creatures cannot cure themselves of their miserable condition: "in vain, men, do you seek in yourselves the medicine for your miseries," says the divine wisdom (fr. 149). This, however, is not specifically Augustinian, perhaps just incompatible with the extreme version of Pelagianism. To say that "man is not worthy of God but not incapable of becoming worthy" (fr. 239) does not go beyond the standard interpretation of original sin. What is specifically Augustinian is neither the dogma of original sin (at least in the most general sense that mankind was corrupted as its result) nor the general belief that, being what we are, we cannot be justified without grace; it is rather the doctrine which states that the distribution of grace has nothing to do with human merits, that grace is gratuitously given to the elected few without the slightest contribution on their part, and that it works infallibly. This was indeed "harsh" and difficult to swallow for many believers. And this specifically Augustinian tenet, which was Pascal's own (as it appears from the *Écrits sur la Grâce*), is simply absent from the *Pensées*, at least in an articulated form. We do not know how he would have produced a "suave" presentation of it and made it appear delightful to readers.

Still, he did, of course, want to convert people—to God, not to his peculiar Augustinian portrait—regardless of the troubling problem of how to do this given that conversion is reserved for God only and that we are unable to resist his will if he wishes us to be saved. And he came up with a method which, once explained, is striking in its simplicity, but could have been devised only against the background of the Pascalian scientific, philosophical, and theological perspective.

This method is expounded in the Wager, the *pari* (fr. 418). It is rightly considered the core of the *Pensées* as we know them. Those three pages are of such incomparable celebrity (or perhaps comparable only to the short Part IV of the Cartesian *Discours*) that it is awkward to quote them. But they can be misleading and did, indeed, mislead some readers. Let the summary be brief.

Since the purpose of the *pari* is to dispose us to enter on the path to Christian faith, it starts, fittingly, by giving a reason (not the main reason, as it appears later) why we naturally resist God's appeal. This reason is simply the incomprehensibility of God. "Our soul is thrown into the body where it finds number, time, dimension; it is about them that it reasons and calls them nature, necessity, and it cannot believe anything else."

"Thrown into the body"—this Augustinian (indeed, quasi-gnostic) and non-Thomist expression is meant to explain our *intellectual* disability: our imprisonment in the body induces us to believe that body is all there is in the universe. *Horror corporis.*

God is thus incomprehensible by not being a body. But he is incomprehensible, above all, because he is infinite. "A unit added to infinity does not augment it"; "the finite is reduced to pure nothingness in the face of infinity. So is our mind in the face of God and so is our justice in the face of divine justice."[52]

Then we have two sentences which might easily have occurred to the writer at this point but do not seem properly to belong to his reasoning and may be set aside: "God's justice must be as immense as is his mercy. His justice towards the damned is less immense and should shock us less than his mercy towards the elect"; in other words, if we go to hell, it is by justice, and if to heaven, by mercy: a standard Jansenist view. What we are to do with the "immensity" of both the justice and the mercy of God is not clear; it seems that no practical conclusions about our behavior can be inferred from this knowledge.

Then there is a somewhat perplexing fragment on infinity, of the nature of which we are ignorant while we know that it exists. "It is true that there is infinity in numbers but what it is we do not know; it is false that it is even and false that it is odd because its nature is not altered at all when a unit is added. It is a number nonetheless and every number is even or odd. True, this applies to any finite number."

The fragment is perplexing insofar as it suggests that, according to Pascal, there is such a thing as the mysterious highest number, a number higher than any other number. Yet it is unbelievable and impossible that Pascal the mathematician should have confused the simple and obvious fact that the series of numbers is infinite with the false idea that there is a highest number. Indeed the *Esprit géométrique* clearly denies the concept of a highest number.[53]

But even assuming that there was a false premise in his explanation, it is not essential to his argument, because his point is only our mental helplessness in the face of infinity. "And so one can know that there is a God without knowing what he is." But, unlike in the case of infinite extension, of which we know the existence (because we are extended) but not the nature, "we know neither the existence of God nor his nature because he has neither extension or limit. But we know his existence by faith and his nature we shall know by glory."

So far, the Wager confirms what we know from other fragments of the *Pensées*: there is no reliable way to God either from the natural order of the universe or from human nature.

That Christians cannot provide reasons for their creed is not grounds for blaming them, because they say precisely that: their religion is *stultitia*, folly, when they reveal it to the world. "If they proved it they would not be keeping their word."

Now come the crucial moment. "God does or does not exist; but which side are we going to take? Reason can decide nothing on the issue, an infinite chaos separates us." It is heads or tails.

Counter-argument: since we are incapable of deciding, the right thing to do is not to bet at all.

Counter-counter-argument of the highest importance: "yes, but one has to bet. It is not up to you to decide, you are committed" (*cela n'est pas volontaire, vous êtes embarqués*). Pascal does not explain why it should be compulsory to opt either for or against God's existence but an answer that would be in keeping with his thinking is easy to imagine. The answer would be: if you say that you cannot decide because of the shortage of reasons, you have already made your decision, most probably *against* God; you must not delude yourself; once you say "I cannot know whether God does or does not exist," you will prefer to live as if there were no God because it is so much more convenient; and then, if God does exist, you will be judged correspondingly.

But is it not possible to say "I do not know whether God does or does not exist but I prefer to live *as if* he did"? Yes, it is feasible. The implicit commitment is an intellectual assent not to a belief but to a way of life which can be either against or for God; I cannot have both and I cannot have neither. There is no way to avoid the decision in practical behavior even if it is possible to suspend theoretical judgment on the fundamental question: does he exist or not? And all the time we have to keep in mind that once we die, *les jeux sont faits, rien ne va plus*. "The last act is always bloody, no matter how beautiful the rest of the play might be. At the end they throw earth on the head and that is that, forever" (fr. 165).

That the option *for* God is open, even if we suspend judgment, is the argument of the remaining, perhaps the most striking, and the most famous part of the *pari*. We ought to behave as in a game of chance and weigh the stake we put on the table against the expected gain or loss. If, compelled as we are to gamble, we risk one life against the possible gain of three lives, we would be unreasonable not to risk, it if the chances of winning and losing are equal. But in this case it is not three lives that can be gained but an eternal life of infinite happiness. In this case, even if there were infinitely many chances of losing against only one of winning, it would be reasonable to bet on God, considering that a finite amount is at stake while an infinite reward may be won. "And so when one is compelled to gamble one should be renouncing reason by preserving one's life rather than risking it for infinite gain, which is as likely to come about as the loss of what is nothing." And it would be vain to argue that the gain is uncertain whereas the risk is certain; this is so in any game where the gambler risks with certainty a finite stake in order to gain with uncertainty a finite reward, and does this "without sinning against reason."

The potential addressee replies: "yes, but my hands are tied and my mouth is mute; I am being compelled to bet and I am not free; I am bound, and I am so made that I am incapable of believing. What do you want me to do?"

The reply to this reply: "true, but you must understand that your inability to believe is due to your passions. Since reason inclines you to believe and yet you cannot do so, do not try to convince yourself by multiplying the arguments for God but by reducing your passions. You want to advance towards faith and you do not know the route." Learn from those who have found it: "they acted *as if* they believed, they took holy water, they had masses said, etc. This will make you believe naturally and will make an automaton of you." ("Vous abêtira"; there is a consensus, after Gilson, about this strange expression, meaning not "will stultify you" but rather "will make you like a beast," that is, an automaton.)

The would-be convert, if he follows Pascal's advice, will soon discover that even his initial perception of gambling was wrong. Pascal assures him that he will gain in this life and will come to realize more and more that he risked nothing to gain with certainty; "at the end you will recognize that you bet on a certain, infinite thing for which you have given nothing." The pernicious pleasures of old will be replaced by other ones.

The *pari* is striking by its rigor and its refusal to look for easy solutions or to seek refuge in vagueness; as usual, Pascal is merciless in searching for truth "to the very end." He does not promise any credible arguments for God's existence, as this is simply impossible. And he appeals—perhaps not quite in keeping with some of the moralistic fragments of the *Pensées*—to the amour-propre of the reader, to his desire for happiness, and to his reason, insofar as reason can be harnessed to the service of self-interest (not any interest, to be sure, but interest in one's own eternal salvation): it is simply reasonable to opt for God, just as it is reasonable to stake an amount of money in a game of chance if the possible gain is great by comparison with what the gambler risks.

The ultimate practical advice to the potential convert might appear rather meager: "take holy water," etc. But both the context of this advice and its philosophical background considerably enrich its meaning.

To an unprejudiced reader the *pari* argument seems uncomplicated; but misunderstandings were once many, even among perceptive readers, and a few explanatory remarks, even if not necessarily original, are not out of place.

First of all, Pascal does not make any probabilistic presuppositions concerning the very existence of God. Probabilistic reasoning is used in the calculation of losses and gains in opting for God; he does not say that the probability of God's being there is the same as that of his absence, he simply says that "reason can decide nothing on the issue." God, let us repeat, as this is a crucial point throughout the *Pensées*, is not an empirical hypothesis of however great or however small a degree of probability. He is beyond the intellectual game.

Still, misreadings of this point were almost unavoidable. Voltaire even thought that Pascal tried to prove dogmas of faith by reason. This is apparently nonsense—Pascal said the opposite many times; but if one writes an apology for Christianity it is impossible simply to leave reason out, in all its functions. Voltaire, however, simply failed to grasp the practical character of Pascal's reasoning and the part reason was supposed to play in his exhortations. He says that it is obviously false to argue that if you do not opt for God you opt for his nonexistence; this would be false if Pascal spoke of intellectual acceptance of "'a religious statement," but he spoke of betting or opting in practical conduct, where it is not obviously false. The *pari*, according to Voltaire, is "indecent and childish" because one cannot believe in something for no better reason than that one wishes it to be true.[54]

But Pascal is not guilty of this charge. He does not say, absurdly, "if God exists, this is very good news, therefore you should believe in God." He says, rather, if you admit that God's existence would be a great promise of eternal happiness but you feel you cannot believe, you should take practical steps that will lead you to faith and start by recognizing that the root of your inability is your unwillingness to tame your passions, not the lack of rational arguments (even though it is true that there are no credible rational arguments).

Therefore—and this is the second important point—the person to whom the *pari* might be addressed has to meet some conditions; he cannot be anybody. To be touched by the argument one has to have at least a minimal "will to believe" and to admit that God's existence, albeit undemonstrable, has a degree of plausibility. A convinced atheist, entrenched in his incredulity, would easily shrug off the apologist's appeals because, in his view, the chance of winning in the terrible game is simply nil. Even if he admits that his earthly passions might have something to do with his unbelief, this is a matter of causal connection, having no bearing on the validity of arguments for or against. Our life is finite, he would say, and so are its pleasures, but that is everything we have. Since there are no convincing reasons to believe, it would be foolish to waste one's life on hunting for a chimera.

Thus, to a rationalist, Pascal's effort is futile if he really has not retained in his mind a grain of doubt about his godlessness, a grain of the will to live in a God-ordered world, a slender residue of faith.

This applies, for that matter, to most of the stuff the *Pensées* are made of, because a rationalist will always argue that in order to be moved by the arguments one has to be a believer already, that is, not only to admit *in abstracto* the principle "credo ut intelligam" but actually to believe. Voltaire, by no means a die-hard atheist but a rationalist all the same, reveals time and again his inability to absorb the real sense of the *Pensées* as the author must have conceived it. If Pascal perceives the superiority of Christianity in its obscurity, this implies that in order to be believed it is enough to be incomprehensible; and why should the history of original sin, this "roman théologique," explain human misery and greatness better than the tales of Prometheus and Pandora? If the prophetic texts have always had a double meaning, this amounts to saying that God deceives us. And what is wrong with divertissements that are in fact a natural medicine for our suffering?

Everything boils down to this: Pascal believes that human destiny and God's self-concealment are made intelligible by the history of the Fall. A rationalist will always reply that he sees no reason to believe the biblical story and that even Pascal does not explicitly accept this story as a credible hypothesis. And so we turn in a circle: once you are a believer, everything makes sense, but you cannot infer the content of faith from facts; it is rather the other way around: armed with your faith, you project meaning onto the facts.

Pascal knew this, and addressed himself to people in whom a willingness to believe can be traced. Reason works to remove the obstacles laid by rationalists: for religion in its *content* does not violate reason. Like Jansenist writers, for that matter, Pascal speaks not to incurable materialists but to people of little faith whose religious allegiance is feeble and insignificant in their daily lives; he speaks to the "tepid" about whom the Scriptures say what they say.

The third point is that faith is not a deist's religion, an act of asserting; it is an act of total commitment, including love and trust and submission of one's will to God. And Pascal does not advise his reader to behave *as though* God existed and to expect an eternal reward as a result. This is not an insurance policy ("just in case, follow the supposed divine instruction; perhaps hell is not a fable after all"). Holy water or even sinless conduct do not bring us gratuitously distributed salvation. Why holy water and similar exercises nevertheless pave the path to faith—and thus to heaven—is explained elsewhere in the *Pensées*. "We are automata no less than minds. Therefore demonstration is not the only tool to convince people. How few things can be proved! Proofs convince only the mind; it is habit that makes the strongest proofs and those that are most believed. It inclines the automaton, which draws the mind unconsciously behind it" (fr. 821). And this applies to the relationship between behavior and real virtue or, possibly, between the "external" signs and faith. "One gets accustomed to internal virtues by external habits" (fr. 912). "External repentance inclines us to internal repentance, as [acts] of humiliation incline us to [real] humility" (fr. 936; cf. 944).

How an animal body, an automaton, is joined to the soul is, Pascal admits, incomprehensible (it is indeed incomprehensible on Cartesian grounds); but it is also incomprehensible that we are soulless automata. We have to admit that a mysterious link couples and makes one thing of two incompatibles, at least in our earthly life; therefore it is reasonable to suppose that by acting on the body one may influence the soul and that bodily training affects our "interior." This is a philosophical point in Pascal and it explains his advice that purely mechanical piety might bring about real faith. Again, we do not learn from the *Pensées* how it is possible to obtain grace, given that grace can never be a recompense for proper conduct. But that is, it seems, the best we can do.

Did Pascal himself achieve faith by following this advice, by "wagering"? This seems quite unlikely. When he says "learn from those who were bound like you and who now stake everything they have" there is no reason to suppose he speaks of himself (as Goldmann has suggested). His great night of fire, the sudden conversion, had nothing to do with a wager, to judge from his *Mémorial* (fr. 913). When he mentions himself in the *pari* ("this discourse . . . is made by a man who before and after fell on his knees to pray to this infinite, indivisible being to whom he submits everything he has, to submit to him likewise everything that is yours, for your own good and for his glory") the peculiar "method" of the *pari* is not mentioned or involved.

It has been pointed out that the Wager was not without antecedents even though Pascal might not have heard of them. The Jesuit father Antoine Sirmond (a target of Arnauld's ferocious attack and a nephew of the better-known Jacques Sirmond, S.J., sometime confessor of Louis XIII) suggested in his treatise on the immortality of the soul (1637) an approach which seems to have much in common with the *pari*:[55] a preacher or an apologist should appeal to the selfish interest of unbelievers, convince them that it is reasonable, in terms of the balance of risk and gain, to behave as it suits a good Christian—even without proper faith—and to observe the commandments with hope of celestial reward.

The analogy might be suggestive except for one major snag. Its author is the same Father Sirmond who infuriated Arnauld[56] by averring that it is possible to lead a good Christian life, and thus to obtain salvation, merely by complying with the external requirements of the Church, without loving God. This is consistent with the Molinist belief in grace as a legitimately expected requital for proper conduct. But this is certainly not Pascal's method. Yes, his addressee should start with a mechanical observance of what is right after a cold calculation of his chances of risk or gain. But what he can expect is not heavenly reward, for otherwise a beast, the automaton which he is going to become for a while, could be saved. These mechanical operations are good insofar as they might influence the heart (how?—we do not know, we know only that there is a mysterious link between mind and body) and result ultimately in a real conversion, and the "genuine conversion consists in annihilating oneself before this universal being whom one has angered so many times and who can justly destroy one at any moment, and in recognizing that without him one is helpless and that one deserves nothing from him except his wrath" (fr. 378).

No, Pascal cannot properly *promise* salvation to anybody who will try his way; salvation is in God's hands only, but Pascal wants to show that it is worth trying. "I would soon give up pleasures, they say, if I had faith. And I tell you: you would soon have faith if you gave up pleasures. It is up to you to start. If I could, I would give you faith. I cannot do that, nor can I know if what you say is true, but you can well give up your pleasures and see whether or not what I say is true" (fr. 816).

There is an ambiguity in Pascal to the extent that he does not mention what is so fundamental in Augustinian theology and relevant to his exhortation: the unmerited distribution of grace. But he never forgot the distinction between mechanical obedience and faith. Indeed, the belief that one can smoothly pass from nature to the realm of grace—intellectually or morally—is the chief target of the *Pensées* (to reach God by the use of natural light; to be saved as a result of moral effort based on our natural powers). The unbridgeable gap between the human and the divine—unbridgeable by our powers, that is—is not only an inevitable effect of our depravation but is "metaphysical," so to speak, resulting from the very nature of the realities involved, from the infinite distance between the finite and the infinite. "All bodies, the firmament, the stars, the earth and its kingdoms, are not worth the least of minds, because the mind knows all this and knows itself, and bodies know nothing. All bodies together and all the minds together and all their creations are not worth the slightest stirring of charity. This is of a infinitely higher order."

"From all bodies together one could not produce one little

thought. This is impossible, this is of another order. From all bodies and minds one could not wring a stirring of true charity. This is impossible, this is of another, supernatural order" (fr. 308).

This unforgettable confrontation of the three orders[57] does not imply a contempt for the mind, *esprit*; *esprit* is all we have to distinguish ourselves from the mute, mindless, inert universe, from body. *Esprit* has its own rules that have to be observed, for they, too, come from God: the rules of intellectual procedure, the rules of natural justice. But the confrontation is good enough to humiliate us, including our reason and our natural virtues; for in terms of what really matters they are worthless.

Pascal's concept of the three orders expresses concisely and distinctly what is eminently characteristic of Jansenist piety: that there is no continuity between human values or natural virtues and the world of faith, no intermediary steps leading us from earthly goods to heavenly ones, as there are in what Brémond calls "humanisme dévot," which includes some Jesuit writers and of which François de Sales is the most prominent master. *Humanisme dévot* may have followed the example of Plato's *Symposium*: one discards lower delights for more sublime ones, but there is a continuity in the spiritual itinerary, rather like climbing up a ladder; indeed, earthly love is a pale reflection of perfect love directed toward the Being, who is identical with Truth, Goodness, and Beauty. Not so in Jansenist piety. Here, the world is just a mass of filth. By taking us out of the abyss of sin, grace, as it were, inflicts a benevolent violence on the sinner. The values of the world are not simply left behind with every step on the path toward something higher; there is nothing in the world that could serve us as a support on this path, everything has to be annihilated.[58]

Pascal's Modernity

Has anybody been converted to Christianity by following the instructions in the Wager? We do not know. For all the importance the *pari* has in Pascal's strategy, the message that really mattered to modern *Pascalisants* seems to have been similar to the ideas that were to be elaborated, closer to our time, by some Catholic modernists: do not worry about being unable to prove God's existence by rationally reliable means; do not try to prove God, trust him and obey him and you will recognize that he is there, beyond doubt. But the modernists did not believe in the literal, perennial truth of dogmas as they had been codified in the Church's teaching.

In the seventeenth century the dominant tendency in the Church favored on the one hand the by then obsolete scholastic rationality in religious matters and, on the other, employed the authority of its office and of Holy Writ—as interpreted by this very office—to repress science.

This policy was self-destructive on both accounts; it seemed to make religious truths more and more dependent on the increasingly dubious efficiency of scholastic syllogisms, and it repelled the growing educated classes, to whom the Church must have seemed more and more like overbearing Ignorance on an oppressive throne. And the time was long past when the educated class meant, practically, the clergy; the process of emancipation of the urban "intelligentsia" could not be reversed, nor could the spirit of the new science be permanently stifled, occasional condemnations notwithstanding. By failing to work out a policy that would make peace with, and eventually assimilate, the new spiritual order, the Church risked losing what had been its precious asset: the ability to maintain as narrow as possible a gap between the faith of simpletons and the faith of the learned.

The importance of Pascal in the Catholic world was that he undermined the prevailing tendency of the Church on both sides simultaneously. This was what made him signally "modern," for this tendency was to last for the next long historical epoch, up to, and including, the beginning of the twentieth century. Had he only degraded the role of secular reason, he would have been in the company of eleventh-century antidialecticians or early Protestant preachers; had he simply defended the right of secular reason against the encroachments of ecclesiastical power, he would have joined the ranks of deists or the advocates of natural religion. Yet he protected both faith and reason against each other; he argued that the former did not need the fragile support of the latter because it is not the business of our limited intellectual powers to grant validity to Christian truth; and he argued that the latter has its own legislation and that it is not the business of the pope or the Holy Office to issue decrees concerning physical theories or historical facts.

But clearly what mattered was not just the separation of secular reason from faith according to their respective subjects. The
distinction between the order of faith and that of knowledge, albeit
differently drawn, had always been a part of Christian philosophy;
it belongs to its very definition. In the late Middle Ages and after,
the separation of the realm of the profane from the world of faith
was mainly an instrument whereby philosophy, science, and secular
politics were to be sheltered from theocratic aspirations. In our
time, it is the other way around: the separation serves religious life,
which needs protection from the voracity of the general spirit of
scientism, rationalist doctrines, and the prevailing habit of measur-
ing the validity of spiritual creations by their usefulness.

But if Pascal was both *defensor fidei* and *defensor rationis*, if he
refused to convert faith into philosophy, into second-rate knowledge, and to reforge science into a meek servant of papal verdicts,
this was not simply in terms of laying down the borderline between
their respective territories in order to achieve a lasting truce. Faith
and knowledge are not defined by their subject matters, the question of the movement of the earth belonging to the latter, the question of the Holy Trinity to the former. Faith and charity and moral
submission to God are one and the same thing in human life, and
charity is "of an infinitely higher order." The distinction is ontological, so to speak: it refers neither to the taxonomy of knowledge nor even to the hierarchy of values, even though it is true that
faith, thus fused together with charity and moral obedience into a
single alloy, is by comparison infinitely more important, as it decides about our eternal life, unlike mathematics, which is only "a
craft," however superb. The distinction is ontological in that it is
not made between two areas that lie on the same plane; they are
incommensurable; people deprived of faith, for whatever reason,
are dwellers in a different universe than the faithful. It is a part of
the distinction between two "irreconcilable enemies," God and the
world, incapable of making peace with each other.

It might be said therefore that the transition from the kingdom of reason to that of faith is not simply logically unsound; it is
ontologically impossible, perhaps like making a body from many
two-dimensional planes (but this comparison is clumsy, too). Reason cannot provide faith with legitimacy, as this would amount to
suggesting that love and virtue as effective qualities of human life,

as spiritual events, could be logically deduced from some mathematical axioms—a perfect absurdity.

The inverse movement is unfeasible, too. There is no way to infer from faith-charity a rule for deciding whether Aristotelian or Galilean mechanics is reliable.

Perhaps nobody in the seventeenth century expressed this incongruity between the life of faith and the secular life better than Pascal. The distinction has, of course, its "cognitive" side, in that we perceive the world differently once faith is given to us. But there is no smooth transition. Those who want "to prove God ['s existence] from the works of nature" fail to see this. "I would not be astonished by their attempt if they addressed their discourse to the faithful, for those who have living faith in their hearts see immediately that all that there is, is the work of God alone, whom they adore; but for those in whom this light is extinguished and in whom one would like to rekindle it, people robbed of faith and grace, who, when they examine by their light everything they see in nature that might lead them to this knowledge, find nothing but obscurity and darkness; to tell such people that they have only to look at the least thing around them and they will see God there quite clearly, to give them, as the only proof of this great and grave subject, the movement of the moon and planets and to claim that one has thus completed the proof with such arguments, amounts to giving them cause to believe that the proofs of our religion are very weak; both reason and experience tell us that nothing is more likely to cause them to feel contempt for our religion. The Scriptures, which have better knowledge of things divine, do not speak this way. On the contrary, they say that God is a hidden God and that after the corruption of nature he left men in their blindness, from which they can escape only through Jesus Christ, without whom all commerce with God is cut off" (fr. 781).

Again: when we live in faith we see God everywhere with certainty, but one cannot—as a matter of principle—provide a faithless person with this kind of wisdom by logically compelling persuasion (". . . we cannot convince the unbelieving. And they cannot convince us . . ." [fr. 237]). Does this mean that faith is "irrational"? That is not the right way of putting it; this very ambiguous and threatening word was not used in this context, lexicographers tell us, until the mid-nineteenth century, and its meaning is, as a rule, pejorative: to say "your belief is irrational" usually implies "you are silly." But that is obviously not what Pascal wants to say. He would rather have said, if he had known the adjective, that it is silly to say "your love is irrational," thereby suggesting that love can ever be "rational" and that we know what it means. But such descriptions, in his perspective, are simply inapplicable. Faith cannot be assessed in these terms, it belongs to another reality, and to ask whether or not it is "rational" is like asking whether a number is red or green.

Thus, Pascal offered Christians a way to dismiss the challenge of the incredulous: "How do you know that God exists?" He admits that an unbeliever is not only impervious to possible arguments but that he is *rightly* so, for on his own terms the arguments are bound to be powerless; a person with faith, however, is right as well because it is not such arguments that confer legitimacy or credibility on his faith. But then faith, with its separate ontological status, can gain legitimacy only from the world in which it is immersed, that is, from God; it cannot defend itself by reference to a vague feeling or by any "secular" support, because it is not a mundane event.

Therefore in theological terms a heavy price had to be paid for making faith impenetrable to assault from "the world." As God's presence in our hearts, faith is no less than a miracle; the elect obtain it without merit. That only a few enjoy this undeserved privilege is perhaps not directly deducible from the very fact of its arbitrariness (it is, after all, in God's power to give grace to as many as he might wish), but it is strongly suggested by the very fact that it is a miracle, a supernatural intervention, and it is normal to think that it cannot be promiscuously offered to legions. ("There are few true Christians" [fr. 179]). This is confirmed by experience, which reveals how rare is observance of the commandments; and morally impeccable conduct, while not the cause of election, is nonetheless its visible, though not infallible, symptom. The Jansenists' concept of election is thus linked with their strong belief that the gate to heaven is indeed very narrow.

The peculiar Augustinian image of the sovereign God is of course at the center of this religiosity. To the Jansenists, the God of the Jesuit laxists was a nice fellow who is lenient, who understands our weaknesses in the face of so many temptations and with whom a bilaterally advantageous contract can always be arranged—unlike their own stern avenger who dispatches most of mankind, including all unbaptized babies, to everlasting tortures. This is Brémond's description—malicious but not inaccurate—of the Jansenists' God: "this remote God, mute and terribly uncaring, this grace which is necessary but hangs on sinister whims, this Christ, mean and merciless, who counts on the cross the few predestined whom he wants to save. . . ."[59]

This was not to be an unavoidable either/or, and many theologians, including Jesuits, chose the middle way that was eventually adopted by the Roman Church. The image of God is neither that of a complacent friend nor that of a jealous, exacting, and inexorable guardian of a labor camp. In the usual teaching of the Church God orders us to take his rules very seriously, without looking for easy excuses, but he rewards our sincere efforts; his mercy and love are immense. By rejecting the Augustinian concept of grace and election, the Church entered a path which would have horrified Pascal. Moral rigor allowed for gradation: if you were not a character like Saint-Cyran this did not necessarily mean that you were a laxist; there was plenty of room in between. But there was no gradation in matters concerning election and grace. On this point if you were not an Augustinian, you were a semi-Pelagian, at least if you tried not to suspend this crucial question in ambiguity: grace is either gratuitous or not, given to all or not, irresistible or not, there is nothing in between. Theologically, the Church did not, indeed could not, take a Pascalian shape.

Or imagine Arnauld, carrying his treatise on *Frequent Communion*, visiting a Catholic church today and seeing a crowd during Mass queuing up to a priest who lavishly dispenses holy bread without asking whether they have confessed and received absolution, without even asking whether they were baptized; "sanctum canibus" would probably be his comment.

A Note on Politics

Does secular political life enjoy a kind of independence from religion and the Church as well as a validity analogous to that enjoyed by secular reason? The most striking and frequently cited arguments for a negative answer come from several Montaignesque *dicta* in the section on "Misère" in the *Pensées*; they strongly suggest that what passes for justice and right on earth is a matter of usurpation and custom. "We see nothing just or unjust that would not change its quality with the change of climate; three degrees more from the pole turns upside down the entire jurisprudence, one meridian decides what is true. A ludicrous kind of justice, its limits drawn by a river. Truth on this side of the Pyrenees, falsity on the other. . . . No doubt there are natural laws, but this nice corrupted reason of ours has corrupted everything. According to reason alone, nothing is just by itself, everything shifts with time. Custom is the whole [basis for] equity, for no better reason than that it is accepted" (fr. 60). Laws are necessary, of course, but they do not thereby become just: "It is dangerous to tell the people that the laws are not just, for they obey them only because they believe them to be just. Therefore one ought to tell them at the same time that they should obey them because they are laws, just as one should obey superiors not because they are just but because they are superiors" (fr. 66; cf. 525 on customs). Since peace is the supreme good (fr. 81) and "the worst evil is civil war" (fr. 94), it seems that the very force of a law which prevents people from falling victim to war and chaos is good, whether or not it is just in any other sense; moreover, it seems that it is hopeless to expect that a law would ever become just, except in the sense that "justice is what has been settled" (fr. 645). To be sure, "justice without force is powerless, force without justice is tyrannical," therefore the best way of ruling the state would combine justice with force; but it appears that this is not feasible: "Unable to make strong what is just, we made just what is strong" (fr. 103). The *Trois discours sur la condition des grands*, recorded by Nicole and considered authentic by scholars, confirm Pascal's disbelief in any just order on earth. The dignities and status of kings, nobles, and the rich result from an accident of birth; no "natural greatness" made them great but rather a greatness established by human will. Honors and external signs of respect are due to them but they must not be confounded with the respect one should pay to people because of their "real," intrinsic qualities, like being a great mathematician; "we should speak to kings on our knees; we should stand up in the rooms of princes" as a matter of law.[60]

A number of such remarks lead naturally to the conclusion that, while Pascal accepts the need for political order as a necessary evil, he does not believe that any order can be just (except in a perverse sense); as part of the realm of nature, politics is incurably corrupt and there is no prospect of any improvement in political affairs. His political conservatism (a point strongly stressed by Goldmann) fits well into his fundamental despair about the state of the earthly kingdom which is, after all, the kingdom of the devil.

But some counter-arguments to this interpretation cannot be easily dismissed. Gerard Ferreyrolles, the author of the most comprehensive analysis, and a very instructive one, of Pascal's "politics,"[61] argues that Pascal had a political doctrine which was coherent and original and by no means reducible to gloomy acquiescence in the irremediable rule of Satan over the human city. He accepted the concept of natural law, on which the legitimacy of any regime is based; he believed that a legislator can use evil human instincts for the good order not by forcibly suppressing them but by harnessing them for the benefit of the community; he perceived the providential wisdom that governs historical changes and he demanded respect for the "autonomy" of politics. Unlike the Jesuits, who provided a theoretical foundation for contempt of law and the state if they conflicted with their supreme goal—the power of their Society—and denied the temporal order any autonomy, and unlike other ultramontanists, who fought for theocratic despotism and wanted the pope to hold sway over the entire area of politics, the Jansenists, including Pascal, separated the secular from the spiritual by giving to the former its own legitimacy.

A lot depends on the meaning we attach to the notion of "autonomy." It is true, as Ferreyrolles points out, that in contrast to fragment 60, which appears clearly to deny that there is anything universal in human legislation, we find in the *Provincial Letters* and in the *Écrits des Curés de Paris* a number of references to natural law, natural light, and common sense; they are the source of rules that have been considered valid always and everywhere and are sufficient to condemn the permissiveness of Jesuit laxists. Contemptuous sentences in the *Pensées*, he says, are exaggerations, explicable by the polemical context: unlike the *Provincial Letters*, addressed to the Catholics, the *Pensées* speak to the incredulous, to whom we should reveal the misery and inconstancy of purely human truth and justice in order to make them feel the need for God.

One might argue that some fragments of the *Provinciales* can be likewise explained by their polemical context: it was rhetorically quite convenient to castigate the "probabilists" by showing that they violate rules which have been considered valid even among pagans as a matter of natural law. But this is not an important point. The question is rather: autonomy in relation to what? in what area?

That Pascal cannot accept an autonomous politics in the Machiavellian-Hobbesian sense is more than obvious. Both Machiavelli (in the *Discourses*) and Hobbes (in the *Leviathan*) leave no doubt that to them religion is no more than a tool in the hands of skillful rulers. As to its dogmatic tenets, they mean what the rulers want them to mean; in themselves they mean nothing. It is even misleading to say that politics, on such an assumption, is independent from religion, because it has both religious institutions and dogmas at its service.

But neither can we attribute to Pascal a belief in autonomous politics in Grotius's half-deistic sense. According to Grotius we must distinguish between positive divine law and natural law. In his positive legislation God established, by an act of will, what is just, commanded, or forbidden, and it is his order which makes this or that commanded or forbidden. We would not know this kind of law without revelation. Whereas natural law commands or forbids what is intrinsically obligatory or evil; this law is immutable, known to us by reason alone, and God himself can change it as little as he can cancel the truth that two and two are four.[62] Since to Pascal sins become sins by divine decree, there is no reason to think that he accepted the distinction between natural law and God's positive legislation in Grotius's sense; on this point he was closer to Descartes and to the theologians of the Great Reformation, and differed from Aquinas. If there is natural law, it is causally dependent on God's decrees. We must suppose—Pascal does not say this distinctly—that while we cannot obey moral commandments without special grace, we can know them through revelation, which has been given to all and is, in this sense, an act of universal grace. We simply know that killing, incest, false testimony, etc., are forbidden, as God has told us so. As for pagans who are not familiar with the Holy Scriptures, they can presumably acquire a similar knowledge because, apart from the Book, God inscribed some basic rules into the human mind (or heart) just as he provided us with the natural light which enables us to tell truth from falsity. Pascal failed to elaborate on these issues but we have no grounds for conjecturing that he admitted the independence, either causal or logical, of *moral* natural law from God's orders.

Certainly, God's commandments, being valid by their origin, limit what the legislators of a human kingdom may *validly* do: they cannot make murder or incest lawful without violating divine edicts. This, however, has little to do with the autonomy of politics.

An entirely different question is papal power. Pascal, indeed, did not approve of theocratic regimes; secular sovereigns are not supposed to be at the service of Rome and take orders from the Curia; the pope is to be obeyed in spiritual—moral and dogmatic—matters but not in other provinces. This is a Thomist rather than an Augustinian position, as Ferreyrolles rightly observes. But it is hard to speak of a specifically Pascalian political theory; this was rather a standard Gallican standpoint.

And there is another, logically quite independent question: did Pascal believe that a significant improvement is possible in political institutions? From the small scraps scattered throughout his writings we can infer hardly more than a few uncontroversial commonsense tenets: tyranny is bad, and so is anarchy; civil war is horrible; a state in which law is enforced is preferable to lawlessness, etc. This does not amount to a political theory, let alone to a proclamation of the autonomy of politics. Politics seems rather to be a kind of technique in a particular area of terrestrial life, like, say, medicine; if a better medicament is available, it is reasonable to take it, but it will not shelter us from death, and it is death that really matters in life. Did Pascal believe in progress in the organization of the polis? There is nothing in his writings to suggest this. Did he believe that some real "values" emerge in the field of politics? Only in the sense that this applies to all the domains of our life in the flesh: it is right to protect people from hunger, and it is right to protect them from the abuse of power by royal officers. No doubt we all have duties related to the temporal realm. This neither invalidates the general truth that our short sojourn on earth is only a preparation for eternity nor makes the goods that sustain the body (in the most general sense, contrasted with the two higher "orders," those of the mind and of charity) self-dependent values. "Render unto Caesar. . . ." But this does not imply that Caesar is the creator of the real good.

There are indeed no good reasons to claim (as Goldmann does) that there was a radical break or a third conversion between the *Provinciales* and the *Pensées*. But in neither do we find an original political theory or an assertion of the autonomy of politics, except for a general anti-ultramontanist attitude.

Divine justice is inscrutable, human justice is at the mercy of fashions, customs, and prejudices. If Jesus had died in the hands of justice, rather than in an unjust riot, we might even suppose that, in terms of human justice, *the crucifixion was just*; a rather uncomfortable conclusion.

The beautiful aphorisms on Cleopatra's nose and the grain of sand in Cromwell's body (fr. 413, 750) suggest that history— profane history, to be sure—is prey to trivial accidents that can unpredictably slant the course of events. On the other hand we should always remember that the world is under the constant tutelage of its maker and that providence leaves nothing to chance; ultimately everything is arranged to serve God's glory. Does Pascal contradict himself? Not necessarily. Of course, a Christian must trust God; he must never complain about his personal fate and the adversities of life but rather welcome them as a just punishment, a trial, an exercise in humility, an occasion for improving his moral standards. This is expressed in various of Pascal's notes and letters, especially in the moving *Prayer for the Good Use of Illnesses*.[63] "O Lord, . . . you are so merciful that not only the good things but the very misfortunes which befall your elected result from your mercy. . . . You are no less God when you afflict and punish than when you comfort and make use of your indulgence. . . . Make me incapable of enjoying the world . . . make me adore in silence the order of your adorable providence in the conduct of my life. . . . I feel that I cannot love the world without displeasing you, without harming and disgracing myself. . . . Make me accept, my God, all kinds of events in equanimity, because we do not know what we ought to ask of you and I cannot wish this rather than that without presumption, and without making myself a judge and responsible for the effects that your wisdom justly decided to conceal from me. I know, Lord, that there is only one thing I know: that it is good to follow you and evil to offend you. Other than that, I do not know what is best or worst in anything. . . . I adore your providence and I do not want to fathom it."

That pious people should accept in advance whatever might happen is a general Christian precept, because everything is under God's control and aims at the greatest possible good. To say that we must forbear from inquiring into the hidden reasons of any particular event is to go further, and such abstemiousness (*non est nostrum scire. . .*) was by no means normal among theologians and preachers. Bossuet was to compose *ad usum Delphini* his *Discourse on Universal History* (1682) in which, following Augustine, he managed to disclose God's secret purpose in major historical events. But to Pascal such curiosity was futile and unbecoming to a pious soul. Therefore, apart from general confidence in divine wisdom, he could not have any philosophy of history, any method of finding the meaning in a historical fact. No such meaning is accessible to us; to the human eye history is just that: the nose of Cleopatra, a senseless tale, a series of absurd accidents, a pathetic display of human vanity and blindness.

In the same prayer Pascal confesses, in the Saint-Cyranian spirit, that he made his past life hateful to God "by a complete waste of time, which you gave me only to adore you." Political issues ultimately fall in the same category of our profane concerns, chores, and affairs; any importance they might have vanishes by comparison with the worship of God and personal salvation—the only thing that is worth remembering.

If there is a good summary of Pascal's thinking on politics, it is perhaps this: "All men naturally hate each other. We have used concupiscence as best we can to make it serve the common good, but this is only pretence and a false image of charity, because at bottom it is only hate. We have created and drawn from concupiscence admirable rules of government, morality, and justice, but, at root, this evil root of man, this *figmentum malum*, is only covered up; not pulled up" (fr. 210–11).

PART TWO

Pascal after the Pelagian Conquest

If we ask the ritual and usually not very helpful, because equivocal, question, "What is alive in Pascal's legacy?" the tentative answer should refer to his sensibility rather than to identifiable doctrinal tenets. The question might mean "Why do people keep reading Pascal?" but then the probable answers are of little interest: people read him because he was an exquisite French writer, because he is a part of the curriculum, because he was an amusing hammer at the Jesuits, because people like reading ingenious and paradoxical dicta.

As a theologian Pascal was not original (nor did he aspire to be), and apart from a few particularly well-turned, inimitable sentences his, that is, the Jansenists', doctrine, is largely forgotten and has stopped being a viable option for theologians and preachers. As an apologist for the Christian faith (not necessarily of the Augustinian variety) he was, of course, superb, not only in giving those believers who are exposed to libertine or skeptical strictures a reliable and well-shaped shield but by his talent in using dramatic rhetorical cuts that lent traditional doctrine a striking freshness. That Jesus Christ's passion and humiliation opened up to us a liberating path to God had been a part of the established teaching of the Church; but it took a special spiritual skill to phrase it in this way: "Jesus will be in agony until the end of the world. One must not sleep until then" (fr. 917), or to say, "Jesus Christ did not want to be killed without the forms of justice because it is much more ignominious to die by justice than in an unjust riot" (fr. 940). Reduced to their purely dogmatic content, Pascal's words would be uninteresting and he would be quite lost in such a reduction.

The whole of Christian philosophical, theological, and moral teaching is ultimately about a single question: how is the reality of our worldly experience related to the primordial, creative, infinite divine reality which in the realm of finite things is both manifested and concealed? That our mundane business and chores do not count in the face of our supreme goal, our eternal destiny, and God, is not a matter for discussion in Christian terms; that these chores and business and interests are simply worthless is less patent. An Augustinian-Jansenist-Saint-Cyranian thinker's attitude was clear: apart from God and eternal life nothing really matters;[64] nothing is real, properly speaking; everything is short-lived and trifling. But it does not follow that we may use this truth as a pretext for disregarding our earthly duties or that the proper way of life is to escape from the world. We must escape in the moral sense, by not letting ourselves become infected by the sinful habits of pagan or psuedo-Christian society; but we must try to implement Christian norms among our fellow men even though we know that evil cannot be eradicated, that it is bound to be victorious on earth, and that no Christian utopia will ever be built.

This last point deserves attention when we ask in what sense the legacy of the Pelagian-Augustinian quarrel is still of relevance to our time.

It is relevant but ambiguously so. It has been pointed out more than once that the entire history of European millenarian and utopian thinking, from the sixteenth century onwards or even from its medieval sources, has depended, consciously or not, on the Pelagian mentality, on the refusal to admit that the evil cannot be rooted out on earth by human effort, that we are incurably tainted by radical evil of which only God can cleanse us if he so wishes. According to this view our modernity is fundamentally Pelagian and this includes its Promethean hope for a perfect human city without evil. And that is a belief in man-made redemption.[65]

Viewing the Pelagian image of man with suspicion is no doubt justified after the spectacular disasters that utopian dreams have brought upon European civilization in our century, and it is plausible to perceive in the utopian will a symptom of morbid hubris. That there are no lasting obstacles built into human nature to the heavenly city on earth is a dangerous and potentially calamitous fantasy, and this has been amply confirmed by our experience. There is much in this experience to bear out the deep conservative mistrust of all-encompassing utopian projects and the belief that evil is inherent in our world, and that therefore all progress and improvements in human affairs must be paid for, sometimes very dearly, sometimes intolerably so.

But we must not forget Pascal's wise dialectical remark that "everything is true in part, false in part . . . nothing is purely true and thus nothing is true in the sense of pure truth" (fr. 905). The essential dogmas of the Church, according to him, combine two truths that seem incompatible (e.g., that the Eucharist is an act both of real transubstantiation and of commemoration, or that Jesus Christ is God and man); heretics are heretics precisely because they unilaterally pick one of the two while rejecting the other (fr. 733). "Two contrary reasons. We must start there, otherwise we understand nothing and everything is heretical. And even at the end of every truth we must add that we keep in mind the opposite truth" (fr. 576). The conversation with De Saci on the respective merits and faults of Montaigne and Epictetus is a striking example of this "method." So is his remark on the Stoics, who advise us to seek rest within ourselves, while others find it in the outer world. Both are wrong. "Happiness is neither outside nor in us; it is in God, both outside and in us" (fr. 407).

Thus, while it is true that the Pelagian mentality, especially once it had "secularized" itself and assumed the form of utopian politics, is deservedly discredited nowadays, it may well have played a liberating role in the history of modern Europe. It put into circulation a belief in human freedom conceived as an unconstrained ability to choose between good and evil; it made possible the habit of trusting in our spiritual prowess and our unlimited potential to better our lot, to enquire fearlessly into the secrets of nature, to create and to expand, to apply our curiosity to anything we can think of. If it brought disasters in our age, it also made possible the great achievements of modern European civilization in the arts, the sciences, and social institutions. And so, let us accept, in the Pascalian manner, "two contrary truths."

If Europe had lived indefinitely under the umbrella of the Augustinian tradition, the greatest minds and the most splendid creations of modern centuries would probably never have appeared. This tradition consistently and frequently condemned the sin of *curiosity* and thereby the disinterested scholarly search for knowledge. It elaborated a specific, positive concept of freedom according to which we are free not by making a choice between good and evil but by effectively choosing good (through divine inspiration). And this concept is still upheld, though ambiguously, in the Roman Church, its professed de-Augustinization notwithstanding.[66] It has therefore justified any kind of coercion that robs individuals of their ability to make a choice; it has justified the oppressive and potentially totalitarian idea that we can, and should, be good under compulsion. The very concept of religious freedom is unthinkable in Augustinian terms, for it would amount to deliberately opening room for falsity, heresy, and sin to spread with impunity. Early Calvinist theocracy was based on this theology. And, for all the remarkable works and acts of great Jansenists, for all their purity and piety, few people nowadays would like to live under the jurisdiction of a Jansenist church; it would be a highly oppressive regime.

Let us rather admit that there is no idea, however attractive and however promising, that by its very content is invulnerable to the infiltration of evil and cannot become prey to the dark side of human nature. This applies to Pelagian humanism no less than to the conservative, pessimist Augustinian wisdom; infernal powers are capable of seizing anything that is great, holy and noble.

But Pascal was much more than a champion of efficient grace and predestination. He was reacting to the libertine, skeptical spiritual environment in which, he felt, the Christian virtues of old were rapidly declining and the Christian tradition was being eroded step-by-step in favor of faithless naturalism, a post-Cartesian contempt for history as a source of wisdom and authority, a frantic search for temporal blessing. Certainly, the lament over the growing corruption of morals and the downfall of piety had been heard throughout the history of the post-Apostolic Christian Church. But never before had the hostile anti-Christian army had such powerful intellectual and literary backing, never had it expressed itself so boldly, aggressively, openly, and frequently. Most scholars agree that a cultural mutation or "qualitative change" occurred in this respect in France in the first quarter of the seventeenth century.

Despite all changes and revolutions in mentality and in institutions, we inhabit a world (post-Nietzschean rather than post-Cartesian) which increasingly displays the same characteristics and produces the same worries as those which drove Pascal to desperation. To deplore oblivion to God might seem banal in Pascal but to combine it with his other, all-pervading topic of the absence of God, was not; both resulted from our sins, but it is not absence that causes oblivion, it is rather the other way round.

His peculiar sensitivity may perhaps be summed up in the words of George Herbert a generation earlier:

> Philosophers have measured mountains,
> Fathom'd the depths of seas, of states, and kings,
> Walk'd with a staff to heaven and traced fountains:
>   But there are two vast, spacious things,
> The which to measure it doth more behove:
> Yet few there are that sound them; Sin and Love.
>
>   (*Agony*)

This is about oblivion to God. But Pascal's most urgent message to his contemporaries was: if you scratch the surface—and not very deeply—you will see that everybody is unhappy. The reasons for human misery are uncountable; but then there is perhaps only one: people have lost their ability to trust God and thereby to trust, to accept, and to absorb their own destiny. This makes them so vulnerable that the slightest failure produces in them a helpless despair. Our insecurity and anxiety are built into our very existence (cf. fr. 583).

The message, thus phrased, still touches the enlightened mentality of our age, a godless mentality which refuses to recognize that the absence of God continues to torment it. The most legitimate heirs of Pascal, if often unaware of their legitimacy, are nowadays not preachers of the "religion of feeling" and not those who speak of the undefinable "leap of faith" but rather those who display to us the absurdity of a world abandoned by God. When Eugene Ionesco says that it is absurd to call his work "the theater of the absurd," because, he says, it is a theater of the search for God (he attributes, perhaps groundlessly, the same intention to Samuel Becket), he appears as today's Pascal *redivivus*.

Those who seek God will find him, says Pascal (fr. 781), he even says that he who searches for God has already found him (fr. 919); but he also says that those who search and do not find are unhappy. He promises them good news; he is himself—with his strangely appropriate name—a carrier of this news; he knows or pretends to know how to make the message efficient by "preparing the machine" (fr. 11). But he also knows that it is not up to him to make it efficient. "Faith is not in our power" (fr. 703).

Was Pascal an "Existential" Thinker?

Comparisons have been made fairly frequently between Pascal's thought and twentieth-century existential philosophy. The analogy is plausible to some extent but not without important restrictions. There is no undisputed description of what existential philosophy is supposed to be, unless it is defined by inspiration rather than content: "existential" in this sense is a philosophizing from the personal, from irreducible individual existence, or, to speak in Heideggerian parlance, from being to whom its own being is at issue ("dem es in seinem Sein um dieses Sein geht"). The celebrated definition of existentialism devised in Sartre's popular manifesto ("existence precedes essence") is by no means universally accepted.

There is, as has been mentioned, a deep-seated similarity between Heidegger's description of a human being as a "Sein-zum-Tode" and the persistent topic of the *Pensées*: death and finitude. Both point out the fundamental difference between death as a natural phenomenon, an event in animal life, and the specifically human death, which everyone anticipates and nearly everyone tries to forget, to remove from everyday memory. Heidegger's empty chatter ("das Gerede") into which we disperse our existence in order not to face reality is clearly a Pascalian theme. Pascal certainly had no doubts about immortality, but immortality, albeit the most important matter of all, is not necessarily implied in his reflection on the human—as opposed to the animal—fear of death. And Heidegger says that his analysis of death is valid irrespective of the question of an afterlife. This attempt to compel people to realize their inescapable condition, instead of seeking refuge in "divertissements," displays the kinship of two souls, separated from each other by almost three centuries. Miguel de Unamuno who, in his *Tragic Sense of Life* (1913), quotes Pascal, takes up, perhaps in a more genuine way, his perspective: the absolute inability of man to accept total annihilation.

But formal similarities are uninteresting and sterile. One may pick at random two European philosophers and find in them something similar and something that made them different; this leads us nowhere. What matters is the confrontation not of "statements" but of meaning that either has not been made explicit, or, even if explicit, requires rephrasing if we are to understand it. And this meaning has to be looked for against the historical background of thought; to find it, we must reflect on the "spiritual situation of the age."

Pascal was responding to the Cartesian-libertine mentality that robbed the world of purpose, meaning, and life. He defended Christianity from a position which, he knew, could not be reinforced by appeals to scholastic rationalism (he would, perhaps, reluctantly have accepted Heidegger's belief that philosophy is by nature a-theistic, that is, alien to the "problem of God," at least in the sense that it is helpless in the search for the real God who matters). A scientist, he saw the world, like his contemporaries and unlike Renaissance naturalists, as a machine or as an indifferent dead mass, and he opposed the unshakable faith of the elect to the religious indifference of the enlightened and to the seeming bravery of God-killers. Behind the veil of the optimistic worship of Reason he disclosed the unacknowledged fear and self-deception of people who avoid the real issues of life. He assimilated the new science and greatly contributed to it, but he fought against the Enlightenment of his age, which, in his eyes, produced despair in disguise.

Heidegger, too, fought against the Enlightenment of his own century, and of two previous ones. None of the "existentialists," our contemporaries, was a scientist (Jaspers had medical training, to be sure, but his interest as a doctor was in general psychopathology, which is half-philosophy, rather than medicine). But they—especially Heidegger and Jaspers—were reacting to a world dominated by technical progress, obsessed by the hope for the endless conquest of nature which brings about both ever greater comfort and the satisfaction of "maîtres et possesseurs"; metaphysical meditation and the quest for an elucidation of the metaphysical status of man fell into oblivion. We might feel happy in our spiritual self-mutilation and find this voluntary impoverishment quite convenient. Neither our technical prowess nor our scientific achievements produce meaning, and if the meaningless world keeps us satisfied, this is *mala fide*: philosophy is there to remind us of our duty to be human, to live in dignity, to bring back into our minds the forgotten metaphysical side of existence.

It may thus be said that existential thought is, in a limited sense, a continuation of the Pascalian effort. In both cases the target is the Enlightenment. In both cases the point is to translate into philosophical idiom the hidden panic (variously miscalled rationality, science, progress, etc.) we carry deep in our hearts when we face the world we have emptied of sense. In vain do we pretend to be cheerful. And it is this anti-Enlightenment thrust that makes Pascal our contemporary.

The difference in philosophical context is obvious and there is no need to dwell on it. Pascal was a Christian, Heidegger was a pagan, trained in Christian philosophy. To Heidegger "die Sorge" includes death and guilt; guilt is ontological, not historical, as in Pascal. Pascal had a conventional idea of time even though he reflected on our mental attitudes to the past and future and experienced the irreality of what is perishable (but he did not quote Augustine's treatise on time in the *Confessions*; neither did other Jansenists, it seems). To Heidegger past and future are modalities of *Dasein*, and time itself seems to be *Dasein*'s specific form of life. Meaning is conferred on the world rather than found ready-made, and if Being is opening itself to us, this seems to be because our existence is somehow embedded in its very constitution. Heidegger's ontology is unfinished and often opaque but on this point he is perhaps more in debt to the legacy of German pantheist thought than to orthodox Christianity; to the former there was a kind of necessary coupling between God and our minds, and God himself achieved self-realization through his creation, the human soul in particular.

To Pascal, however, God is the unique meaning-giver, and as far as we are concerned the meaning is there, not created by us. God's will—not our deeds, as in semi-Pelagian soteriology—is the only source of salvation. In Heidegger we find a strange Ersatz of salvation: authenticity, in which our dignity is restored. But authenticity is a half-gnostic project of self-salvation, with no prospect of eternity. Heidegger lived in what we, rightly or wrongly, believe to be a post-religious or post-Christian age. Unlike Pascal, Heidegger did not want to rescue God from oblivion. A similar worry seems to have tormented both, but nothing can be farther from the Augustinian spirit than the idea of self-salvation. Ultimately, Heidegger would be, in Pascal's eyes, one more example of a "philosopher" in a perjorative sense, a false prophet, a spokesman for incurable human hubris, a man who, in his attack on the Enlightenment, assimilated the essence of this very Enlightenment, its passion for self-deification, its attempt to assassinate the Creator, its stooping to the sacrilegious "ye shall be like gods."

Another typically Pascalian topic still relevant to our time is his insistence on irreligion's being the matter of "passions," rather than reason: not as though people, as he claimed, fear that religion could be true because this would force them to adopt an ascetic way of life. The point is rather that the considerable enfeeblement of faith and the spread of indifference in European civilization does not seem to result from the logical incompatibility of Christian tenets with the content of modern science; neither can this indifference be attributed to the failure of religion in rational arguments. To find reliable support by insisting unconvincingly on the rationality and provability of the doctrine theologians brought to light the very gap between science and religion that they wished to bridge. To the extent that popular teaching encouraged, or at least failed to oppose, the magical and technical interpretation of the sacraments, prayers, and rituals, the distinction between them and technical measures could only be manifested more glaringly. It became patent already in Pascal's time—and he knew this—that scholastic reason was irredeemable in terms of the reason that science had codified by then, not without his own assistance. He also knew that sacraments and prayers do not necessarily bring miraculous responses from heaven to satisfy our wishes and whims. Science and technique have been increasingly trusted because of their efficacity and predictive power. But communication with God was increasingly mistrusted not because of its mundane inefficiency alone—in this respect it had always been so—but because whatever was not thus efficient was regarded with more and more indifference. In other words it was a profound mutation in human mentality that brought about contempt for everything that was not beneficial in the sense that science and technique were. For Christian preachers this is a lesson not yet fully assimilated.

A Note on Skepticism and Pascal's Last Word

Pascal's remarks, which scholars analyzed so extensively, on Pyrrhonism and Stoicism (in the conversation with de Sacy[67] and, later
on, in various parts of his *Apology*, especially fragment 131) repeat
or anticipate, in historical context, Pascal's reflections on human
greatness and misery, two sides of our condition that we have to
know jointly in order to avoid both pride and despair. Pascal quotes
Montaigne, but there is no evidence that he was acquainted with
Sextus Empiricus or other skeptics. Skepticism, or Pyrrhonism, is
for him not an epistemological question, separated from the general problem of our destiny, suspended as it is between original sin
and redemption. The frailty of reason; the uncertainty of all our
intellectual endeavors; our inability to establish the foundation of
knowledge and to grasp what matters more than anything else—
infinity; the dependence of our thought on the accidents of history,
on local customs, climate, passions—all those sad facts of human
mental life are there to bear out the miserable status of man;
thereby they reveal that we have fallen from a higher position to
our present wretchedness. To this extent Pyrrhonism is an ally,
even though it stops at the negative side, at humiliating us and de-
nouncing our sinful confidence in our intellectual prowess. And
Pascal, as he acknowledges, simply likes to see presumptuous reason defeated. Stoicism (that is to say, Epictetus' *Handbook*) teaches
us that everything is in God's hand, that we therefore ought to accept without a murmur whatever happens, and that we have divinely imposed duties; to this extent it is an ally, too, but not when it
tells us that we are equal to the task and can use our freedom and
moral strength to acquit ourselves perfectly of our obligations.
Both "greatest defenders of the two most famous sects in the
world" are pagans but their reasonings may justly (and jointly) be
employed in the cause of Christianity. "If Epictetus fights against
slackness, he induces us to feel pride and thus he can be most helpful to those who do not see clearly that even the most perfect justice
is corrupted if it does not come from faith. And Montaigne is absolutely pernicious to those who are inclined to impiety and vices."[68]
The reading of both is edifying to the extent that they lead us, by
their respective unilateral truths, to the realization of the full

Christian truth which alone provides us with our understanding of the roots of our wretchedness and with the hope of salvation.

Two un-Christian doctrines may therefore provide negative support for Christianity but not, it seems symmetrically. Pyrrhonism appears to be the stronger helper. Even the presence of its enemies promotes its cause because "man's weakness is more conspicuous in those who do not know it than in those who do" (fr. 34). In other words, when we boast of our intellectual powers we display thereby our infirmity and reinforce the skeptics' arguments.

While we have reason to doubt everything and, apart from faith, there are no firm grounds for knowledge, we are incapable of being consistent in our uncertainty; "there has never been a really perfect Pyrrhonist"; "Nature confounds the Pyrrhonists and Reason the dogmatists" (fr. 131). Still, since the "natural sentiment" is not compelling and cannot remove rational grounds for doubt, Pyrrhonism is in this sense invincible.

Descartes comes naturally to mind when we reflect on these dramatic hesitations. Pascal seems to have inherited the destructive part of Descartes' doubt. But not his solution. He did not believe either in the Cogito or in the Cartesian proofs of God's existence. He admitted that in strictly rational terms we cannot, despite our "natural sentiment," overcome the dream argument (we know that we are not dreaming in our waking state, yet we cannot prove that we are not) or even find an unshakable foundation for mathematics. His last word appears to be: within the natural light nothing can really be proven. But this is only a part of his last word. Skepticism is a pillar on which confidence in the Bible can be built: the weakness of human reason reveals the truth of original sin. Epistemology, the quest for certainty, is not a self-contained problem; it makes sense only as a part of our attempt to discover the meaning of human life: who are we, where did we come from, whither are we going? This amounts to admitting that, strictly speaking, there is no epistemology at all. At the end of our search we are left only with the advice: "Listen to God."

Like all great (or minor, for that matter) philosophers, Pascal reveals in his opus not only the "opinions" at which he arrived after rational reflection but some characterological traits of his personality as well. His belief that whatever is perishable ought to be seen as having perished already is less a metaphysical tenet than an expression of the peculiar way he perceives the world and time. Like Plotinus and like Augustine he experienced the unreality of everything that is time-bound and of every "now"; and every "now" is about to vanish, and vanishes in the very moment we try to grasp it. Only the eternal is real. Others simply feel it differently. To Bergson, only what is now is real, even though the past is stored in the indestructible memory. This is not a confrontation of metaphysical doctrines of which the rightness or wrongness could be ascertained by logically sound arguments, but rather the expression of two opposite kinds of experience, both of which may be called mystical insofar as the ultimate truth about the world is touched (and not just asserted) in them. Descartes, too, went through the experience of the unreality of the world but he managed to get rid of it. Pascal did not. His scorn for everything that belongs to the earth and is thus perishable by definition, goes beyond the traditional Christian concept of life as a preparation for everlasting happiness or agony. This image of life does not necessarily imply that whatever is temporal is unreal; yet Pascal felt that it did. He is said to have always had the feeling that there was an abyss on his left side[69] (a symptom of lunacy, according to Voltaire). This squares with his life and thought, with his feeling of the incurable fragility of existence and the conclusion that we ought to abandon "the world" and its illusory joys, and wait for liberating death, which detaches the soul forever from the dirty body.[70]

This is what the *Pensées* are about. The author says (fr. 532) that he deliberately avoids order in his writing because he would be paying too much honor to the subject by imposing order on it; the subject is not fit to be ordered. If so, what *is* the subject? Not religion; he could not make such a disparaging remark about religion. The subject is human misery, the vanity of life and its chaos, displayed in the very disorder of writing about chaos. Not a new subject in his time, of course, and not obsolete in ours.

Going back to the question of whether the *Pensées* are a Jansenist text, we may hazard a provisional answer. There is nothing in this work that runs counter to the fundamental tenets of Jansenist theology. Some of those tenets, indeed, are prominent, in particular the concept of faith as the actual operation of grace in the human soul, the sovereignty of God, and original sin as a constitutional fact of the human condition. The necessity of grace is not specifically Jansenist, and the five propositions (as interpreted by Arnauld and purportedly cleansed of heretical contamination) are hardly present. Of the few sentences about Jesuits, most were probably not to be included in the Apology, and after the *Provinciales* they are not of great interest anyway. Whereas what is uniquely Pascalian, most distinctive, most inventive and unforgettable, is not characteristically Jansenist: the Wager, the three orders, the order of the heart, "greatness and misery," *divertissements* (in Pascal's peculiar sense), the two infinities, the virtues and vices of Pyrrhonism, clarity and obscurity in the way God reveals himself, the *esprit géométrique* and the *esprit de finesse*, the "hateful I". . . . While he saw Jansenist piety as a genuine expression of Christianity, Pascal worked on an apology for the Christian religion, not an apology for Jansenius's theology. He was speaking not to priests, not to Jansenists or Jesuits, and not to simple believers, well-entrenched in their unreflective faith ("la foi du charbonnier," as the French say) but to educated skeptics, incredulous or uncertain. The bulk of the *Pensées* is not recognizably Jansenist and if we were to remove only a small part of it (perhaps in the manner analogous to Condorcet's edition) and ignore the author, we would not have a clue strong enough to state that it is a Jansenist's text.

We are, in Pascal's perception, inevitably torn asunder not only between two poles that attract us, the divine and the natural (or the sacred and the profane, as people now say) but between two parts of our nature as well. Of the three orders—body, mind, charity—only the last is uncorrupted and incorruptible; but it is not a part of nature, it is a gratuitous gift and it cannot be earned by human effort. Body and mind, although created by God, make up the two parts of our natural existence. How they are linked with, and influence, each other is incomprehensible (cf. fr. 199). We do not have two souls, as Pascal observes (fr. 629; perhaps an allusion to Augustine's anti-Manichean treatise *De duabus animabus*), but we are a compound of two incongruous halves. Their corruption is self-inflicted but not self-curable; it springs from one common source called concupiscence. It is not the case that the corruption of the mind is always caused by the depraved body; the mind suffers its own pollution: *libido sciendi* and amour-propre, the idolatrous adoration of the odious "I."

The line dividing nature from God is by far, indeed infinitely, more important than that which separates mind from body, as it corresponds to the distinction between the temporal and the eternal. Or so it appears. However, there is an ambiguity on this point. The "I" might be hateful and is hateful as an object of special attachment (frs. 220, 373, 577), as a moral issue (vanity, selfishness, ambition, the craving for others' respect, etc.). But the soul is immortal, whether we wish it or not. Pascal speaks of the immortality of the soul, never of the immortality of the "I." What distinguishes the two entities? *"What* is the 'I'? . . . If one loves me for my judgment, my memory, does one love me? The *I*? No, because I can lose those qualities without losing myself. Where then is this I if it is neither in the body nor in the soul? And how can one love the body or the soul unless one loves them for those qualities which are not what makes up the I, as they are perishable? Would one love the substance of the soul of a person, abstractly, no matter what qualities it might have?" (fr. 688).

And so it is seems that the "I" is eternal, not merely a Cartesian "substance" whose qualities are perishable. But the "I" is evasive, conceptually unattainable. And since nothing matters more to us than our eternal destiny, we have to conclude that this hateful "I" is, and ought to be, the center of our concern after all. But then we learn that "the universal Being" is in us, and "this is true of all of us." "The kingdom of God is in us. The universal goodness is in us, it is ourselves and not ourselves" (fr. 564).

That God is "in us" is certainly not meant in the sense mystics or pantheists would have it; it cannot refer to a potential, let alone an actual ontological union; the infinite gap that separates us from God is not bridged. Pascal did not explain. But his expression would be consistent with Augustinian theology if it meant that God is in us in the sense that he operates "from inside," that grace is "internal." This applies, however, to the elect and occasionally, to the "justes temporels." What about the other, those who do not enjoy God's attention? Is God "in them" in the sense that he is an idle observer of their rotten souls? No explanation.

Pascal experienced strongly the dramatic split both within our nature and between our nature and God. The former is incurable; the body is irredeemable and our task is only to tame it as much as possible. The soul may be healed by God's will. But as long as we live in the body, the *guilt* is in us; we are guilty not by doing something but simply by being there. Neither Pascal nor any other Jansenist writer came properly to grips with this dreadful question; the guilt is unavoidable, and this seems to run counter to the normal concept of guilt.

One may argue that unavoidable guilt is the stuff tragedy is made of. But the analogy is fragile. A tragedy in the traditional sense is a situation in which the actors are morally wrong whatever they do. But what produces the tragic impossibility of a morally good choice is the situation, not their inherited guilt; and the actors have a choice, even though any choice is morally wrong for one reason or another. In the Augustinian worldview we are always morally wrong if we act by our own will and always morally right if we are guided by grace. Unlike the tragic situation, this doctrine contradicts our usual intuitions about guilt. In this sense the Augustinian-Jansenist world is not tragic, it is only sad, and it has made many Christians wonder why divine justice should be called justice at all. It may be called "tragic" only in the loose sense in which any irreversible disaster is so called.

In Pascal's eyes the human world is a funny farce played out at Golgotha. Because Pascal felt sheltered by God, he pretended to be happy himself, and pretended to perceive a higher justice in both temporal and eternal pain. But he was certainly sensitive to the immense mass of human woe. Whatever God does is just because it is done by him, and not by virtue of any standard of justice we might have borrowed from our world, our imagination, our history, our moral feeling, our legal tradition. But how this divine justice is just, is incomprehensible. Since this justice encompasses everything temporal and eternal, we must conclude that the world is altogether incomprehensible; there is a meaning in everything but we have no access to it except by faith, and faith, while it provides us with a general certainty about the meaning being there, cannot confer meaning on anything in particular. Consequently, Pascal's universe, insofar as it is accessible to all, is meaningless—to him and to us.

To say that ultimately everything—our eternal and temporal destiny, the meaning of the world and the meaning of any particu-

lar event, our souls and our bodies—depends on providence, might
sound banal in Christian terms, but it was left to Pascal to reveal
and depict the full dramatic dimension of this truth. It is not only
what actually happens that is divinely controlled; to us it is even
more important to realize that how we perceive the world, and
what we know about it, hinges on faith; and the latter, let us repeat,
is not the acquiescence in the assertion "God exists," but the effective operation of grace in the human "heart." Can anybody be certain that he is in fact a blessed beneficiary of faith? And if one does
feel such certitude, is this feeling infallible? Can it not result from a
convenient self-deception? (The virtuous life is not a sign immune
to error, as some pagans did live virtuously.) Pascal did not answer
these questions. But if certitude of living in faith is accessible to us,
it cannot be conveyed to others; I cannot convince another person
either that I am living in faith or that the content of my faith, insofar as it can be expressed in the form of an assertion, is true. And so,
communication in this matter, the most important of all, is closed.
This is not banal. Faith is an act in which only God and the human
"heart" takes part, not the Church, and not a priest, however important they might be; faith is not part of an institution. The latter
can neither produce it nor give perfect assurance of its reality. Everyone would like to have this assurance, no doubt, but this precisely seems impossible. For all his genuine attachment to the
Church, Pascal was unable to say to his readers: "in matters of faith
(as opposed to dogmas and moral rules), you may safely rely on the
Church." The Jesuits knew better. They supplied their flock with
what it needed—a comforting knowledge of the route one should
take to be saved. Pascal's religion was not tailored to the needs of an
ordinary decent Christian; it was for people who were able to bear
never-ending suspense and uncertainty about the only thing that is
really serious. It was rightly treated with suspicion. All his protestations about the happiness of those who "have found God" notwithstanding, it was a religion for unhappy people and it was designed
to make them more unhappy.

Notes

PART ONE

1. The work quoted here is from the edition of Rouen: Cornelii Iansenii episcopi iprensis *Augustinus seu doctrini a sancti Augustini de humanae naturae sanitate, aegritudine, Medicina adversus Pelagianos et Massilienses*, Rothomagi, 1652. (On the copy I used, a reader or a librarian had produced the anagram: Cornelius Iansenius—Caluini sensus in ore.)

2. The literature on Jansenism is enormous. The general history of the movement can be found in Augustin Gazier, *Histoire générale du mouvement Janseniste depuis ses origines jusqu'à nos jours*, vols. 1–2 Paris, 1922. While instructive and valuable, this work is written with a very strong pro-Jansenist and anti-Jesuit bias. The classic *Port Royal* by Sainte-Beuve (1840–59) is another fundamental survey of the movement (like all later historians, he makes the distinction between Jansenism and Port-Royal). It is quoted here from the excellent edition by Maxime Leroy in the Bibliothèque de la Pléiade in 3 volumes, 1952–55. The author's sympathy with the Jansenist movement—and even more his loathing of Jesuits—are obvious, but the work cannot be seen as uncritically apologetic. A very good critical modern work of a general character is Antoine Adam's *Du mysticisme á la révolte. Les jansenistes du XVII-e siècle*, 1968. Henri Bremond's *Histoire littéraire du sentiment religieux en France*, 12 vols, 1916–36, when the author deals with the subject, is hostile to Jansenism. The most detailed analysis—and defense—of the Jansenist, or rather Arnauld's, theory of grace in modern literature is to be found in the second volume of Jean Laporte, *La doctrine de Port-Royal*, PUF, 1923.

3. *Mémoire sur le dessein qu'ont les Jésuites de faire tomber la censure de cinq propositions sur la véritable doctrine de S. Augustin*, in *Oeuvres de Messire Antoine Arnauld*, vol. 19, Paris, 1778, pp. 197–207.

4. *Augustinus*, vol. 3, l. III, c. 13, p. 133. Cf., 1. I, c. 7; "Opus enim

199

bonum omnis creaturae etiam intergerrimae supernaturae est; cum tamen ad illum operandum nulla Christi gratia vel Angeli vel Adamus indigerint, et sine illius ope opera bona exercurerint" (vol. 3, l. I, c. 7). "Omnia infidelium opera, quantumcunque speciosa, et ex philosophica virtute profecta videantur, sint vere et proprie dicta peccata" (ibid., c. 5). As for divine law, its presence makes us worse sinners because it renders us conscious of being sinners but does not provide us with strength to avoid sinning (ibid., c. 9–12). That nature could produce in us good "cogitationes" is a Pelagian "hallucinatio" of the Jesuit Vasquez (ibid., c. 18).

5. Ibid., vol. 3, l. 3, c. 13.

6. Ibid. The proper quotation from Augustine (*De gratia et libero arbitrio*, c. 10): "iubet aliqua quae non possumus ut moverimus quid ab illo petare debemus."

7. Sermo 3, c. 8.

8. *Augustinus*, p. 136.

9. Ibid., p. 139. St. Augustine states: "Per hanc gratiam fit, ut sit homo bonae voluntatis, qui prius fuit voluntatis malae. Per hanc gratiam fit, ut ipsa bona voluntas, quae iam esse coepit, augeatur et tam magna fit, ut possit implere divina mandata" (*De Gratia*, c. 15).

10. *Summa Theol.*, 2a 2ae, qu. 2, c. 5, ad 1.

11. *Cont. Gent.*, 3, 160.

12. *Considérations sur l'entreprise faite par Maître Nicholas Cornet* . . . , in *Oeuvres de Messire Antoine Arnauld*, vol. 19, Paris, 1778, pp. 16–22, and *Réponse au P. Annat, provincial des Jésuites touchant les cinq propositions*, ibid., pp. 152–58. Cf. *Tertium scriptum circa gratiam sufficientem quae vulgo dicitur Thomistarum*, ibid., pp. 79–145. After quoting Augustine's sentence (*De Gratia et lib. arb.*, c. 16) "Certum est nos mandata servare si volemus; sed quia preparatur voluntas a Domino, ab illo petendum est ut tantum volimus quantum sufficit ut volendo faciamus," Arnauld comments: "Quid aliud his verbis significatur, nisi gratiam ad plene volendum et ad faciendum sufficientem, eam esse ac dici quae magna et efficacissima est, et prater quam alia ad plene volendum, ad operandum, et ad praeceptum perficiendum non requiritur?" (p. 82). One should always remember that the debate is somewhat obscured by the Molinists' use of the expression "sufficient grace"; it is sufficient for us to employ our free will for good acts but it is not sufficient to cause those acts by itself. The Augustinian "efficient grace," on the other hand, is sufficient for those acts to be actually performed.

13. Jurieu rightly, it seems, censures Arnauld's rendering of the Reformed creed, and he sums up the latter by saying, "qu'il n'y a point d'homme régénéré, qui puisse, avec les degrez ordinaires de la grâce, parvenir jusqu'au dernier des degrez qui sont refermés dans le commandement" (i.e., the commandment to love God with all our heart); Pierre Jurieu, *L'esprit de M. Arnauld* . . . , Deventer, 1684, vol. 1, p. 311.

14. Ibid., p. 340.

15. *Cavilli iansenianorum contra latam in ipsos a sede apostolica sententiam* . . . , A. P. Francisco Annato, S. I., Paris, 1654, pp. 52, 58–59. The genuine Catholic doctrine, which both Thomists and Jesuits accept, says, according to Annat, that "talem esse gratiam quae pracepta facit esse possibilia, ut ei resistere vel obtemperare liberi arbitrii sit" and that "nunquam subtrahitur gratia quare necessaria est ad habendam potentiam vel immediate servandi praeceptum, vel orandi sicut opportet ad impetrandum quod deest."

16. *Augustinus*, vol. 2, l. II, c. 4, pp. 40–43.

17. Ibid., c. 23, p. 78.

18. Ibid., c. 24, p. 79.

19. Ibid., p. 82.

20. *Considérations* . . . , p. 23; cf. *Réponse au P. Annat*, p. 159, and *Tertium Scriptum*, pp. 85–88.

21. *Cavilli* . . . , p. 53.

22. *Augustinus*, vol. 3, l. VI, p. 387.

23. Ibid., c. 24, p. 300.

24. Ibid., p. 301.

25. In the bull *Ex omnibus afflictionibus* (1567), Denzinger, *Ench. Symb.*, 1039 and 1966.

26. *Augustinus*, vol. 3, l. VII, p. 305.

27. Ibid., l. VIII, c. 19, p. 366. It even appears that in the case under scrutiny "free" and "necessary" mean the same; if the will wills something "cum tanta determinanatione ita ut oppositum velle non possit," then, "hoc ipso quo voluntas est quae vult necesse eam esse in potestate, et hoc ipso quo est in potestate, esse liberam" (ibid., l. VIII, c. 19).

28. Ibid., vol. 2, c. 24, p. 269.

29. *Considérations*, p. 24; *Réponse au P. Annat*, p. 161.

30. *L'esprit* . . . , vol. 1, pp. 354–62.

31. *Cavilli*, p. 60.

32. *Augustinus*, vol. 3, l. II, c. 15, p. 62.

33. Ibid., vol. 1, l. VIII, c. 6, p. 186.

34. Ibid., vol. 3, l. X, c. 1, p. 419.

35. *Considérations*; pp. 25–26; *Réponse*, p. 164.

36. *L'esprit*, p. 363.

37. *Cavilli*, p. 55, 61.

38. *Augustinus*, vol. 3, l. III, c. 20, pp. 162–65. Cf. p. 163: "omnibus vero illis pro quibus sanguinem dedit, et quatenus pro eis fundit, etiam sufficiens auxilium donat, quo non solum possint, sed etiam reipsa velint et faciant, id quod ab eis volendum et faciendum esse decrevit. Nam per illa occutissime iusta et iustissime occulta consilia sua, quibusdam hominibus dare praedestinavit fidem, charitatem et in ea perseverantiam usque in finem, quos absolute praedestinatos, electos et salvandos dicimus; aliis

charitatem sine perseverentia, aliis fidem sine charitate. . . . Pro istis in aeternum vivificandis mortuus est, pro istis ab omni malo liberandis rogavit
patrem suum, non pro caeteris, qui a fide et charitate deficientes in iniqui-
tate moriuntur." It is difficult to be more explicit. Christ died for all those
for whom he died, namely, the elect.

39. *Considérations*, p. 27; *Réponse*, pp. 165–73, 191–94.

40. *L'esprit*, vol. 1, pp. 365–71; vol 2, pp. 32–35, 41ff., 54.

41. *Cavilli*, pp. 56–57, 62–63.

42. Cf. Arnauld, *Relation Abrégée sur le sujet de cinq propositions*, *Oeuvres*, vol. 19, p. 78.

43. *Cavilli*, p. 26.

44. *L'esprit*, vol. 1, p. 401. Like Arnauld, Pierre Jurieu was a man of
bellicose character, but far more malicious and violent; occasionally he was
not above spreading slanderous rumors about his "papist" enemies (cf.
Elisabeth Labrousse, "Note sur Pierre Jurieu," *Revue d'Histoire et de Philosophie Religieuse*, n. 3, 1978); the preachers of religious tolerance among his
own Protestant brothers, like Bayle, were the target of attacks on his part
that were hardly less hateful. A remark on tolerance in his anti-Arnauld:
"c'est une chose etrange que les Papistes abusent à ce point de la tolerance
et de la patience de leurs souverains, qu'ils osent publier et faire imprimer
dans les Pais, òu nous devrions être maîtres, des Ouvrages uniquement des-
tinez à nous déchirer, à nous faire passer pour des rebelles, pour des enemies du genre humain, pour des meurtiers des Rois, pour des Sociniens,"
etc. (*L'esprit de M. Arnauld*, vol. 1, p. 6). It was Jurieu whom Bayle had in
mind when he said that if the Protestants established an inquisition of their
own, one would long for the Roman one. As a Calvinist warrior, Jurieu had,
of course, a strongly fideistic approach to religious issues, but when, oblivious of Augustine's celebrated remark, he assails Catholic authors' claim
that the divinity of Scriptures can be believed only on the Church's authority, he says: "la voye d'autorité est une voye de tyrannie, à laquelle l'esprit
humain resiste naturellement. Il est libre, cet esprit, et il ne peut se re-
soudre à se rendre qu'aux *lumières de la raison*" (emphasis mine). Calvin
would have spun in his grave at such a remark from the pen of his zealous
follower. He argues as well (*L'esprit*, vol. 2, pp. 143ff.) that the dogma of the
Holy Trinity is perfectly compatible with reason: the three dimensions of a
body differ from each other but all are identical with the body itself. Did
Jurieu, too, unwillingly participate in the miraculous process whereby the
Reformation transmuted itself into the Enlightenment? It may be noted,
however, that, unlike the Jansenists, he did not consign all unbaptized infants to hell.

45. *Abregé de l'Histoire de Port-Royal*, in Racine's *Oeuvres complètes*,
Bibl. de la Pléiade, vol. 2, pp. 67ff.

46. *Mémoires*, choisies par Y. Coirault, , 1990. pp. 183–97.

47. A. Gazier, *Histoire générale du mouvement janseniste*, vol. 1, Paris, 1922, pp. 79–92.

48. *Les imaginaires ou lettres sur l'heresie imaginaire*, vol. 1 par le Saint Domvillier (Pierre Nicole), Liège, 1667, and *Les visionnaires ou Seconde partie des lettres sur l'heresie imaginaire*, Liège, 1667.

49. Gazier, *Histoire général*, p. 82.

50. *Le siècle de Louis XIV*, ch.37, in *Oeuvres historiques*, Bibl. de la Pléiade, pp. 1063ff.

51. Sainte-Beuve, *Port Royal*, vol. 1, pp. 573ff.

52. Denzinger, 2020.

53. Sainte-Beuve, *Port Royal*, vol. 2, p. 626.

54. The story of the *formulaire*, with all its intricacies, is to be found in all general studies on Jansenism.

55. Pascal, OCL, p. 368.

56. *De incoacta libertate Disputatio quadripartita . . .* , auctore P. Francisco Annato, S.I., Rome 1652, pp. 6, 16.

57. Ibid., p. 22.

58. Ibid., p. 25. Augustine says, indeed: "Nemo peccat in eo quod nullo modo caveri possit"; but Annat's interpretation—"Ergo ad liberatetem quae necessaria est ad peccandum requisit Augustinus ut qui peccat possit non peccare: quod est indifferentem habere liberatetem ad peccandum et non peccandum" (p. 30)—is clearly false. To Augustine a sinner "can" abstain from sin, that is, he can do so if grace is given to him; in other words he is not under a "compulsion" to sin but only under a "necessity" (cf. discussion on prop. 4).

59. Ibid., pp. 55ff.

60. The text of the constitution is included in Gazier, *Histoire général*, vol. 2.

61. Augustine expressed these views on grace and predestination on innumerable occasions; this was one of the main topics of his theology. Jansenius's work includes thousands of quotations to support his—apparently irrfutable—interpretation. A sample may suffice for the purpose of this essay:

That justifying grace cannot be deserved, that it is not a reward for good works, is for Augustine tautologically true, as it is for Paul (Rom. 11: 5–10); if grace is not gratuitous, it is not grace, by definition: "Quomodo est ergo gratia, sinon gratis datur? Quomodo est gratia si ex debito redititur?" (*De Gratia Christi et peccato orginali*, XXIII, 24). The Pelagian heretics "omnino laborant, ostendere gratiam Dei secundum merita nostra dari: hoc est, gratiam non esse gratiam" (*De Gratia et libero arbitrio*, VI, II). Nobody is worthy of grace, indeed our corrupt nature produces nothing that is good, therefore God could not be accused of injustice even if he saved no one; one cannot be saved without faith—explicit, not just implicit—in God and the Savior, and faith is God's gift. Both the beginning of faith and its completion is an act of divine mercy, conferred on some, denied on other. "Fides igitur, et inchoata et perfecta, donum Dei est: et hoc donum quibusdam dari, quibusdam non dari. . . . Cur autem non omnibus datur, fidelem movere non debeat, qui credit ex uno omnes isse in condemnationem, sine dubitatione iustissimam, ita ut nulla Dei est iusta reprehensio, etiam si nullus inde liberaretur" (*De praedestinatione sanctorum*, VII, 16). ". . . sine ea [gratia] nullus prorsus sive cogintando, sive volendo et amando, sive agendo faciunt bonum" (*De correptione et gratia*, II, 3). "Haec enim omnia operatur in eis, qui vasa misericordiae operatus est eos, qui et elegit eos in Filio suo, ante constitutionem mundi per electionem gratiae. . . . Profecto et electi sunt per electionem, ut dictum est, gratiae, non praecedentium meritorum suorum; quia gratia illis est omne meritum" (ibid., VII, 13, cf. *Civ. dei.*, XIV, 26). "Quoniam cuius vult miseretur, et quem vult obdurat; sed miseretur, bona tribuens; obdurat, digna retribuens" (*De praed. sanc.*, VII, 14). " 'Sed cur', inquit, 'gratia Dei non secundum merita hominum datur?' Respondeo: Quoniam Deus misericors est. 'Cur ergo', inquit, 'non omnibus?' Et hic respondeo: Quoniam Deus iudex est" (*De dono perseverantiae*, VIII, 16; cf. *Enchiridion*, 98). Men are justly condemned because it is their will which leads them to sin; but it is not their will which produces good acts; "Voluntate autem sua cadit, qui cadit; et voluntate Dei stat, qui stat" (*De dono pers.*, VIII, 19).

The Pelagians, like the Jesuits later on, occasionally quoted Augustine's early treatise *De libero arbitrio* in which it is asserted that it is up to our will to live according to God's will. But in the *Retractations* Augustine puts the record straight: this early work was directed against the Manicheans, not against the Pelagians, who did not yet exist. What he then said is true, he explains, because if we do good, we do it willingly and we can avoid sin, but the will itself is then shaped by God, and without grace it cannot improve itself: "Quis, inquam, peccat in eo quod nullo modo caveri potest? Peccatur autem: caveri igitur potest": but "voluntas ipsa nisi Dei gratia liberatur a servitute . . . recte pieque vivi a mortalibus non potest." But even in this early work he wrote that God is the author of all good acts, small or great: "non solum magna sed etiam minima bona non esse posse nisi ab illo a quo sunt omnia bona, hoc est Deo" (*Retractationes*, IX, 3–4). "In potestate quippe hominis est mutare in melius voluntatem; sed ea potestas nulla est nisi a Deo datur" (ibid., XXII, 4).

The will, to Augustine, is not the ability to make a choice, including in particular a choice between good and evil, but rather the sheer faculty of doing what one actually wills, and therefore both in doing evil and in doing good our will is active, except that in doing evil we follow our own will and in doing good we follow God, who infallibly directs our will. God withdraws grace temporarily from just men, as he did in the case of Peter: "Ipsam charitatem apostolus Petrus nondum habuit, quando timore Dominum ter negavit. Timor enim non est in charitate . . ." (*De gratia et lib. arb.*, XVII, 33). ". . . quia utique ipsa obedientia munus eius [Dei] est; quae necesse est ut sit in eo cui charitas inest, quae sine dubio ex Deo est" (*De corr. et gratia*, V, 8). Peter could avoid his crime, and so can everybody, on the sole condition that his will is informed by grace, the giving or refusing of which is God's decision. "Quibus autem datur [adiutorium], secundum gratiam datur, non secundum debitum, et tantum amplius datur per Iesum Christum Dominum nostrum, quibus id dare Deo placuit, ut non solum adsit sine quo permanere non possumus, etiam si velimus, verum etiam tantum ac tale sit, ut velimus" (ibid., XI, 32). ". . . unde est in hominibus, charitas Dei et proximi, nisi ex ipso Deo? Nam si non ex Deo, sed ex hominibus, vicerunt Pelagiani" (*De gratia et lib. arb.*, XVIII, 37). "Certum est nos velle cum volumus; sed ille [Deus] facit ut velimus bonum. . . . Certum est nos facere cum facimus; sed ille facit ut faciamus, praebendo vires effacissimes voluntati" (ibid., XVI, 32).

The election, quite independent from human merits, is decided by God eternally, before the creation of the world; it is arbitrary (in the human sense), irrevocable, and just by definition, because God made it; "Quos enim praedestinavit, ipsos et vocavit: illa scilicet vocatione secundum propositum: nec alios, sed quos ita vocavit, ipsos et iustificavit; nec alios sed quos praedestinavit, vocavit, iustificavit, ipsos et gratificavit, illa utique fine qui non habet finem" (*De praed. sanct.*, XVI, 34). "Elegit Deus in Christo ante constitutionem mundi membra eius" (ibid., 35). Those who are elected and predestined *cannot* perish, they are saved necessarily: "Illi ergo electi, ut saepe dictum est, qui secundum propositi vocati, qui etiam praedestinati atque praesciti. Horum si quisque perit, fallitur Deus; sed nemo perit, quia non fallitur Deus" (*De corr. et gr.*, VII, 14). "Quicumque ergo in Dei providentissima dispositione praesciti, praedestinati, vocati, iustificati, glorificati sunt, non dico nondum renati, sed etiam nondum nati, iam filii Dei sunt, et omnino perire non possunt" (ibid., IX, 23).

There is no doubt that grace (internal) is irresistible; once it is given, it is not in our power to reject it. Before his fall, Adam needed divine aid to be good but he was able to spurn it by his free choice; this is no longer possible after the Fall: ". . . sed haec [gratia] potentior est in secundo Adam. Prima est enim quae fit ut habeat homo iustitiam si velit; secunda ergo plus potest, quae etiam fit ut velit, et tantum velit, tantoque ardore diligat, ut carnis voluntatem contraria concupiscentem voluntate spiritus vincat" (*De corr. et gr.*, XI, 31). We must make the distinction between "being able not to sin" and "not being able to sin" (ibid., XII, 33). "Aliud est adiutorium sine quo aliquid non fit, et aliud est adiutorium quo aliquid fit. . . . Nunc vero sanctis in regnum Dei per gratiam Dei praedestinatis, non tale adiutorium perseverantiae datur, sed tale ut ei perseverantia ipsa donatur: non solum ut sine isto dono perseverantes esse non possint, verum etiam ut per hoc donum non nisi perseverantes sint" (ibid., XII, 34). "Qui autem cadunt et pereunt, in praedestinatorum numero non fuerunt" (ibid., 36). "Subventum est igitur infirmitati voluntatis humanae, ut divina gratia indeclinabiliter et insuperabiliter ageretur. . . . Infirmis servavit [Deus] ut ipso donante invictissime quod bonum est vellent, et hoc deserere invictissime nollent" (ibid., 38). "Non est itaque dubitandum, voluntati Dei qui in coelo et in terra omnia quaecumque voluit fecit, et qui etiam illa quae futura sunt fecit, humanas voluntates non posse resistere, quominus faciat ipse quod vult" (ibid., XIV, 45). "Haec itaque gratia, quae occulte humanis cordibus divina largitate tribuitur, a nullo duro corde respuitur; ideo quippe tribuitur, ut cordis duritia auferatur" (*De praed. sanc.*, VII, 13).

Sometimes it might even seem that God predestines most of mankind to damnation not only by leaving them to their corrupted will, i.e., by omission, but by positively causing their fall: "non solum bonas hominum voluntates quae ipse facit ex malis, et a se factas bonas in actus bonos et in aeternam dirigit vitam, verum etiam illas quae conservant saeculi creaturam, ita esse in Dei potestate, et eas quo voluerit, quando voluerit, faciat inclinari, vel ad beneficia quibusdam praestanda, vel ad poenas quibusdam ingerendas, sicut ipse iudicat, ocultissimo quidem iudicio, sed sine ulla dubitatione iustissimo" (*De gr. et lib. arb.*, XX, 41). On the king Amaziah: "Ecce Deus idolatriae peccatum volens vindicare, hoc optatus est in eius corde cui utique iuste irascabatur, ut admonitionem salubrem non audiret sed ea contempta iret in bellum, ubi cum suo exercitu caderet" (ibid., 42). However, we should not build a new interpretation on the basis of a few expressions of this kind, since Augustine on innumerable occasions stresses that the damned are victims of their own depravity, and God, by not calling them to glory, simply leaves them without aid (cf. *Civ. dei*, XX, 1). Ultimately, there is no distinction in God between predestination and foreknowledge: "sine dubio enim praescivit, si praedestinavit; sed praedestinasse, est hoc praescisse quod fuerat [Deus] ipse facturus" (*De dono persev.*, XVIII, 47).

The divine law is of no help without grace; indeed, it can be an obstacle (*De gr. Christi et pecc. origin.*, VII, 9); law and doctrine work from outside, whereas grace is God's operation in the human heart: "non lege atque doctrina insonante forinsecus, sed interna et occulta, mirabili ac ineffabili potestate operari Deum in cordibus hominum, non solum veras revelationes, sed bonas etiam voluntates" (ibid., XXIV, 25). "Quae [gratia] si desit, ad hoc lex adest, ut reos faciat et occidat" (*De corr. et gr.*, I, 2). Neither can miracles convert those who are not among the predestined; if the inhabitants of Tyre and Sidon had witnessed Jesus' miracles, they would have believed, but "nec illis profuit quod poterant credere, quia praedestinati non erant ab eo, cuius inscrutabilia sunt iudicia" (*De dono pers.*, XII, 28). Moreover, those who simply do not know divine law by no fault of their own, will not avoid eternal fire: "Sed nec ipsi sine poena erunt qui legem Dei nesciunt. . . . Sine fide enim Christi nemo liberari potest. . . . Sed et illa ignorantia quae non est eorum qui scire nolunt sed eorum qui tamquam simpliciter nesciunt, neminem sic excusat, ut sempiterno igne non ardeat, si propterea non credidit quia non audivit omnino quod crederet; sed fortasse ut minus ardeat" (*De Gratia et lib. arb.*, III, 5; cf. *De corr. et gr.*, VII, 12). Thus, if we ask why Jesus came so long after the creation, the answer is clear: He wanted to spread his teaching then and there, when he knew there would be people who would believe in him; if the Gospel was not preached at any other time and place, this was because Christ knew that nobody would believe him, no matter what miracles he performed (*De praed. sanct.*, IX, 17). He knew this because God had decided not to include people from earlier generations or other areas in the number of the predestined. Again: there is no difference between foreknowledge and predestination.

There is nothing surprising, therefore, in the fact that very few are elected by comparison with the future dwellers of hell: "Tam multos autem creando nasci voluit, quos ad suam gratiam non pertinere prescivit, ut multitudine incomparabili plures sunt eis quos in sui regni gloriam filios promissionis praedestinare dignatus est, ut etiam ipsa reiectorum multitudine ostenderetur quam nullius momenti sit apud Deum iustum quantalibet numerositas iustissime damnatorum" (Ep. 190 ad Optatum, III, 12). This is, of course, the question of the distribution of grace: "Quod ergo pauci in comparatione pereuntium, in suo vero numero multi liberantur, gratia fit, gratis fit, gratiae sunt agendae quia fit" (*De corr. et gratia*, X, 28). And Jesus shed his blood for those whom he redeemed, not for others (*Enchir.*, 61). While the apostle says that God wants the salvation of all people, this word "omnes" refers to the fact that among the elect there are people of all nations, conditions, sexes, ages, etc.; it does not mean all individuals (*Enchir.*, 103; cf. *De corr. et gr.*, XIV, 44: "Hoc dictum est: omnes homines vult salvos fieri, ut intelligantur omnes praedestinati: quia omne genus hominum in eis est").

It needs stressing that the election, however sparse, is not for the sake of the elect but only for God's own glory; it is not the blessedness of the lucky few that is intended but the display of the Creator's greatness: "Et tamen propter ipsum nomen meum, inquit [Deus], quod profanastis vos, ego faciam vos bonos, non propter vos" (*De gratia et lib. arb.*, XIV, 30); "Conficitur itaque gratiam Dei non secundum merita accipientium dari, sed secundum placitum voluntatis eius, ut qui gloriatur, nullo modo in se ipso, sed in Domino glorietur: qui hominibus dat quibus vult, quoniam misericors est; quod et si non dat, iustus est; et non dat quibus vult, ut notas faciat divitias gloriae suae in vasa misericordiae" (*De dono persev.*, XII, 28).

God, then, it seems, loves himself, and whatever good he does for the predestined, he does for himself. And we ought to imitate him; we must not love other people for their own sake but for Christ only (*Civ. Dei*, XXI, 26).

Even though faith which leads to salvation is God's gift, it is not true
that converting and exhorting others is useless, because only a few receive
the doctrine of salvation directly from God or angels; most are enlightened
by the intermediary of men, even though it is God alone who makes the
exhortation useful and efficient (*De dono persev.*, XIX, 48; *Civ. Dei*, V, 10; *De
corr, et gratia*, V, 8).

There is no doubt that the entire heretical doctrine of Jansenism is
faultlessly derived from Augustine's theology. The antihumanist and, it is
not unfair to add, anithuman Jansenist teaching is genuinely Augustinian.
In Catholic historical works the hardness—or cruelty—of Augustine's
doctrine of predestination is often mitigated by omission; this applies even
to Gilson's classic *Introduction à l'étude de saint Augustin* (1950) and to the
most valuable commentaries on the bilingual edition of Augustine's
Oeuvres, edited since 1950.

62. Cf. Arnauld's *Tertium Scriptum*, 1. c.: "Gratiae sufficientes actu-
ales voluntati externae sunt, contemplatio mundi ac operum Dei, eiusque
Providentiae qua universas creaturas regit et administrat consideratio;
legis documenta; Prophetarum oracula; miraculorum signa; praedictio
Evangelii; exhortatio, correctio; exemplum vitae et mortis Christi et Sanctorum; castigationes divinae, et alia adiuncula externa."

63. Even Jansenist doctrine was occasionally employed for such purposes, as is mentioned by René Pintard, *Le libertinage erudit dans la première
moitié du XVIIe siècle*, 1943, vol. 1, pp. 8f.

64. Cf. *Adv. Haer.* IV, 37–39. Hilarius and John Chrysostom were
semi-Pelagians in the same sense.

65. Cf. the most interesting and instructive study by B. R. Rees, *Pelagius: A Reluctant Heretic*, Boydell Press, 1988 (with copious bibliography).
The author points out that "Pelagianism" as a distinct body of doctrine is
not to be attributed to Pelagius alone; a number of other theologians, his
contemporaries, contributed to it (Rufinus, Celestius, Julian of Eclanum).

66. Denziger, 621.

67. Ibid., 628.

68. This question has a philosophical significance going beyond historical investigations. The same objection, that it would be outrageous to
think that justice can be defined by God's commands rather than by the
intrinsic validity of moral rules, is frequently uttered by the same rationalist critics who assert that there is no such thing as intrinsic validity of moral
rules.

69. "Tolle liberum arbitrium, et non erit quod salvetur; tolle gratiam, non erit unde salvetur. Opus hoc sine duobus effici non potest: uno a
quo fit, altero cui vel in quo fit. . . . Tam absque consensu esse non potest
accipientis, quam absque gratia dantis. . . . Consentire enim salvari est"
(S. Bernard, *De gratia et libero arbitrio Tractatus. . .* , Migne, *Patr. Lat.*, vol.
182, p. 1002. "Velle quidem inest nobis ex libero arbitrio, non etiam posse

quoad volumus. Non dico velle bonum aut velle malum: sed tantum velle. . . . Itaque liberum arbitrium nos facit volentes, gratia benevolos. Ex ipso nobis est velle, ex ipsa bonum velle" (ibid., p. 1010).

70. *Summa Theol.*, Ia 2ae, qu. 82, arts. 1–4.

71. Ibid., qu. 85, art. 2.

72. Ibid., Ia, qu. 23, arts. 1–2.

73. Ibid., art. 4.

74. Ibid., art. 5.

75. Ibid., art. 6.

76. Ibid., art. 8.

77. Ibid., Ia 2ae, qu. 109, art. 2.

78. Ibid., arts. 3–5.

79. Ibid., art. 7.

80. Ibid., qu. 111, art. 2.

81. Ibid., qu. 113, art. 3.

82. Ibid., qu. 112, arts. 2–3. The last three quotations are in the translation of A. M. Fairweather in his excellent anthology of Aquinas's writings, *Nature and Grace*, Philadelphia, 1964.

83. *Cont. Gent.*, III, 160.

84. Ibid., 70.

85. Ibid., 73.

86. Ibid., 149.

87. Ibid., 151–53.

88. "Licet aliquis per motum liberi arbitrii divinam gratiam nec promereri nec acquirere possit, potest tamen seipsum impedire ne eam recipiat. . . . Et quum hoc sit in potestate liberi arbitrii, impedire divinae gratiae receptionem vel non impedire, non immerito in culpam imputatur ei qui impedimentum praestat gratiae receptioni," ibid., 159.

89. *Les imaginaires*, vol. 1, p. 97, cf. ibid., 251.

90. Can it be argued that the image of God as an inexorable judge, established by the Reformation, emerged as a result of great calamities, wars, and plagues (cf. Jean Delumeau, *Le Catholicisme entre Luther et Voltaire*, Paris 1971)? It is doubtful. Certainly Augustine, the main source of this image, did live amidst misfortunes and wars. But then, were there between him and the Reformation many generations which did not experience wars, famine, and great miseries? And psychologically would it be less plausible to expect that at a time of terrible trials people, instead of seeing God as a merciless revenger, would rather look for hope and consolation in him as a benevolent father? Human experience suggests that the reactions might go both ways.

91. Ignatius in his "Rules for Thinking with the Church" (rules 14, 15, 17) recommends that the brothers should avoid speaking of, or be very cautious in talking about, predestination and grace in order not to encourage people to believe that their deeds have no significance in terms of salva-

tion or to exclude free will (in *Spiritual Exercises* of Saint Ignatius of Loyola, trans. Anthony Mottola, Image Books, 1964).

92. I discuss these questions in more detail in a book on various sides of the second Reformation and Counter-Reformation, written in Polish and subsequently published in French translation: *Chrétiens sans église*, Paris, 1969. It should be noted, however, that of three great wars Augustine waged—against Manicheans, Donatists, and Pelagians—Luther continued the last one, not the two former.

93. A sample, chosen almost at random, of Calvin's teaching can show that he faithfully followed Augustinian theology and that the Jansenists were in a most awkward position when they tried to point out the enormous differences between his "abominable doctrine" and their own.

"Man is not possessed of free will for good works unless he be assisted by grace, and that special grace which is bestowed on the elect alone in regeneration. . . . Then man will be said to possess free will in this sense, not that he has an equally free election of good and evil, but because he does evil voluntarily, and not by constraint" (*Inst. Rel. Christ.*, III, II, 6–7). "That grace, as Augustine teaches, precedes every good work, the will following grace, not leading it. . . . It is wrong to attribute to man a voluntary obedience in following the guidance of grace" (ibid., 3, 7). "I deny . . . that sin is the less criminal because it is necessary; I deny also . . . that it is avoidable because it is voluntary"; "a man is righteous, not in himself, but because the righteousness of Christ is communicated to him by imputation" (ibid., III, 11, 23). "Man cannot without sacrilege arrogate to himself the least particle of righteousness" (ibid., 13, 2). "With respect to justification, faith is a thing merely passive, bringing nothing of our own to conciliate the favour of God" (ibid., 13, 5). "Even the most splendid works of man not yet truly sanctified . . . are accounted sins" (ibid., 14, 8). "The kingdom of heaven is not the stipend of servants but the inheritance of children, which will be enjoyed only by those whom the Lord adopts as his children, and for no other cause than on account of this adoption" (ibid., III, 18, 2). "By an eternal and immutable counsel, God has once for all determined, both whom he would admit to salvation and whom he would condemn to destruction. . . . This counsel, as far as concerns the elect, is founded on his gratuitous mercy, totally irrespective of human merit" (ibid., III, 21, 7). "These two propositions, that the holiness of believers is the fruit of election and that they attain it by means of works, are incompatible with each other. . . . The holiness they were in future to possess had its origin in election" (ibid., III, 22, 3). "The will of God is the highest rule of justice; so that what he wills must be considered just, for this very reason, because he wills it" (ibid., III, 23, 2). (Quoted from *A Compend of the Institutes of the Christian Religion*, ed. H. T. Kerr, Philadelphia, 1964).

"It seems harsh to many to think that God chooses some and rejects others and does not consider man's worth, that by his own free will he chooses whom he pleases and moreover rejects others. But what is this scruple except a desire to call God to order and subject him to their judgment? . . . There is no real difference among men, except in their hidden election. . . . But since in Adam all are sinners, deserving the eternal death, it is obvious that nothing but sin will be found in men" (*Comment.* on Mal. 1: 2–6). "Election does not give men any occasion for license. Impious people blaspheme saying 'Let us live as we please. We are safe. For, if we are elect, it is impossible that we should perish.' But Paul protests that it is vicious to separate holiness of life from the grace of election; because those whom God elects, he also calls and justifies" (*Comment.* on Eph. 1: 4–6). The last fragments quoted from Calvin, *Commentaries*, trans. and ed. Joseph Haroutunian, Philadelphia, 1958.

It is clear that to Calvin grace is gratuitous, that it has nothing to do with human merit, that it is irresistible, that its distribution was decided eternally, that necessity is not compulsion, and that we may speak of human free will not as an ability to choose between good and evil but only in the sense that we always do evil when our own will is working and always do good when our will is propelled by grace. All this is perfectly Augustinian; all this is Jansenist doctrine.

94. Denzinger, 1452, 1453, 1481, 1482.

95. Ibid., 1520–83.

96. Arnauld asserts that the Tridentine verdict to the effect that free will may refuse to assent to grace means only that there is in the human will a power of resistance; but this resistance can never be effective (*Considérations*, p. 31). He shares this exegesis with some Dominican theologians; it is difficult to see, however, how it is supported by the text.

97. Denzinger, 1927, 1935, 1940, 1925, 1920, 1937, 1965, 1954, 1967, 1968, 1939, 1952 resp.

98. Cf. J. S. Spink, *French Free Thought from Gassendi to Voltaire*, 1960.

99. Denzinger, 2021–65, 2101–67.

100. Bossuet, *Oeuvres*, Bibl. de la Pléiade, 1961, pp. 44–46.

101. Cf. Gazier, *Histoire générale*, vol. 1, p. 19.

102. *Oeuvres de Messire Antoine Arnauld*, vol. 27, Paris, 1778, p. 201.

103. Ibid., p. 210.

104. Ibid., p. 253.

105. Ibid., p. 620.

106. Ibid., p. 88.

107. Ibid., p. 100.

108. Ibid., p. 129.

109. Denzinger, 1676–78.

110. Ibid., 2315, 2460, 2454 resp.

111. Ibid., 2307.

NOTES TO PAGES 74 - 75

112. *Mémoires touchant la vie de Monsieur de S. Cyran*, by M. Lancelot, 1738, vol. 1, p. 39. On the author, see Louis Coguet, *Claude Lancelot. Solitaire de Port-Royal*, Paris, 1950.

112. *Mémoires touchant la vie de Monsieur de S. Cyran*, by M. Lancelot, 1738, vol. 1, p. 39. On the author, see Louis Coguet, *Claude Lancelot. Solitaire de Port-Royal*, Paris, 1950.

113. Jean Orcibal, *Saint-Cyran et le Jansenisme*, 1961, p. 46.

114. About one-quarter of the fourth volume of Henri Bremond's gigantic opus (*Histoire littéraire du sentiment religieux en France*, vol. 4, *L'école de Port-Royal*, 1925) deals with Saint-Cyran's peculiar kind of piety. The author assumes as a matter of course that the five propositions stand firm in Jansenius's masterpiece; he is right, I think, on this point, even though it might seem strange that he did not bother to discuss the issue, so crucially relevant to his work. Neither does he ask what is the relationship between the Jansenist heresy and the Augustinian legacy. He might be justified to the extent that his work does not purport to be a theological dissertation but only to depict, within the framework of the history of literature, the religiosity and mentality of the Port-Royal school; appropriately, the texts he uses most are letters. Jansenism is to him an execrable, heretical, schismatic, rebellious sect, but he is generous enough to recognize some good, i.e. Catholic, sides in Saint-Cyran and in Mère Agnès in particular, and he even regrets some exaggerations of Father Rapin and other Jesuit historians or critics of Jansenism; he makes the distinction between the first generation—misguided but not yet schismatic—and the mature, self-consciously anti-ecclesiastical revolt. Saint-Cyran is to him a "megalomanic" (the epithet is repeated time and again), a "sick brain," a pathetic failure, "grand homme manqué, plus digne de pitié que d'admiration ou colère" (p. 38), a childish mind, an *illuminé*, obsessed by the idea of a grandiose mission. "Ce constant souci de se peindre en saint, cette sorte de charlatanisme dévot" (p. 49); "une hérédité psychopathique assez accusée" (p. 50); "ce déséquilibre mental éclate jusqu'à l'évidence" (p. 51); a dreamer incapable of action, "pauvre imaginaire"; "imagine-t-on vanité plus niaise, égoisme plus répugnant?" (p. 66); "ce qu'il rêve de faire est pur artifice, autosuggestion, vie d'emprunt; tout cela incohérence et faillite" (p. 68); "ce malheureux, ce malade, bavard et dissimulé tout ensemble" (p. 101); "incontinence verbale; la faiblesse de ses nerfs" (p. 103); "porté aux ingéniosités puériles" (p. 157); this is a sample of Bremond's analysis. He states nonetheless that real Jansenism, starting with the publication of *Fréquente Communion*, and organized as a "formal sect," developed after Saint-Cyran's death. The latter's confused and diseased mind unintentionally created a certain spiritual climate that was to grow into the horrible heresy. One might wonder how this morbid character, this "mégalomane au cerveau brouillé" (p. 111), could be so venerated by a number of undoubtedly great minds, by the pious and humble nuns of Port-Royal, by so many people who fell under his charm. But Bremond finds some alleviating circumstances. He admits that the lunatic had some humane aspects that gained people's hearts. While some of his writings announce the intoler-

able Jansenist rigorism, others are expressed in the suave manner of François de Sales. Unlike his great disciple, he did not imbue Holy Communion with an air of dread and terror. Occasionally, in his prayers and spiritual advice, he is not far from a "humanisme dévot." Not a sinister conspirator, rather an irresponsible fantasist who dreamt about a "catholicisme purement intérieur, dans lequel on s'unirait directement à Dieu, sans récourir à la grâce des sacraments et sans dependre de l'autorité de l'Église' (pp. 149–50). In other words, Saint-Cyran, without realizing the nefarious results of his preaching, laid the foundations for a new religion in which only "onction de l'Esprit" matters, not sacraments or the Church. "Ni église, ni prêtre, ni dogme, rien que Dieu et moi. Il semble du moins que l'on ait le droit de construire ainsi la philosophie qui a agité, à l'état de larve, dans les dernières retraites de cette conscience" (p. 154). He prepared the schism efficiently but without thinking of it (p. 174). How this contempt for the sacraments (let us reread the *Fréquent Communion*!), for the priesthood and the Church (should we quote the innumerable Jansenist texts extolling the greatness of the priesthood, of the apostolic succession, of the Church and its hierarchy?) could develop into a dangerous "sect" is incomprehensible. And it is no less incomprehensible how Bremond, a man of immense learning, could devise such an astonishingly partial and prejudiced caricature of the Jansenist movement. A reader who has perused some of Saint-Cyran's writings and the magisterial study of Jean Orcibal cannot believe that this was the same person Bremond was talking about.

On Arnauld: "Une machine à syllogismes, une mitrailleuse théologique en mouvement perpétuel, mais tout à fait denuée de vie intérieure" (p. 286).

"Quand on est capable d'une telle inconscience, on n'est plus homme" (p. 290).

Bremond even knows Arnauld's eternal fate: "Le P. Rapin lui ouvre l'enfer. Non, sa place est aux limbes, parmi les enfants éternels" (p. 287).

On Jansenism in general: "Le jansenisme historique est pour moi un véritable monstre" (p. 317).

115. Orcibal, *Saint-Cyran*, pp. 119–28.

116. Sainte-Beuve (*Port Royal*, vol. 1, pp. 362, 364) thus depicts Saint-Cyran's attitude: "il ne fléchit sur rien d'accessoire, il ne s'en préoccupe pas; il semble ne point chercher de résultats extérieurs et de developpements manifestes sur la terre. L'âme humaine, individuelle, chaque âme une à une, naturellement et incurablement malade par le péché, cette âme à sauver par Jesus-Christ et par lui seul, voilà son oeuvre; il s'y concentre; à droite et à gauche, rien. . . . Le monde d'une part, et les affaires qui sy'y agitent, grand abîme de perdition; de l'autre l'âme humaine, une âme particuliere à guerir et à sauver, sans s'inquiéter de ce qu'elle paraîtra et fera par rapport aux yeux d'ici-bas. . . Nulle distraction vers la nature. . . M. de Saint-Cyran n'a point de fenêtre de ce côté."

117. See Jean Orcibal, *Jean Duvergier de Hauranne, Abbé de Saint-Cyran et son temps*, Louvain-Paris, 1947, pp. 598f., 665ff.

118. Soliloquia, 1, 2, 13.

119. Lancelot, *Mémoires*, vol. 2, pp. 493ff.

120. Cf. *Jansénisme et politique*, Textes choisis et presentés par Réné Tavenaux, 1965. The author argues that from about 1650 Jansenism looked like an opposition party. A critic, Morande, says (in 1654), first, that every religious novelty tends to form a party; second, that Jansenists have frequent meetings, as the Calvinists used to; third, that some of them preach the total refusal of the world on the assumption that all human acts coming from reason or custom are evil. It was not the new bourgeoisie (says Tavenaux), promoters of capitalism, which supported the movement but rather the old one, educated in the humanities and morally austere. On the clientele of Jansenism and of anti-Jansenism see also Orcibal, *Jean Duvergier de Hauranne*. On the political background of Saint-Cyran's imprisonment, cf. the six-volume-long eulogistic biography of Richelieu: G. Hanotaux et Le Duc de la Force, *Histoire du Cardinal de Richelieu*, vol. 6, 1947, pp. 181ff.

121. Lancelot, *Mémoires*, vol. 2, p. 493, Lancelot adds that Saint-Cyran was privy to some details of Richelieu's life that were not publicly known and this was one of the reasons for the persecution.

122. Orcibal, *Saint-Cyran*, pp. 682ff.

123. Cf. the comparison of François de Sales's preaching, especially as it was displayed in his *Traité de l'Amour de Dieu*, with the spirit of Saint-Cyran, in Sainte-Beuve, *Port Royal*, vol. 1, pp. 258ff.

124. A digression is not out of place here. My knowledge of the history of the Jesuit order is rather scanty, but I have noticed that whatever book on the subject I happened to come across, it was usually either aggressive or evasively defensive. Both Jesuit and anti-Jesuit literature is immense. But the standard image of the society was molded by *Les Provinciales* and, closer to our time, by such well-known works as the courses of Michelet and Quinet, Eugène Sue's novel or, in our century, by popular books like Fülop-Miller's *Die Jesuiten. Geheimniss ihrer Macht*. Such works established the image of the order as a sinister and ruthless world-wide conspiracy aiming at the conquest of the earth and shunning no means to achieve this goal. As to Jesuit theology, Henry Bremond's work might have redressed the balance, but it was tainted by a strong anti-Jansenist bias. Michelet's objection that the order failed to produce a real genius is hardly worth discussing as proof that it was, throughout its history, spiritually sterile and interested only in power, not in religion. It might not have Pascal in its ranks (which religious order can boast of having "produced" a similar figure in the seventeenth century or later?), but its history teems with great theologians and scholars—from Francisco Suarez and Bourdaloue to such twentieth-century figures as Henri de Lubac, Stanislaw von Dunin-

Borkowski, Teilhard de Chardin, Jean Daniélou, Karl Rahner—not to speak of a gallery of martyrs. The Jesuits' enormous contribution to the spread of education in the seventeenth century is beyond dispute. Depending on one's polemical needs, one attacked the order either for its extreme, unprincipled flexibility, the readiness to accept anything that might be politically useful, or for its extreme rigidity, which left no room for personal expression; either for cultivating the medieval mentality to serve theocracy or for being carriers of dangerous novelties, ruinous for the Church; on one occasion they were ferocious enemies of freedom, on another frivolous promoters of everything that undermined social order and moral discipline. The Jesuits' strong esprit de corps was used to depict them as a malignant mafia and their entire history was supposed to be summed up in the notorious and endlessly quoted "perinde ac cadaver."

125. The intransigent and sectarian spirit of the Jansenists may be illustrated by a letter, quoted by Sainte-Beuve (*Port Royal*, vol. 2, p. 791), of the abbé de Pontchâteau's, which tells a horrifying story of a Jesuit priest who assisted a soldier-heretic, about to be executed, and publicly prayed for him, hoping for his salvation; instead of demanding the abjuration of heresy, the Jesuit only wanted the victim to pronounce the act of faith and of love toward God, as well as read the seventeenth chapter of Saint John, "Il fallait encore ce digne couronnement aux excès qu'ils [i.e., Jesuits] commettent." Sainte-Beuve's comment: "Il serait à souhaiter que les Jésuites n'eussent jamais commis de plus énormes excès."

126. *Augustinus*, vol. 1, chaps. 4–8.

127. "Panem doloris manducant qui veritatis cognitionem (haec enim mentis panis est) extra veri Dei cognitionem et extra Ecclesiam summis quaerunt laboribus, ut fuerint philosophi, et nunc adhuc sunt heretici, Judaes, et infideles, quorum omnia studia pro invenienda veritate vana sunt, eo quod a Dei non pendeant illuminatione." Cornelii Iansenii episcopi gandavensis *Paraphrasis in omnes psalmos Davideos*, Antwerp, 1619, p. 284; similar remarks are to be found in the same author's commentaries on Ecclesiastes, Proverbia Salomonis etc.

128. A good recent exposition of Arnauld's philosophy is to be found in Steven M. Nadler, *Arnauld and the Cartesian Philosophy of Ideas*, Princeton, 1989. To discuss Arnauld's polemics with Malebranche, Leibniz, etc. is beyond the scope of the present essay. It needs stressing, however, that his critique of Malebranche is quite in keeping with the Jansenist approach; apart from accusing him of undermining the very idea of providence by the contention that God works through general laws rather than particular acts of will (and thus necessarily), he spots the semi-Pelagian heresy in Malebranche's belief that God does everything to save people but human will determines the outcome of the operations of grace. Malebranche indeed rejected the idea of efficient grace in the Jansenists' sense and could be plausibly suspected by them of semi-Pelagianism. He says, e.g.: "toute grâce de

Jésus-Christ est efficace, quoique'elle ne convertisse pas entièrement le coeur. Elle est toujours efficace par rapport à la volonté qu'elle excite et qu'elle meut, quoiqu'elle ne soit pas efficace par rapport au consentement de la volonté qui lui resiste. Et toute grâce est suffisante pour convertir entièrement le coeur, lorsqui'il est bien préparé à la recevoir. . . . En un mot on peut dire que toute grâce de Jésus-Christ est efficace par elle-même en ce sens qu'elle y produit physiquement l'amour naturel du bien. Mais elle n'est pas efficace par elle-même en ce sens qu'elle y produise physiquement notre consentement au bien, ou l'amour libre du bien: car il dépend de nous de consentir ou de ne pas consentire au bon mouvement qu'elle produit en nous." *Conversations chrétiennes* . . . IX, in Malebranche, *Oeuvres*, ed. Geneviève Rodis-Lewis, Paris, 1979, vol. 1., p. 1293.

129. *La Logique on l'art de penser*, IV, 12.

130. Augustine deals on many occasions with the question of the eternal damnation of unbaptized infants. This topic appears frequently in *De natura et origine animae*, and the Pelagian author Vincentius Victor is the main target of the treatise. Augustine's point is simple: all who have been affected by original sin, i.e., all human creatures, deserve damnation unless the stain is washed away by baptism. "Si enim quaeram quare damnari mereantur si non baptizantur, recte mihi respondetur: Propter originale peccatum; item si quaeram unde traxerint originale peccatum, iste respondebit: Ex carne utique peccatrice" (*De nat. et orig. animae*, I, XI, 13). And it is wrong to suppose, as the Pelagian heretics do, that there is a separate place between hell and the heavenly kingdom where such children can enjoy a natural happiness: "non baptizatis parvulis nemo promittat inter damnationem regnumque coelorum quietis vel felicitatis cuiuslibet atque ubilibet quasi medium locum. Hoc enim etiam heresis Pelagiana promisit" (ibid., I, X, 10).

The Pelagian merciful feelings toward the innocent babies deserve only derision: "sed merito inoboediens misericordia vel misericors inoboedientia reprobata atque damnata est, ut caveat homo ne ab illo misericoridam mereatur homo contra eius sententiam a quo factus est homo" (ibid., II, XII, 17). It is absolutely forbidden to offer the dominical sacrifice for such children (ibid., I, XIII, 14–15; II, IX, 13). The main biblical foundation of this theory is, of course, John 3:5, quoted innumerable times. It is true that often, when pious parents hurry to get their newborn children baptized, *God's will* prevents them from doing so, while children of the unfaithful happen to be baptized and saved from eternal death (*De dono perseverantiae*, XII, 31). Why one infant is accepted by God and another rejected is a matter of the inscrutable judgment of God, like the question why, of two just adults, one receives the gift of perseverance and the other does not (ibid., IX, 21). Anyway, it is utterly wrong to think that this results from God's foreknowledge of sins that the unbaptized children would have committed later in life, if they had reached adulthood (*De praedestinatione sanctorum*, XII, 24–5): "cum moriuntur infantes, aut merito regenerationis transeunt ex malis ad bona, aut merito originis transeunt ex malis ad mala." Augustine admits that he once had doubts about the eternal damnation of infants but eventually he saw the truth (*De dono pers.*, XII, 30; cf. *De gratia Christi et de peccato originali*, II, XIX, 21; XX, 22; XXI, 23; *De correptione et gratia*, VII, 12). However, the eternal punishment of those children will be less severe than of adults who added their own crimes to original sin, as Augustine explains in a letter: "si ergo, parvuli cum baptizantur, non inaniter dicitur, sed veraciter agitur, ut inter credentes habeantur, unde etiam nova proles ore Christianorum omnium nuncupantur, profecto, si non crediderint, condemnabuntur ac per hos, quia nihil ipsi male vivendo addiderint ad originale peccatum, potest eorum merito dici in illa damnatione minima poena, non tamen nulla (*Epist.* 184 A, CSEL, vol. 44, pp. 732–33). And he adds again that there is no intermediary place "inter regnum et supplicium."

131. *Augustinus*, vol. 1, pp. 5–10, 46, 65.

132. Ibid., vol. 2, c. 6, p. 8; c. 20, p. 158.

133. *Tractatus de statu parvulorum sine baptismo decedentium*, ex hoc iuxta sensum B. Augustini compositus a F. Florentio Conrio, Rothomagi, 1652. Pascal once mentions this author in *Écrits sur la grâce*.

134. In *De la necessité de la foi en Jesus-Christ pour être sauvé*, Arnauld attacks the criminal doctrine according to which pagans who knew God by reason alone, without revelation, could be cleared of sins and original sin could be effaced in their children. "Aujourd'hui, selon la créance de l'Église Catholique, les enfants des Chrétiens les plus saints ne sont point sauvés s'ils ne reçoivent le Baptême, lequel souvent on ne leur peut conférer" (Arnauld, *Oeuvres*, vol. 10, p. 266). Elsewhere he says that even some Jesuits admit that Jesus did not want to save children who died unbaptized (*Considérations sur l'entreprise faite par Maître Nicolas Couret, Oeuvres*, vol. 19, p. 26).

135. *Pensées*, 131.

136. *Seconde lettre de M. Arnauld à un duc et pair de France*, in: *Oeuvres*, vol. 19, pp. 487ff.

137. *De natura et origine animae*, I, IX, 12.

138. "Nullorum hominum perversitate perversum fieri dici sacramentum Dei quod etiam in perversis fieri declaratur" (*De Baptismo*, III, X, 16); "in ista quaestione de baptismo non esse cogitandum quis det sed quid det, aut quis accipiat sed quid accipiat, aut quis habeat sed quid habeat" (ibid., IV, X, 16); "baptismum Christi nulla perversitate hominis dantis sive accipientis posse violari" (ibid., VI, I 1). "Sicut autem bono catechumeno baptismus deest ad capessendum regnum coelorum, sic malo baptizato vera conversio" (ibid., IV, XXXI, 28). Augustine quotes Ambrose to prove that his teacher did not believe in the salvation of good catechumens (even though Ambrose might have been inconsistent on this point).

139. Henri-Charles Puech, *En quête de la gnose*, vol. 1, 1978, pp. 185–213.

140. Hans Jonas, *The Gnostic Religion: The Message of the Alien God and the Beginnings of Christianity*, Boston [1963].

141. "Au delà de la Renaissance 1580–1630. Genése d'une modernité," in Jean Mesnard, *La culture du XVIIe siècle*, PUF, 1992, pp. 27–42.

142. In the *Seconde lettre, Oeuvres*, vol. 19, pp. 335–563, Arnauld produces a list of fundamental issues in which Calvin's doctrine is glaringly opposed to Augustine's. This confrontation, too, is less than convincing. According to Arnauld, Calvin makes God the cause of original sin—something that Calvin repeatedly denied; he is accused of absolutely denying free will, whereas in fact he asserts that men have no free will to perform good acts without grace (*Institutions*, II, 2,6). Calvin does, indeed, say that whatever pious men do deserves condemnation in God's eyes, but then he adds that everything praiseworthy in our works comes from God (*Inst.*, III, 14, 11; 15, 3) and he stresses on various occasions that, while we are not justified by works, we are not justified without them, etc. It is true that the belief in the certainty of salvation is not Augustinian; but on the crucial issue of efficient grace one is hard put to find a difference between the heretical teaching of Calvin and the most orthodox (as Arnauld would have it) Augustinian theology.

143. *Pensées*, 900.

144. P. François Garasse, *La doctrine curieuse des beaux esprits de ce temps ou pretendu tels*, Paris, 1623, pp. 494–99.

145. Martinus Becanus, *Compendium manualis controversiarum hujus temporis de fide et religione*, 1623, I, 1, 6–7.

146. Lucien Goldmann's *Le Dieu caché. Étude sur la vision tragique dans les Pensées de Pascal et dans le théatre de Racine*, was published in 1955. I then wrote a long and detailed review of the book in a Polish philosophical journal (*Studia Filozoficzne*, 3/1957). The review was by no means uncritical but as a whole it was positive if not laudatory. I would now take a more censorious approach (which I took in part in a chapter on Goldmann in the third volume of my *Main Currents of Marxism*, 1978). My criticism then affected, first, the a priori ideal of Jansenism whereby sundry variants of the movement are measured to yield the conclusion that the most consistent and fully developed variety is to be found in Pascal's *Pensées*, in the writings of de Barcos, and in Racine's *Phèdre*. Second, the model, apart from not being built on empirical evidence, is arbitrarily deduced from the peculiar class situation of the noblesse de robe. Goldmann claims that this class, in the process of transition to absolute monarchy, was step by step losing its position and influence to the new centrally controlled bureaucracy and was becoming more and more "alienated" from political reality, but it could not oppose the monarchy which was the economic condition of its very existence; hence its ideology was expressed in the "vision tragique," which im-

plied that genuine Christian values cannot possibly be realized in the existing world order, even though it is a Christian's duty to fight for them in this very world. The "hidden God" who plays such a prominent role in the Pascalian description of the human condition is supposed to be the most striking expression of this "vision tragique." Goldmann thus assumes, as a matter of Marxist dogma, a strict one-to-one correspondence—without any mediating cultural life-forms—between the actual situation of a social class and its ideological self-assertion. This correspondence, in addition, is established in causal terms. Therefore he neglects factors so fundamental in the history of Jansenism as the conflicts within the Church, the tensions between secular and regular clergy, the gallican-ultramontanist quarrels, the weight of pre-Cartesian philosophical tradition, the very war with the Reformed churches, etc. Those arbitrary presuppositions led him, further, to the invention of the third and most important of Pascal's conversions that occurred between the *Provinciales* and the *Pensées* (the *Provinciales* do not fit into the model) and even to the assertion that Pascal was a Catholic, rather than a Calvinist, by a fully conscious act of choice, determined by the "vision tragique." But there were many cases in history when a social group was tied, by its economic position, to the existing political system but felt uncomfortable in it (did not the lower nobility suffer during the growth of absolutism?); but to our knowledge in no other case were a *Pensées* or *Phèdre* produced on such occasions. Goldmann's study is one of the most ingenious products of Marxist philosophical historiography, but it suffers from the baseless Marxist assumption that products of human culture can be completely explained and understood by their role in the "class struggle."

He took from Lukács the concept of "zugerechnetes Bewusstsein," of a global world-outlook corresponding exactly to the needs of a social class and deducible not from any empirical material but from the knowledge of those very needs conceptually concocted by a Marxist historian. Nor is Goldmann's attempt to insert the *Pensées* into the history of dialectics (leading to Marx and Lukács) convincing. He believes that, since God is accessible neither to reason nor to experience, his existence is established by a practical gamble, a *pari*, just as Marxian socialism is the target of a *pari*. Therefore, he claims, the *pari* is not addressed—as it ostensibly is—to a libertine but is rather Pascal's own monologue. This amounts to saying, contrary to everything that the text suggests, that Pascal in the *pari* tried to convince himself of God's existence; and to maintain that socialism was to Marx a practical gamble and not a scientific certainty, deduced from his knowledge of "historical laws," runs counter to Marx's own innumerable and unequivocal assertions. Goldmann's theory is certainly worth studying, and my criticism does not imply that there is anything wrong with taking up the "hidden God" as the organizing principle in reading Pascal (there are many others, though, equally legitimate). It is aimed at a socio-

NOTES TO PAGES 94 · 97

logical explanation. In such matters a lot depends on intellectual fashions. (I happened to read a book that attempted to show that Pascal's great merit was in being a forerunner—incomplete, to be sure—of Mr. Jacques Derrida; today "post-structuralism" is more in fashion than Marxism.) As an explanatory device Goldmann's work remains in the realm of attractive imagination, a number of very interesting remarks notwithstanding. As to the connection between Jansenism and noblesse de robe, the matter seems to be less established than Goldmann believed; cf. Gerard Ferreyrolles, *Pascal et la raison du politique*, PUF, 1984, chap. 1, and Tavenaux, *Jansénisme et politique*, pp. 20–21. The social background of Jansenism is discussed in Adam's book, *Du Mysticisme à la Révolte*.

147. *Instructions théologiques et morales sur le premier commendament du Decalogue* . . . par feu Monsieur Nicole, vol. 1, Paris, 1723, pp. 23–25.

148. Ibid., p. 47.

149. *Les visionaires ou seconde partie es lettres sur l'heresie imaginaire*, Liège, 1668, p. 463.

150. *Instructions*, p. 106.

151. Ibid., vol. 2, p. 324.

152. Ibid., p. 72.

153. Ibid., p. 167.

154. Ibid., p. 388.

155. Ibid., p. 457.

156. *Dictionnaire*, vol. 3, p. 501.

157. *Les visionnaires*, p. 22.

158. Ibid., p. 51.

159. Ibid., p. 455.

160. Ibid., p. 493; cf. Pascal's remark on painting in *Pensées*.

161. See Racine's *Oeuvres complètes*, Bibl. de la Pléiade, vol. 2, 1966, pp. 13–31. Jean Mesnard in his beautiful essay on "Jansenism et littérature" (in *La culture de XVIIe siècle*, PUF, 1992, pp. 247–61) stresses the great contribution of Jansenism to literature and even says: "On peut se même demander si sa destinée n'a pas été surtout littéraire." Surprisingly (considering the heading) he discusses neither Racine's tragedies nor Nicole's condemnations but praises instead the beauty of Robert Arnauld d'Andilly's religious poems and the clarity of language in the writings of Antoine Le Maistre, Le Maistre de Sacy, and in the *Provinciales*.

162. *Instructions*, pp. 16–18, 78, 90.

163. *Les visionnaires*, pp. 137ff., 314ff.

164. It is known that Nicole mitigated the harshness of the Jansenist theory of grace by a number of curious distinctions, and mollified the stiffness of Jansenist moral doctrine by common sense. A meticulous analysis of his theory of grace, including his ambiguities, changes, hesitations, and inconsistencies is to be found in E. D. James, *Pierre Nicole, Jansenist and Humanist*, The Hague, 1972, and in Bremond *Histoire littéraire*, vol. 4,

pp. 418–588. The latter author calls Nicole a "janséniste malgré lui" and claims—with convincing arguments—that "son génie le voulait moliniste" (p. 428). Nicole boldly attempted to reconcile the Jansenist concept of efficient grace not only with neo-Thomist but even with Molinist doctrine. There is, according to him, a general grace given to all men: not only external grace, like the very act of creation, the revelation of divine law, the ability to know the truth, etc. (which Augustine and Jansenius did not deny, of course), but an interior grace that enables us to perform meritorious works. That is, it is simply not true that in the absence of another grace, given to few, we can produce nothing but evil. There is a universal God-given "illumination" which affects not only the mind but "the heart" as well. There are no sins that result from insuperable ignorance. Occasionally, Nicole suggests that efficient grace can be resisted actually, not merely "in principle." He does not exclude the reality of "pagan virtues" and he rejects the Augustinian doctrine according to which no acts or thoughts are good unless they spring from supernatural charity. To claim that those clearly semi-Pelagian tenets are ultimately Jansenius's own, required making a number of most unconvincing distinctions on which it is beyond the scope of the present essay to dwell.

On Nicole's anti-mysticism, cf. James, *Pierre Nicole*, part 3, and Bremond, *Histoire littéraire*, vol. 4, pp. 501ff.

165. Included in Pascal's *Oeuvres complètes*, vol. 3, ed. Jean Mesnard, 1991, pp. 1135–98.

166. Lancelot, *Mémoires*, vol. 2.

167. On disinterested love and the "disappropriation" of Christian souls in Saint-Cyran, in connection with the affair of the *Chapelet secret* by Mère Agnès Arnauld, see Orcibal, *Jean Duvergier de Hauranne*, pp. 310–34.

168. *Dict. hist. et crit.*, 4th ed., 1730, pp. 830ff.

169. Cf. Gazier, *Histoire générale*, vol. 2.

170. The Jesuits extracted from Quesnel's work, *Réflexions morales*, 155 false statements. When they protested to the pope that only 101 had been ultimately condemned, he allegedly said that he had promised them to condemn over one hundred statements, which he did (Gazier, *Histoire générale*, p. 243). Is this how dogmas are made?

171. Denzinger, 35th ed., p. 490. The comment deserves quotation: "neque tamen in casu discrepantiae sive verae sive apparentis inter decreta Magisterii ecclesiastici et doctrinam Augustini homo vere catholicus, ad modum Calvini, Baii, Iansenii, Augustino auctoritatem quasi infallibilem et absolutam attribuet, cui illius decreta subiuganda sint, sed sibi persuasum erit, omnem Augustini auctoritatem pendere a concedente et interpretante Ecclesiae magisterio, sicut lux lunae a sole. Infelix illa exaggeratio auctoritatis Augustini maxime in Iansenismo funestissimos fructus produxit."

172. On the effects of *Unigenitus*, see Gazier, *Histoire générale*, vol. 2, pp. 252–75.

173. Tavenaux (*Jansénisme et politique*, pp. 40ff.) and other historians stress the importance of the underground weekly *Nouvelles ecclesiastiques* (published from 1728 until 1803) which brought political Jansenism to the masses and contributed strongly to molding the democratic mentality, even though it is true that Quesnel himself had no well-developed political ideas, apart from preaching the anti-ultramontanist principle of unrestricted obedience to the monarch.

174. Cf., e.g., Friderici Spanhemii F., *Selectiorum de Religione Controversiarum . . . Elenchus Historico-Theologicus*, Lugd. Batav, 1687, pp. 66–69, 78–79.

In the impressively erudite and instructive collection of studies by Bruno Neveu (*Erudition et religion au XVIIe et XVIIIe siècle*, Albin Michel, 1994), which I had the opportunity to read only after completing my essay, we find an excellent description of the position of Augustine in the seventeenth-century Church (see, in particular, the chapters on "Augustinisme Janséniste et magistère romain" and "Le statut théologique de saint Augustin au XVIIe siècle," pp. 451–490). The author confirms that *Augustinus*, which was obviously a work of positive theology rather than a historical analysis, deserves its title and is genuinely Augustinian. He does not discuss in detail the five propositions or the question of whether they reproduce faithfully the Augustinian doctrine. He quotes instead a number of contemporary or later theologians; some of them argued that the teaching of the great doctor could not be considered an absolute norm for the Church and that he erred on some important points in the theory of grace, whereas others believed that what the Holy Office condemned was not the Augustinian theology as such, only its exaggerated, "fundamentalist" or "extremist" interpretations. The opinion of the former seemed to gain in credibility in the second half of the seventeenth century.

Jansenius, says Neveu, "est lui aussi attaché entièrement à la *mens sancti Augustini*, à cette difference près avec le gros des théologiens qu'il fait de s. Augustin l'interprète de la foi de l'Église et non de l'Église l'interprète de s. Augustin" (p. 481).

175. Denzinger, 3817.

176. See the very interesting study of the Polish theologian Waclaw Hryniewicz, OMI, *Nadzieja zbawienia dla wszystkich (The Hope of Salvation for All)*, Warsaw, 1989.

PART   TWO

Pascal's works are quoted either from Lafuma's edition: *Oeuvres Complètes*, Editions du Seuil, 1963 (referred to as OCL) or from the still incomplete edition by Jean Mesnard: *Oeuvres complètes*, Desclée de Brouwer, vol. 1, 1964; vol. 2, 1970; vol. 3, 1992 (referred to as OCM). These three volumes, an almost incomparable monument of editorship, do not include the *Pensées* or the *Provinciales*. References to the *Pensées* are given directly in the text of this essay as "fr." with the number of Lafuma's edition. We owe the now standard English translation to A. J. Krailsheimer, Penguin Books, 1966, and many later reprints. This is an excellent translation but the present author prefers to use his own words even, if possible, in quotations.

Among Pascal's biographies one should mention Fortunat Strowski, *Pascal et son temps*, 3 vols., 1907–8, and Jean Mesnard, *Pascal*, 1962. In English we have an illuminating study by Ernest Mortimer, *Blaise Pascal: The Life and Work of a Realist*, 1959.

1. OCM, vol. 3, 1991; the introduction to the *Écrits*, pp. 487–641, the text pp. 642–799.

2. In the *Prayer for the Good Use of Illnesses* Pascal makes it quite clear that in the beginning of a conversion nothing at all depends on human effort, it is entirely God's work. "Mais je reconnais, mon Dieu, que mon coeur est tellement endurci et plein des idées, des inquiétudes et des attachements du monde, que la maladie non plue que la santé, ni les discours, ni les livres, ni vos Ecritures sacrées, ni votre Evangile, ni vos mystères les plus saints, ni les aumônes, ni les jeûnes, ni les mortifications, ni les miracles, ni l'usage des Sacrements, ni le sacrifice di votre corps, ni tous mes efforts, ni ceux de tout le monde ensemble, ne peuvent rien du tout pour commencer ma conversion, si vous n'accompagnez toutes ce choses d'une assistance tout extraordinaire de votre grâce . . . je ne puis attendre aucune grâce que de votre miséricorde, puisque je n'ai rien en moi qui vous y puisse engager, et que tous les mouvements naturels de mon coeur, se portant vers les créatures ou vers moi-même, ne peuvent que vous irriter" (OCL, p. 363).

This is a prayer, not a theological treatise. But its Augustinian-Jansenist background and tenor are manifest.

3. Cf. a much earlier letter (5 November 1648) to Pascal's sister Gilberte: "Ainsi la continuation de la justice des fidèles n'est autre chose que la continuation de l'infusion de la grâce, et non pas une seule grâce qui subsiste toujours . . . il faut continuellement faire des nouveaux efforts pour acquérir cette nouveauté continuelle de l'esprit, puisqu'on ne peut conserver la grâce ancienne que par l'acquisition d'une nouvelle grâce" (OCL, p. 274).

4. Strowski (*Pascal et son temps, 1907–1908*, vol. 2, pp. 358ff.) has suggested that the young Pascal had previously believed in the "God of philosophers" and that the great conversion brought him to the biblical Creator. Gouhier (o.c., p. 43) disagrees with this interpretation and thinks rather that Pascal felt abandoned by God and the conversion made him experi-

ence his assistance. Gouhier's reading seems to conform more to the testimonies of Gilberte and Jacqueline.

5. OCL, p. 394.

6. Pascal was not an erudite. E. Baudin remarks (*Études historiques et critiques sur la philosophie de Pascal*, vol. 1, Neuchatel 1948, p. 28) that there is no trace in Pascal's texts of his acquaintance with St. Thomas, Duns Scotus, Suarez, or the Augustinians of old and that his knowledge of ancient philosophy was based on Epictetus and Montaigne. The quotations from the fathers give the impression that he took them from anthologies like M. de Luynes, *Sentences tirées de l'Écriture Sainte et des Pères*. Baudin's study is rarely referred to in Pascal scholarship, perhaps because it was written from the conservative-Thomist perspective and is therefore far from enthusiastic about Pascal; and it is somewhat flat and pedantic. This is, however, a solid, analytically sound, and penetrating study with a lot of interesting remarks.

On Pascal's attitude to philosophy, see a most interesting study by Vincent Carraud, *Pascal et la philosophie*, PUF, 1992. Unfortunately, I read this book after already having composed mine. The author argues convincingly that Pascal, while all the time employing Cartesian concepts, produced a subversive text which de-philosophizes his discourse. Carraud discusses in detail Pascal's refutation of metaphysical proofs of God's existence (pp. 347–92).

7. J. Laporte (*Le coeur et la raison selon Pascal*, 1950) suggests that the despair of a skeptic threw Pascal into irrational faith or "fideism." This is not plausible. In fact the opposite might be closer to the truth. What we know about his skepticism comes from texts written after the great conversion. It was the conversion which turned his mind toward reflections on the fallibility of reason.

8. *Lettres philosophiques ou lettres anglaises*. Avec le texte complet des remarques sur les Pensées de Pascal. Introduction, notes by Raymond Naver, 1956, p. 147.

9. Cf. Jean Mesnard, *Les Pensées de Pascal*, 1976, pp. 158–59. Augustine himself made this point, cf. *De Correptione et gratia*, V. 8.

10. Filleau de la Chaise, *Discours sur les Pensées de M. Pascal*. Introduction and notes by Victor Giraud, Paris, 1922, pp. 38–39. Lafuma argues convincingly (*Recherches Pascaliennes*, 1949, pp. 83–92; *Histoire des Pensées de Pascal*, 1954, pp. 33–34) that Filleau de la Chaise, who was a member of the committee preparing the edition of Pascal's notes (along with Arnauld, Nicole, and Etienne Perier, among others) must have had the manuscript at his disposal when he was drafting his report from the lecture of 1658. He is less convincing when he maintains that the unnamed person who was supposed to have attended the lecture was a product of Filleau's imagination because the text mentions "histories de la Chine," whereas a book with

this very title was to appear shortly after Pascal's presentation. Albert Beguin, another Pascal scholar, in his introduction to Lafuma's *Recherches*, does not accept this conclusion. Both of Lafuma's studies provide a detailed description of Pascal's manuscripts and copies which resulted in Lafuma's, now standard, edition of the *Pensées* with their division into "papiers classés" (ordered by the author himself), "papiers non classés," the section on miracles (written before the plan of the *Apology*) and fragments not registered in the copy. On the logical order of the *Apology*, cf. also *La disposition des matières* by Anthony Rugh in *Pascal: Thématique des Pensées*, ed. Lane Heller and Ian Richmond, Paris, Vrin, 1988.

11. Filleau de la Chaise, *Discours*, p. 69.

12. Ibid., p. 80.

13. Ibid., p. 83.

14. Ibid., p. 37.

15. Ibid., pp. 40–41.

16. Ibid., p. 50.

17. Ibid., p. 53.

18. Ibid., p. 56.

19. Ibid., p. 57.

20. Ibid., p. 61.

21. Ibid., p. 74.

22. Ibid., pp. 94–102.

23. The preface to the first edition of the *Pensées* (1670) is usually reproduced with the text; it is also included in the cited edition of Filleau de la Chaise by V. Giroud, pp. 157–89. It was written after the *Discours* and hardly adds anything to it. The first edition was slightly, but not excessively, bowdlerized.

24. OCL, p. 266.

25. OCM, vol. 1, p. 590. According to a well-known anecdote, Pascal, as a baby, was gravely ill, as a result of a spell cast by a malicious witch, and he was near death (eventually the witch, under the father's threats, transferred the spell onto a cat; the animal duly died); during his illness the child could not suffer to see his father and mother together, only separately (OCM, vol. 1, pp. 507, 1091). A Freudian's delight.

26. It is not clear to the present author whether the saying "what a happy life which one gets rid of like a plague" (fr. 147) is meant ironically, with reference to Seneca, just quoted, or expresses Pascal's own (Augustinian, in fact) craving for death; it is in keeping with his religiosity to see life in the body as a curse and, at the same time, to claim that this kind of feeling brings pious happiness.

27. OCM, vol. 1, p. 577.

28. Ibid., pp. 631–32.

29. The Augustinian theology of death was summed up in the deserv-

edly famous letter—in fact a small theological treatise—written by Blaise to his sister in October 1651 after the demise of their father (OCM, vol. 2, pp. 845–63).

30. OCL, p. 290.

31. *Lettres philosophiques ou lettres anglaises*, p. 141.

32. Ibid., p. 293.

33. Cf. David Finch, *La critique philosophique de Pascal au XVIIIe siècle*, Philadelphia 1940; Jean Ehrard, *Pascal au siècle des Lumières*, in *Pascal présent*, 1963; Jean Mesnard, "Voltaire et Pascal," in Jean Mesnard, *La culture du XVIIe siècle*, pp. 589–99.

34. Pascal almost said this in the essay on imagination (44): "Le plus grand philosophe du monde sur une planche plus large qu'il ne faut, si'il y a au-dessous un précipice, quoique sa raison le convainque de sa sûreté, son imagination prévaudra. Plusiers n'en sauraient soutenir la pensée sans pâlir et suer."

Jeanne Russier in her detailed and meticulous study, *La foi selon Pascal*, PUF, 1949 (pp. 8ff., 83) says that some of the most memorable fragments expressing dread or dismay in the face of the mute universe (like 201, 427, 429, 194) were to be subsequently put into the mouth of his atheist interlocutor in a dialogue (cf. also Jean Mesnard, *Les Pensées de Pascal*, p. 340). This is possible but by no means certain, considering that none of his libertine friends—or any known libertines, as far as we can say—expressed in their writings this sort of emotional attitude toward the godless world. René Pintard, whose seminal and splendid work (*Le libertinage érudite dans la première moitié du XVIIe siècle*, 1943) provides an inexhaustible source of information on the mentality of the libertine milieu, says in a separate study (*Pascal et les libertins*, in *Pascal présent*, pp. 105ff.): "Le désarroi que Pascal prête à son interlocuteur (427, 68, 201), n'essai-t-il pas de lui inspirer plutôt qui'il ne le constate, tout comme il s'attache à faire naître en lui, à l'égard de sa vie terrestre et de son destin d'outre-tombe, des préoccupations qui ne l'effleuraient pas?"

But let us read, as an *instantia crucis*, fragment 198:

"En voyant l'aveuglement et la misère de l'homme, en regardant tout l'univers muet et l'homme sans lumière abandonné à lui même, et comme égaré dans ce recoin de l'univers sans savoir qui l'y a mis, ce qu'il y est venu faire, ce qui'il deviendra en mourant, incapable de toute connaissance, j'entre en effroi comme un homme qu'on aurait porté endormi dans une île déserte et effroyable, et qui s'eveilerait sans connaître et sans moyen d'en sortir."

This fragment ends with a comforting certainty: "Je vois plusieurs religions contraires et partant toutes fausses, excepté une. . . . Chacun peut se dire prophète mais je vois la chrétienne et je trouve des prophéties, et ce que chacun ne peut pas faire." We see "je" at the beginning and "je" at the end. Is it likely that it is two different persons who speak, a godless man in despair and then Pascal, who has found God? No, this is the same person; this is Pascal's real experience, not a rhetorical device.

35. The famous *Mémorial* is a text found on Pascal's body after his death, sewn up in his clothes (published for the first time in 1740 and then included in the addenda to the *Pensées*). It relates the extraordinary experience Pascal went through on the night of 23 November 1654. It has been analyzed many times in religious, historical, psychological, and psychiatric terms. It cannot be summarized. It refers to a joyful encounter with God and the firm promise never to abandon him. It marked the so-called second conversion, which was decidedly to shape Pascal's life from that time on. Henri Gouhier in his essay "Le mémorial est-il un texte mystique?" (reprinted in his *Blaise Pascal: Commentaires*, Vrin, 1984, pp. 48–57) replies negatively to the question. His main point is that in genuine mystical experience all the natural human faculties, including reason, are suspended, and the mystic's soul remains passive; all thoughts about oneself are excluded, God is loved for himself, disinterestedly (*amour pur*). The *Mémorial* does not meet those conditions, Gouhier says. Pascal, in his encounter with God, does not for a moment stop caring about his personal salvation, and throughout his experience, as related, memory, reason, and imagination are not set aside or silenced. That memorable night was the culmination of a crisis which ends with the renouncement of the world in order to surrender entirely to God and Jesus Christ; while this is always a part of mystical experience in the Christian world, it is not sufficient to make this particular experience mystical.

Everything in this question depends on the definition of "mysticism." Gouhier's comments are not arbitrary, and considering the standard descriptions of mystical union in the writings of great mystics, he is right. If, however, mysticism is described in a looser and more comprehensive sense which includes any experience that the person interprets as a "direct" encounter with God, independent from intellectual understanding and even quasi-sensual, then Pascal's night of fire belongs to this category. The question, though, is not semantic. Gouhier's analysis confirms what has been noticed by others: Pascal's religiosity is not properly speaking "theocentric," because the question of personal salvation is never put aside and the completely disinterested pure love of God is not his topic. The distinction between Jansenism and Catholic mysticism in the seventeenth century is therefore valid and important. Indeed, it is not the inexpressible union with God but rather the infinite, unbridgeable gap between God and man which is characteristic of Jansenist religiosity (on the definition of mysticism, cf. my *Chrétiens sans église*, Paris, 1969, pp. 31ff.). Gouhier's magnificent work deals with various historical and psychological aspects of the *Mémorial* ("Le mémorial," pp. 11–65, 367–87).

36. Letters aux Roannez, OCL, p. 267.

37. Ibid., p. 355.

38. OCL, p. 350.

39. In the context, this remark on God's "duty" not to deceive us may well hint at what is known as "'the miracle of the holy thorn," of which Pascal's family were beneficiaries. Marguerite Périer, the ten-year-old niece of Blaise and a boarder at the Port-Royal school, had suffered for three years from a very painful disease of the eye, which disfigured her face, produced a constant outflow of putrefactive matter, and caused her bones to rot. The disease was considered incurable by physicians. On 24 March 1656, during a religious celebration in the chapel, a sister from the convent touched her with a reliquary which enclosed the thorn of the Holy Crown, and the child was instantaneously cured, with no traces of the terrible affliction left. Many people witnessed the extraordinary event, which immediately became famous in Paris. Considering the location of the divine intervention, the Jansenists, who were then victims of various chicaneries, threats, and persecutions, saw in it, not surprisingly, a sign of a special providential favor granted not only to the girl but to the convent and, by extension, to the holy cause they themselves defended. The Jesuits, without necessarily denying the miracle, denied, not surprisingly, its meaning as interpreted by their enemies. Ample documentation of the event, including testimonies of witnesses and of the little heroine, the statements of several surgeons, various letters, etc., is to be found in OCM, vol. 3. This is perhaps one of the best-documented of reputedly miraculous phenomena (it was soon approved as such by the archbishop of Paris after the interrogation of witnesses). And what could be more natural, in Pascal's view, than to think that God would have deceived us if he had performed a miracle in such circumstances without having a specific edifying purpose in mind, to wit, the affirmation of the Augustinian truth? The *Apology*, according to Brunschvicg, was conceived as an act of gratitude for the miracle. In 922 we read: "Sur le miracle. Comme Dieu n'a pas rendu de famille plus heureuse, qu'il fasse aussi qu'il n'en trouve point de plus reconnaissante."

40. OCL, pp. 199–215.

41. OCL, p. 466.

42. OCL, p. 467.

43. The most concise exposition of Aquinas's rules concerning the relationship between faith and natural knowledge and their respective areas of competence is to be found in *Contra Gentiles*, I, 2–8.

44. Mesnard, while accepting the concept of the "vision tragique" for reading Pascal, argues that it does not apply to Barcos; cf. *La culture du XVII siècle*, pp. 287–88.

45. OCL, p. 282.

46. Ibid., pp. 360–62.

47. OCL, p. 268.

48. Cf. Mesnard's commentary on Gilberte's *Vie*, in OCM, vol. 1, pp. 566–67.

49. On the concept of the "honnête homme," cf. Mesnard, *Les Pensées de Pascal*, part I, chap. 2, and *La culture du XVIIe siècle*, pp. 142ff., and Edouard Giscard d'Estaign, "Pascal et le bon usage de la raison," in *Chroniques de Port-Royal*, Textes du Tricentenaire, 1965.

50. Letter to Roannez of December 1656, OCL, p. 269.

51. Text in OCM, vol. 1, p. 1002.

52. The fragment opens with two words: "infinity nothing," and in it Pascal is obviously applying his mathematical reflections on infinite values of different orders; in the treatise on the arithmetic triangle (OCL, p. 94) he mentions the fact (not discovered by himself) that a point does not add anything to the line, a line to the surface, a surface to the body. He clearly thought of various orders of infinity and then applied this concept to his "three orders." Cf. Gouhier, *Blaise Pascal*, pp. 287ff.; Mesnard, *La culture du XVIIe siècle*, p. 466 (with a unfortunate attempt to express Pascal's thought in mathematical terms, which, however, are mathematically meaningless).

53. OCL, p. 352.

54. *Lettres philosophiques*, p. 146.

55. Cf. L. Blanchet, "L'attitude religieuse des Jésuites et les sources du pari de Pascal," *Revue de Métaphysique et de Morale*, n. 4, 1919, pp. 477–516.

56. *Theologie morale des Jesuites, Oeuvres*, vol. 29.

57. Cf. Mesnard's analysis of the relationship between fragments 308 and 933 (the latter refers to another order of orders: flesh, mind, will), in *La culture du XVII siècle*, pp. 462–84; Mesnard states that the topic of three orders is the organizing principle of the entire *Apology*.

58. Paul Benichon (*Morales du grand siècle*, 1948, pp. 83ff.) points to the *Délices de l'esprit* (1658) as a characteristic specimen of this theology of gradation which refuses to condemn everything that is done without grace. This was a work of Desmarets de Saint-Sorlin, one of the targets of Nicole's attacks. Balzac is another example and so is, of course, François de Sales.

59. Bremond, *Histoire littéraire*, p. 283.

60. OCL, pp. 366–68.

61. Gerard Ferreyrolles, *Pascal et la raison du politique*, PUF, 1984.

62. *De iure belli ac pacis*, I, 1, X–XV; Leibniz's doctrine is quite similar.

63. OCL, pp. 362–65.

64. Baudin (vol. 2, pp. 130–77) argues that Pascal and the entire Jansenist movement had in fact an "anthropocentric," indeed eudaimonistic, orientation: everything was to be subordinated to human happiness, i.e., eternal salvation; God was seen as an instrument of human aspiration

to heavenly bliss and not a center which deserves love for himself, apart from our good. Religion was supposed to be useful, and purely theocentric piety was inconceivable to this movement. Ultimately, truth in the Jansenist view is at the service of the good, unlike in Aquinas, to whom truth was a value in itself. This explains their disrespect for science and history, and their lack of interest for those chapters of theology which have no direct bearing on matters of salvation; theology is reduced to soteriology, as it is in Luther. This resulted in a strange alliance between Jansenism and libertine humanism, which likewise was interested only in human happiness, however differently conceived, and not in truth. This criticism (also made by Bremond) although not entirely false, is very exaggerated. It is true that salvation was the main theme of Jansenist writings; if the question of grace was central to their theological thinking, this was not because they were driven exclusively by selfish motives but because they found the problem ready-made, as it were; it had been central in the Roman Church since the great Reformation and the emergence of the Molinist doctrine, unlike, say, the question of the Holy Trinity or christological speculations characteristic of early Christianity. The Jansenists were not the first to focus on it. It is true that we hardly find in Jansenist writings the topic of *resignatio ad infernum* (if God dispatches me to hell, I will be happy, as it is his will), but it is not frequent in other currents of devotion either. Pascal's feeling of pain for having offended God so often does not necessarily appear in the context of fear about his own salvation. And Arnauld was a philosopher who can hardly be accused of not being interested in truth for its own sake. It might occasionally be seen that in Saint-Cyran and Nicole the "anthropocentric" perspective is more prominent, but their emphasis on perfect *contritio*, in contrast to the repentance resulting from fear, cannot be forgotten.

65. Cf. Leo Moulin, "Les gauches et le peché originel. Essai de methode comparative," *Revue européenne des sciences sociales*, vol. 19, 1981, nos. 54–55. The topic is fairly frequent among Christian critics of Marxism, like Gustav Wetter. I have also discussed it briefly in "Can the Devil Be Saved?" and "The Death of Utopia Revisited," reprinted in: *Modernity on Endless Trial*, Chicago, 1990.

66. Cf. Encyclical *Redemptor Hominis* of John Paul II and *Catéchisme de l'Église Catholique*, 1992, pars. 1733 and 1742. The catechism is semi-Pelagian rather than Augustinian in that it does not mention the inheritance of guilt, even though it confirms, of course, the doctrine of original sin and the resulting corruption of nature (403–5); it speaks of the freedom of choice between good and evil (1732) without, however, stating that the will is irresistibly shaped by grace or that grace is given only to the few according to God's arbitrary decision. Unbaptized children may be saved (1261); Jesus died for all human beings without exception (605); *attritio*, and not only *contritio*, is a divine gift (1453). There are no condemnations,

but all the five propositions condemned in the anti-Jansenist bull are clearly rebuked.

67. From the very beginning Pascal's *Entretien avec M. de Saci* (published only in 1728) provoked serious doubts: Fontaine, sometime secretary to de Saci, reported the conversation in his *Mémoires*, written more than forty years after the event (which historians place in Port-Royal at the beginning of 1655, shortly after Pascal's great conversion). It was impossible to credit such a prodigious memory. Pascal scholars have advanced various hypotheses about the source of this celebrated text (was it a total fabrication based simply on Fontaine's reading of the manuscript of the *Pensées*? was it composed on the basis of letters exchanged between the learned priest and his younger penitent? or did the author use the notes, now lost, written by Pascal?). It would be really a pity if the *Entretien*, so Pascalian in content, turned out to be a fake. Having meticulously examined all the hypotheses, Mesnard (OCM, vol. 1, pp. 236–50) reached the conclusion that Fontaine had had in hand an essay written by Pascal with remarks made by de Saci in the margins, and then arranged the whole thing in the form of a direct dialogue by simply inserting conversational phrases ("dit-il," "je vous demande pardon, Monsieur," etc.). If so, one can safely believe that Pascal really said what he was said to have said. Fontaine reports the conversation as if he had been a stenographer but he does not say directly that he was actually the witness. Cf. Gouhier, *Blaise Pascal*, pp. 67ff., and Pierre Courcelle, *De St. Augustine à Pascal, par Sacy*, in *Pascal présent*, pp. 131–46.

68. *Entretien*, OCL, p. 297; OCM, vol. 3, p. 157.

69. The information was given in a letter by abbé Boileau (reprinted in OCM, vol. 1, p. 969).

70. Cf. the second version of Gilberte's *Vie*, OCM, vol. 1, pp. 624–25.

Index

INDEX

papal authority, 107, 179
papal politics, 27–29
Pascal, Gilberte, 128
Pascal, Jacqueline, 97
passions, 66–67, 164, 190
Paul V, Pope, 7
Paul, Saint, 25, 86
Pelagius, 36, 208 n. 64
Pelagianism, 5, 7, 52, 56, 183–85
    and elitism, 36
    on grace, 13
    and sovereignty of God, 34
Penance, sacrament of, 67–73
Pensées (Pascal), 118–26
Périer, Etienne, 126
Périer, Marguerite, 228 n. 39
Peter, Saint, 10–11
philosophy, 81–82, 121–22
piety, 51, 160, 170, 194
Pintard, René, 208 n. 63, 226 n. 34
politics, 108, 119, 175–81
Ponchateau, Abbé de, 215 n. 125
Prayer for the Good Use of Illnesses (Pascal), 180
predestination, 33–38, 36–38, 42–44, 51–52
    Augustine, 203 n. 61
    Erasmus, 48
    Luther, 49–50
    Saint-Cyran, 76
prophecies, 142
providence, 135–36
Provincial Letters (Pascal), 61–67, 115–16, 177–78
Puech, Henri-Charles, 218 n. 139

Quesnel, Pasquier, 5, 74, 102–3
Quinet, Edgar, 214 n. 124

Racine, Jean, 27, 96, 202 n. 45, 218 n. 146

Rahner, Karl, 215 n. 124
rationalists, 166–67
rationality, 121–22
reason, 139–40, 145, 155–56, 163, 171–72
Rees, B. R., 208 n. 65
religion, 141–42
repentance, 73–81
Richelieu, Armand Jean du Plessis, Cardinal, 6, 78–79
Rugh, Anthony, 225 n. 10
Russier, Jeanne, 226 n. 34

sacraments, frequency of reception of, 67–73
Saint-Cyran, Abbé, 5–6, 74–81, 108, 175, 212 n. 114
Sainte-Beuve, C. A., x, 28
Saint-Simon, duc de, 27
salvation, 100
scholasticism, 82
science, 151–60, 171–72
scripture reading, 91–92, 106
Séguenot, Father, 78
self-deception, 133
Semaison, Father de, 72
semi-Pelagianism (*see also* Molinism), 13, 38, 56, 108–9
Seneca, 225 n. 26
Sirmond, Antoine, 168–69
skepticism, 191–92
Spink, J. S., 211 n. 98
stoicism, 191–92
Strowski, Fortunat, ix, 223
Suarez, Francisco, 214 n. 124
Sue, Eugène, 214 n. 124

Tavenaux, Réné, 214 n. 120
Teilhard de Chardin, 215 n. 124
theater, 95, 134